The Greatest Calamity

THE GREATEST CALAMITY

Tennessee in the Civil War Era

John D. Fowler

Three Star Series

THE UNIVERSITY OF TENNESSEE PRESS
Knoxville

This series of brief books explores topics of interest to Tennesseans, offering primers on such topics as the Civil War, Native American history, historic homes, and more. A relaunch is underway to revitalize this valuable resource, previously supported in part by the Tennessee Historical Commission.

First Edition.

LIBRARY OF CONGRESS CATALOGING-IN-PUBLICATION DATA

Names: Fowler, John D., 1965- author
Title: The greatest calamity : Tennessee in the Civil War era / John D. Fowler. Other titles: Three star series
Description: First edition. | Knoxville : The University of Tennessee Press, [2025] | Series: Three star series | Includes bibliographical references and index. | Summary: "This is an . . . account of Tennessee during the Civil War. It is the first candidate in our effort to revive the press's Three Star Series, a set of short, introductory books that address significant parts of the state's history and culture. Meant to replace Thomas Connelly's Civil War Tennessee, originally published in 1979, this book brings recent scholarship, especially on the social history of the war, to a new audience. This book is intended as a general-interest title and hopefully will be useful to readers as young as secondary school students"—Provided by publisher.
Identifiers: LCCN 2025015714 (print) | LCCN 2025015715 (ebook) | ISBN 9798895270233 paperback | ISBN 9798895270240 kindle edition | ISBN 9798895270257 adobe pdf
Subjects: LCSH: Tennessee—History—Civil War, 1861–1865 | United States—History—Civil War, 1861–1865
Classification: LCC E531 .F69 2025 (print) | LCC E531 (ebook) | DDC 973.7/1—dc23/eng/20250430
LC record available at https://lccn.loc.gov/2025015714

LC ebook record available at https://lccn.loc.gov/2025015715

★ ★ ★

TO JUDY, BRUCE, PAUL, AND STEVE

Thank you

CONTENTS

Preface xiii

Acknowledgments xix

ONE The Three States of Tennessee 1

TWO Confederate Tennessee 29

THREE 1862 Tennessee: The Struggle for the Rivers 63

FOUR The Fight for Middle Tennessee 111

FIVE The Liberation of East Tennessee 147

SIX The Final Campaign 183

SEVEN Tennessee's Home Front 211

EIGHT Reconstruction 247

Epilogue 289

Bibliographic Essay 295

Index 313

ILLUSTRATIONS

Photographs

John Bell 18
William G. "Parson" Brownlow 18
Isham G. Harris 19
Senator Andrew Johnson 24
East Tennessee Unionists 34
Felix K. Zollicoffer 38
Union Supporters Hanged Outside Knoxville 39
Henry Howe Cook 46
Albert Sidney Johnston 47
Ulysses S. Grant 64
Andrew Foote 64
Bombardment of Fort Henry 66
Capture of Fort Henry by US Gunboats 67
Henry W. Halleck 69
P. G. T. Beauregard 70
William Tecumseh Sherman 85
Don Carlos Buell 86
Battle of Shiloh 92–93
Nathan Bedford Forrest 95
Bombardment of Island No. 10 104
Braxton Bragg 113
William S. Rosecrans 118
Charge of the First Brigade at the Battle of Stones River 130
Men Repair a Single-Track Railroad After the Battle of Stones River 137
Sketch of the Battle of Chickamauga 156

Union Pickets Approached by Rebels in Cedar Bushes Near Chattanooga 169
Sketch of the Battle of Missionary Ridge 175
Battle of Fort Sanders 179
Chattanooga, Tennessee, Ca. 1864 185
Fort Pillow Massacre 187
Battle of Nashville 206
Confederate Camps, Battle of Nashville 207
A Refugee Family Arriving at a Union Army Post in Tennessee 212
Union Refugees Coming into Federal Lines 213
Champ Ferguson Surrounded by Prison Guards 224
Fort Pickering Contraband Camp 231
Hannah and Adam Watkins 232
President Andrew Johnson 251
Pardon of Nathan Bedford Forrest 252
Impeachment of President Andrew Johnson 267
Freedmen's Bureau 274
Teaching the Freedmen 275
Two Members of the Ku Klux Klan 278
The Memphis Riot of 1866 279

Maps

Secession Votes by County 2
Western Theater of Operations 26
Railroads across Tennessee 43
Fort Henry Campaign 65
Fort Donelson, February 15, Morning 71
Battle of Shiloh, April 6 am 88
Battle of Shiloh, April 7 99
The Battle of Stones River, December 30, Evening 126
The Battle of Stones River, December 31, 4 p.m. 131
Tullahoma Campaign, June 24–July 3, 1863 139

Chickamauga Campaign,
August 15–September 8, 1863 155
Sketch of Chattanooga, 1863 160
Wheeler's Raid, September 30–October 9, 1863 161
Chattanooga Campaign, Cracker Line 165
Chattanooga Campaign Battles (Nov. 24–25, 1863) 170
Knoxville Campaign Area, 1863 180

PREFACE

> War with all its horrors, is upon us. I hear and think of little else. This the greatest calamity that could befall us. Who dreamed that we would ever come to this? The United States! The star country! The model government—by which other nations endeavored to frame theirs,—but I fear the star has sunk,—her glory has departed. . . . All is confusion,—no telling what the future will be. . . .
>
> —SALLIE GANNAWAY JAMISON TO HER SISTER-IN-LAW, APRIL 1861

In her letter to her sister-in-law Camilla in Murfreesboro, Sallie Jamison spoke for an entire generation of Tennesseans and, indeed, Americans who were undoubtedly shocked that civil war had entered their world and that the anticipated and inevitable rise of the United States would now be stymied by secession and separation of the Confederacy. But war had come to the nation, and it would eventually encompass the farms, towns, forests, valleys, and mountain coves of the Volunteer State.

This work was written as part of the revised Three Star Series published by the University of Tennessee Press examining the various periods of the Volunteer State's history. As such, it will replace Thomas Connelly's *Civil War Tennessee: Battles and Leaders* (1979). Connelly's book stands as a masterful short volume covering the major military events in Tennessee. This volume is intended to be greater in scope by analyzing not only military events but also political events, the home front, the plight of the freedpeople, and the Reconstruction period. Such a story is multidimensional and could fill many volumes if examined in minute detail. This volume, however, is written not as a comprehensive examination of Tennessee's experience but as an introduction to that experience. As such, it fits well within the mission of the Three Star Series to provide brief, introductory-level works on the periods in Tennessee's history. Those interested in digging deeper are directed to the detailed bibliography of major secondary works contained at the end of this book. Deciding which sources to include proved daunting, not because of a dearth of good sources but because of an abundance of them. The list is not exhaustive. There are scores of other secondary works that cover more esoteric topics. Moreover, theses and dissertations, as well as scholarly articles, were excluded, as were myriad primary sources consisting of letters, diaries, reminiscences, etc. that are available. In sum, this book is designed to provide a gateway for greater exploration of this period of the state's history. It is hoped that, like the original edition for the Three Star Series, this work will aid scholars of various interests (Civil War, Southern history, Tennessee history, local history, etc.) and at the same time offer the general reading public, students, and Civil War enthusiasts an engaging story of Tennessee's important role in the war and how the conflict affected the state.

One can argue that Tennessee was the most important state during the war in terms of strategic value—the "keystone of the Southern arch," as Abraham Lincoln called it. Indeed, the state's significance in the sectional crisis was realized immediately. It boasted two presidents, four presidential candidates, two speakers of the House of Representatives, and a number of influential congressmen and senators before the war. Moreover, Tennessee had earned its "Volunteer State" nickname by providing manpower for the nation's early wars. A strong nationalist impulse within the state had translated into a strong Unionist presence during the secession crisis. Indeed, Tennessee rejected secession after Lincoln's election, and only the president's call for military action following the Rebel attack on Fort Sumter pushed the state into the Confederacy. Even then, Tennessee was the only seceded state to have a significant part of its population remain loyal to the Union (with the notable exception of West Virginia). Yet, in East Tennessee, opposing neighbors and families created a brutal civil war within the Civil War.

Once the state did leave the Union, it quickly became critical to the Confederate war effort. With the exception of Virginia, Tennessee was the most industrialized of the Rebel states and ranked behind only Virginia and Georgia in railroad mileage. Major north–south and east–west lines traversed the state, making its control critical to the transportation of war material, food, and men. The Confederacy also desperately needed the state's manufacturing concerns, ironworks, munitions factories, textile mills, gunpowder mills, and copper mines to wage a modern war. Also, Tennessee proved to be a breadbasket for the Confederacy with its fertile farms and extensive livestock. In terms of manpower, the Volunteer State was even more important. Tennesseans, organized into infantry and cavalry regiments and battalions, artillery batteries, or independent units, provided an aggregated strength of more than 186,000, making Tennessee one of the major suppliers of Rebel troops. The state also supplied more than 31,000 soldiers to the Federal war effort.

The geography of the state made it vital to both sides. Bordering Kentucky and touched by the major rivers of the West (the Cumberland, Tennessee, and Mississippi),

Tennessee served as the gateway to what historian Thomas Connelly famously called the "Confederate Heartland." For four long years, Union and Confederate forces struggled for control of the state, leaving no part untouched and subjecting inhabitants to devastation and death on an unimaginable scale for the period. More than 450 engagements took place in Tennessee during the war, and while most of these were minor in scope and significance, some rank among the major battles of the war. Names such as Forts Henry and Donelson, Island No. 10, Shiloh, Stones River, Chickamauga, Chattanooga, Franklin, and Nashville are all part of the campaigns fought in or near the state that would decide not only the fate of Tennessee but of two nations.

Tennessee also served as a fighting stage for some of the most famous commanders of the war: Henry Halleck, Ulysses S. Grant, William T. Sherman, George Thomas, William Rosecrans, Philip Sheridan, and Don Carlos Buell on the Union side, and A. J. Johnston, Braxton Bragg, James Longstreet, Patrick Cleburne, Leonidas Polk, John Bell Hood, B. F. Cheatham, P. G. T. Beauregard, Nathan Bedford Forrest, and John Hunt Morgan on the Confederate side. Beyond the field commander, important political figures such as John Bell, William Brownlow, and Andrew Johnson also played roles in the unfolding of the nation's great drama.

Tennessee's importance is also magnified by the early events of the war. Though the state was the last to secede, it was the first to fall to Federal arms. Indeed, only eight months intervened between the state's Declaration of Independence and the appointment of Andrew Johnson as the Union military governor of Tennessee. While East Tennessee would not be free of Confederate control until late 1863, much of Middle and all of West Tennessee was occupied by Federal forces in early 1862. These regions, therefore, served as a laboratory of sorts for the Lincoln administration's Reconstruction polices. The resistance of the Rebel population eventually led Union officials to move from a conciliatory policy toward a sterner approach as the war dragged on and casualties mounted.

Tennessee should also be studied in terms of the demise of slavery. It was the only seceded state not mentioned in the Emancipation Proclamation as the state's Unionists attempted to preserve slave property. Yet, as the Unionists gained greater control, it was also the first ex-Confederate state to free its own slaves, adopt the Fourteenth Amendment, and grant voting rights to Black men.

In short, one cannot understand the Civil War without understanding the Volunteer State's role in it, and one cannot understand modern Tennessee without understanding the impact of the war on its history. It is an interesting story and one worth telling.

The story in this book follows a chronological pattern except for the chapter on the home front, which is more thematic. Chapter One focuses on the coming of the war and serves as an introduction to the growing sectional discord during the antebellum period, focusing on Tennessee's role in national affairs as well as the state's economic and political developments. Chapter Two covers the election of 1860 and the secession crisis. The sectional split within Tennessee is also explored in this chapter, as are the state's preparations for war following events at Fort Sumter and the joining of the Confederacy. Chapter Three explores Tennessee as a theater of war from the occupation of Kentucky through the Battle of Shiloh and the loss of West and much of Middle Tennessee to Union forces. Chapter Four examines the Confederate resurgence of 1862 with Braxton Bragg's invasion of Kentucky in the fall and the subsequent struggle for Middle Tennessee at Murfreesboro in the winter. The chapter ends with the fall of Middle Tennessee as William Rosecrans's brilliant campaign drives Bragg out of the region to Chattanooga. Chapter Five examines the struggle for East Tennessee, covering the crucial battles of Chickamauga and Chattanooga as well as the savage internecine struggle in the mountains of the region. Chapter Six recounts John Bell Hood's Tennessee Campaign, the subsequent battles of Spring Hill, Franklin, and Nashville, and the final days of the war.

Chapter Seven covers the home front, examining such issues as life under Federal occupation, wartime conditions, the struggle of East Tennessee Unionists, the plight of the freedpeople, and the collapse of slavery. Finally, Chapter Eight explores the process of Reconstruction in Tennessee, focusing on postwar economic conditions, "Parson" Brownlow's Radical government, the Freedpeople's struggle against paramilitary groups such as the Ku Klux Klan, and the collapse of the Radical regime leading to the "redemption" of the state.

ACKNOWLEDGMENTS

In the research, writing, and publication of a book of such scope, the author is indebted to many people who have given generously of their time, labor, and advice. I have been a professional historian for more than two decades, and I find myself much closer now to the end of my career than the beginning. Still, I often reflect on how I arrived at where I am today. This has been especially true over the past few years as I have had to say goodbye to many of the people who helped shape me as a person and as a scholar.

I arrived on the campus of the University of Tennessee in the mid-1990s, excited to begin work on my doctorate. While my fascination with history stretched back to my childhood, it was only at UT that I finally began the road to reach my goal of becoming a professor. I did not know what to expect in those early days. Little did I realize at that time how fundamentally my life would change or how wonderful the next few years would be.

My wife Sonya and I had an amazing time living in Knoxville. We made friends and memories that will last a lifetime. Indeed, some of my fondest memories are of the students, staff, and faculty in the history department during my time at UT. The members of my dissertation committee stand out among those. Paul Bergeron, Bruce Wheeler, Judy Cornett, and especially my dissertation director Steve Ash all were instrumental in my development as a professor and as an individual. Paul Bergeron's knowledge of nineteenth-century Tennessee politics was unmatched, and I will always be grateful for his willingness to spend time helping me grasp its complexities. He was a first-rate scholar and taught me much, not only about Tennessee but also the profession. He was a dear friend, and I was sorry to lose his influence when he passed away in 2020. From Bruce Wheeler I learned a great deal about teaching and interacting with students. He demonstrated by the way he approached the profession how important it is to help students succeed both inside and outside of the classroom. He possessed a wonderful sense of humor, a deep kindness, and a gift for oratory. I have tried to mimic his classroom presence and easy rapport with students. His sudden passing in 2023 was yet another blow to me. Judy Cornett was the only member of my committee who was not a professional historian. She is a distinguished law professor at the University of Tennessee. While not an expert on the Civil War in Tennessee, she was still a vital addition to my committee. Judy is a local historian of merit and a gifted practitioner of the English language. We connected in our love of words, of the past, and especially of Tennessee.

Steve Ash stood out amongst the others, initially because he was guiding me through the laborious, quasi-medieval process of researching, writing, and defending a dissertation. I was Steve's first graduate student, and he took a strong interest in seeing me succeed. Indeed, he devoted more time and effort to directing and mentoring me than I witnessed from others who were in his same position. This was partly because Steve was a generous man who gave freely of himself and partly because he was a consummate professional who never did anything by halves. He was a dedicated scholar, gifted writer, and inspiring teacher. I was blessed to have him as my mentor, but even more so to have him as my friend. I loved Steve dearly. His passing in 2021 came as a shock and left a deep void in my life. His humor, interest, patience, advice, and kindness created a lasting legacy for me and all of his former students. Under Steve's watchful eye, I completed my dissertation, which soon became my first monograph, and I continued through the years to rely on his expertise in all my publications. He was always gracious enough to help in any way needed. Any contribution this study makes to the fields of Tennessee and Civil War historiography is due primarily to his influence. I spent a career attempting to emulate Steve, and I always believed that if I could be even half the scholar he was, I could consider my career a success.

This book is dedicated to my dissertation committee, especially Steve. I could never repay what they taught me.

I also want to thank the amazing staff at the University of Tennessee Press. I especially want to mention Associate Director Thomas Wells, Editorial Coordinator Jon Boggs, Editorial Assistant Maliea Ruby, and freelance editor Katie Little, all of whom have worked hard to make this book possible. I appreciate their dedication and professionalism. I want to give a special thank you to Scot Danforth, the former director of the press, who recently retired. Scot was patient, supportive, and knowledgeable. He was an outstanding colleague in shepherding this book from idea to finished project. The staff did all they could to make the work the best it could be. Any errors or omissions are solely my responsibility. I owe a debt of gratitude to Dr. Glenna Schroeder-Lein for her help and expertise in indexing this volume. It is not often that one has such a distinguished scholar to assist with a project.

I would be remiss without expressing the deepest appreciation to my wife Sonya. Her patience, sacrifice, and careful reading and editing contributed immeasurably to the quality of this book. Everything I am or ever will be I owe to Sonya's support, understanding, and encouragement.

Finally, I have a deep and abiding love for Tennessee. Although I was born in eastern Kentucky, both sides of my family came from the Volunteer State, and I spent much of my life there. Therefore, I consider Tennessee to be as much my home as my birthplace in Harlan, Kentucky. It is an honor to tell this chapter of her story.

ONE

The Three States of Tennessee

★ ★ ★

MOTORISTS ENTERING TENNESSEE in the 1960s were likely bewildered by highway signs welcoming them to the "three states of Tennessee." These signs, however, were entirely apt. Perhaps no other state is as starkly segmented as Tennessee, and nowhere is such division more accepted and even celebrated by its citizens. The state flag, for instance, features a circular crest containing three stars, one for each of the state's "Grand Divisions"—East, Middle, and West Tennessee. Indeed, Tennessee's sectionalism, predestined by geography and accentuated by subsequent economic and political differences, has had a profound influence on the Volunteer State's history.

This sectionalism was never more evident nor more tragic than during the Civil War era. United by politics and economic self-interest, Middle and West Tennessee overwhelmingly supported secession and alliance with the

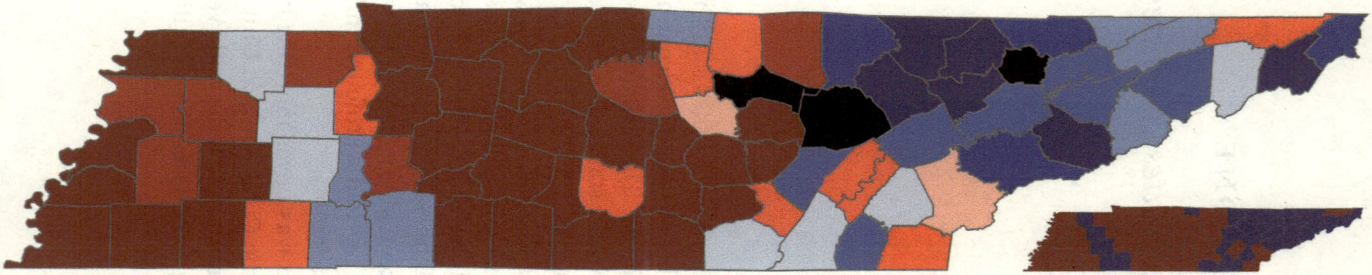

Counties in red voted for secession while counties in blue voted against secession.
Darker shading indicates a heavier vote for or against. Counties in black do not have voter data.

Confederacy. The majority of East Tennesseans, however, refused to renounce their allegiance to the old Union. This stance involved more than just another chapter in the state's ongoing sectionalism; it also involved a rejection of the Confederate South and its values, which made East Tennessee not only a distinctive section of the state but also a distinctive region within the South. Thus, Tennesseans would fight a civil war within the Civil War.

The Land

White settlers began entering what would eventually become Tennessee in the 1770s. The eastern region they first traversed consisted of precipitous and rough mountains covered in dense forests. The Unaka Mountains lie along the eastern border of the region, forming a stout barrier between Tennessee and North Carolina. West of the Unakas lies the Great Valley of East Tennessee, which actually consists of numerous valleys and rugged, parallel ridges. The valley contains the best farmland in the region. Beyond the Great Valley to the west rises the Cumberland Plateau—another steep mountainous region dividing East Tennessee from the rest of the state.

West of the Cumberland Plateau, the region of Middle Tennessee offered earlier settlers better farmland, and once Whites either appeased or drove out the Native Americans, they settled there in large numbers. Also, in contrast to the sharp ridges and mountains of East Tennessee, Middle Tennessee's terrain is quite varied. It includes a Highland Rim of steep ridges that surrounds a great Central Basin of sloping and rolling hills. The limestone soil is rich and fertile and ideally suited for farming and pasture. Moreover, the region is well watered by the tributaries of the Cumberland and the Tennessee Rivers.

The Western Highland Rim forms the boundary between Middle Tennessee and the western portion of the state. Moving westward from the Highland Rim, the land gradually slopes into a great alluvial flood plain stretching to the Mississippi River. This great flood plain, covered in rich top soil, is also crossed by creeks and small rivers. The fertile soil, water sources, and hot climate made West Tennessee perfect for large-scale agriculture similar to that of the Lower South.

Importantly, while Middle and West Tennessee offered abundant quality farmland and connections to other areas of the nation via rivers, the rugged and mountainous landscape of East Tennessee isolated it from Tennessee's other sections and the rest of the nation. Thus, geography was the most fundamental feature distinguishing East Tennessee from the rest of the state. This isolation would greatly affect the region's future economic development.

Antebellum Economic Development

Even before the American Revolution, the land that would become Tennessee attracted White settlers. Following the nation's independence and statehood, more and more families flooded into the state looking to exploit its rich soil and build productive farmsteads. After the War of 1812, the newly formed states west of the Appalachians experienced rapid economic change as the frontier economy based on subsistence farming gave way to a new commercial agriculture supplying growing domestic and foreign markets. Without access to these regional, national, or international markets, large-scale commercial agriculture would not be profitable, and the ability to gain access to these outside markets would further exacerbate the growing distinctiveness of Tennessee's Grand Divisions. Middle Tennessee initially accessed the outside markets via the Cumberland and Tennessee Rivers, which were connected to the Mississippi River. With the invention of the steamboat, the rivers became major transportation arteries that linked the regions to the rest of the nation's markets. Moreover, beginning in the 1830s, a large network of roads connected Nashville, the region's principal city, to areas outside of Tennessee. Eventually, the building of railroads in the 1840s linked Nashville to national markets on an even larger scale. Therefore, because of its access to rivers, roads, and railroads, Nashville became the most important city in Tennessee and one of the most important in the Upper South. Similarly, West Tennessee had early access to Mississippi River travel via the river port of Memphis. Roads and railroads would eventually connect the region's farms and plantations in the hinterland to Memphis and, via the vast Mississippi River and its tributaries, to wider markets. East Tennessee, however, lagged behind its sister divisions. The rugged contour of the region restricted the availability of arable land, meaning that small farms focused on food production rather than larger farms and plantations producing cash crops would be the norm. Even for those with the necessary land and interest in market production, the region's topography hampered attempts to participate in the nation's agricultural boom. To access these lucrative markets, East Tennesseans required a cheap and efficient way to transport their agricultural products. Rough terrain, however, limited the development of road construction, and obstructions in the Tennessee River below Chattanooga interfered with river transportation.

Railroads emerged as the best hope for the inhabitants of East Tennessee. The completion of the East Tennessee and Georgia Railroad in 1855 ended decades of frustration and false starts, providing Knoxville (its northern terminus) and all of lower East Tennessee a reliable and inexpensive connection to the markets of the Lower South. Three years later, upper East Tennesseans witnessed the completion of the East Tennessee and Virginia Railroad, which linked Knoxville to Bristol and beyond. The two rail lines, when connected, established a route through the whole of the valley, offering East Tennessee farmers what their parents and grandparents had dreamed of: greater access to outside markets.

This market access greatly affected the economy of the region. While the traditional exports of corn and hogs could now be shipped more easily, the greatest change was the development of cash crops such as tobacco and wheat. Indeed, the demand for East Tennessee wheat meant that by the mid-1850s, many of the region's farmers had shifted from corn and hog production to the grain.

These new crops also led to an increase in urban development. Although the urban populace of the region remained modest in the antebellum era, numerous villages grew two- or even three-fold during this time. In addition, new communities sprang to life as a result of the railroad. These new railroad towns, along with the older settlements, became the stage for the growth of an urban merchant and professional class that became closely linked to the economy of the wider South.

Adding to the sectional split within Tennessee, these various transportation projects were not designed to connect the Grand Divisions to one another. For example, Middle Tennessee's roads were built with Nashville as the central point or hub. Moreover, all the major railroads with the sole exception of the Memphis and Charleston ran north and south, linking the state's regions to neighboring states but not to one another. In fact, a passenger wanting to travel across the state would have to exit and reenter Tennessee along the journey.

The Importance of Agriculture

Like the rest of the United States, the pre–Civil War Tennessee economy was primarily based on agriculture. It was more "industrialized" than much of the rest of the South, but the vast majority of the twenty-five hundred manufacturing concerns that existed before the outbreak of the Civil War were small establishments in terms of size and number of employees. Moreover, they tended to be related in some way to agriculture or rural life since most were smithies, grist mills, lumber mills, or tanneries. Even the few mines and forges that existed tended to produce for local markets. Agriculture, then, was the economic lifeblood of the Volunteer State, and each region had its own specialty.

East Tennessee's topography, soil, and climate prevented large-scale production of the antebellum South's lucrative cash crops such as cotton. East Tennessee did, however, produce for outside markets when possible. Hog drovers attempted to supply the Lower South with pork, and many farmers tried to produce an overabundance of food crops for Lower South plantations eager to use their own acreage for cotton production. Yet East Tennessee remained a region of subsistence farms except in areas of the Great Valley near the region's few major transportation arteries, such as the railroad. There, some cash crops such as wheat and tobacco were produced in quantity for outside markets. In contrast, the rich soils of Middle Tennessee allowed the farmers to produce corn, wheat, and even some cotton in abundance, while livestock, horses, and mules thrived in the limestone-rich soil. On the great alluvial plain of

West Tennessee, farmers could grow foodstuffs and raise livestock, but tobacco and especially cotton were the chief crops. West Tennessee plantations accounted for 80 percent of all the state's cotton production by 1850, making it one of the major cotton-growing regions of the antebellum South.

Not surprisingly, the planters in West Tennessee specializing in cotton production tended to have larger and more valuable farms than those elsewhere in Tennessee. For example, the median farm size in West Tennessee was a third larger than the farms in Middle Tennessee and more than 40 percent larger than those in East Tennessee. Correspondingly, the median value of West Tennessee crops (principally cotton) was double that of Middle Tennessee farms and triple that of East Tennessee farms. And larger cash crop production meant greater wealth: in a detailed study of antebellum Tennessee agriculture, historian Tracy McKenzie found that the average income generated by West Tennessee plantations and farms was four times that of Middle Tennessee and nearly six times that of East Tennessee.

The Peculiar Institution

Closely tied to agricultural development in antebellum Tennessee was the institution of slavery. In 1860, bondsmen accounted for around one-third of the slave state's population overall. In Middle Tennessee, slaves constituted around one-quarter of the population and in West Tennessee slightly over one-third. In East Tennessee, however, slaves amounted to less than 10 percent of the population, and in no county of that region did the slave population exceed 15 percent. Moreover, the percentage of slaveholders in East Tennessee was quite small. Approximately 37 percent of White families in the South owned slaves in 1860, and the proportion in Middle and West Tennessee stood at one-fourth and one-third, respectively. Yet only one-tenth of White East Tennessee families held slaves.

Clearly, the link between slavery and market production was the key factor in why the slave population of East Tennessee did not match that of Middle and West Tennessee. This meant that while Middle and West Tennessee developed economies tied to the larger Southern economic system with its emphasis on commercial agriculture and slavery, East Tennessee largely remained a land of self-sufficient family farms.

Still, a small but significant number of East Tennesseans, like their counterparts in Middle and West Tennessee, realized that commercial agriculture was key to a more affluent lifestyle. In East Tennessee, farmers producing for the market often earned three to four times more money than subsistence farmers. Why, then, did not all of the region's farmers produce for the market? While some historians contend that many antebellum farmers rejected commercial agriculture on principle in favor of the economic independence of self-sufficiency, this does not appear to be the case in East Tennessee. It was not ideology that hindered the participation of more farmers in the market economy, but rather factors such as soil exhaustion and farm size. Transportation costs, however, were arguably the most critical factor. Only those farmers close to the region's few shipping routes, especially the railroad, could profit by commodity sales. This resulted in an increasing economic disparity among the region's farmers. While the majority of the inhabitants lived in isolated areas, eking out a precarious subsistence lifestyle that often led to poverty, a minority near the valley's rail lines became increasingly tied to the lucrative markets of the Lower South, reaping the benefits of commercial agriculture. In fact, as the Civil

War approached, the townspeople and commercial farmers linked to the Southern economy and the subsistence farmers of the remoter areas began to view one another as different. These feelings of distinction would influence the region's response to the impending crisis.

Antebellum Politics

Not surprisingly, the economic differences among the Grand Divisions of the Volunteer State, along with corresponding differences in wealth, influenced the political development of the state and added to the intersectional rivalry. East Tennessee was the first area of the state settled, and for the first few decades of the state's history, the region dominated the population and subsequent political power. However, as Middle and West Tennessee became more populous and more prosperous, power shifted, especially to Middle Tennessee. This generated resentment among many East Tennesseans. Moreover, the growing reliance on commercial agriculture by the Middle and Western sections of the state meant that their farmers and townspeople were more tied to the rest of the South in the growing network of economic, social, and political matters. In East Tennessee, only those few located near the region's transportation links shared those ties. The rest of East Tennessee remained populated by small subsistence farmers who increasingly shared little in common economically, socially, or politically with Middle Tennessee.

The struggle for power among Tennessee's three sections also had national implications—largely due to Tennessee's political leaders, who wielded national influence. The central figure in Tennessee's antebellum political rise was Andrew Jackson. His desire for national office and eventual election to the presidency changed the political development of Tennessee and the nation forever. Jackson's national image as a common man who rose from poverty to wealth, coupled with his reputation as a military hero of the War of 1812, made him a powerful political force and a household name. Additionally, his political philosophy and rhetoric, which championed the interests of the common man against the interests of the wealthy and well connected, won for him the admiration of middle- and lower-class Americans and allowed him to form a powerful political coalition. Soon Tennessee became the center of the new Democratic Party, led by Jackson and his allies. However, Jackson's populist ideas and his distrust of the nation's commercial interests put him on a collision course with the new developing commercial business class focused more on manufacturing and less on subsistence agriculture. Surprisingly, the core of Jackson's opposition would start in his home state of Tennessee and not in the nation's manufacturing center of the Northeast. Leading Tennessee politicians such as William Carroll, David Crockett, Hugh Lawson White, John Bell, and others were either opposed to Jackson's ideas or felt cut out of his patronage and were major forces in the rise of the anti-Jackson Whig Party.

Tennessee, then, became the center of national politics in the antebellum period and exercised considerable political influence. The Democratic–Whig rivalry in Tennessee grew intense and bitter. As the wealth and political power in Middle Tennessee, Jackson's home and a Democratic stronghold, grew, so did East Tennessee's resentment. Thus, a strong Whig presence developed in the eastern counties during the period in sharp contrast to Middle Tennessee's Democratic political tradition. West Tennessee split, with most supporting a Whiggish ideology, which served to create a nearly equal balance of voters on both sides. This meant the antebellum period witnessed close elections between two evenly matched parties.

It is worth noting that personal economic interests alone cannot explain Whig or Democratic Party affiliation. Myriad factors such as kinship, residence, and tradition are certainly key elements. Nonetheless, generally speaking Whigs were in favor of increased manufacturing and commercial development supported by the federal government. Democrats, however, feared this would create a powerful economic and political elite that would dominate society, thus threatening the liberty of the common man. Therefore, whether it was the debate over governmental power, internal improvements, tariffs, the Bank of the United States, or any number of associated issues that created the party divide, at the core were the intertwined factors of economic development and political power. Naturally, an individual's financial well-being influenced his position and helped determine party affiliation.

Contrasting economic visions of the two parties, as well as republican ideology, enhanced this spirited regional rivalry. Republicanism, a product of the Revolutionary era, forewarned Americans that both internal and external foes threatened their liberty. Only the constant vigilance of the American people provided security against despotism. This fearmongering led political leaders and their constituents to view their opponents not as a legitimate opposition but as a threat to the existence of free government and the Republic itself. East Tennessee's Whiggish political legacy would play a crucial role in the region's response to the growing sectional crisis.

The Specter of Disunion

Although sectional rivalry was the primary factor in Tennessee politics, it was not the same as the growing national sectional rivalry being driven by the issue of slavery. While slavery and the debate over its expansion gradually but inexorably came to dominate national politics, that was not the case in Tennessee. White Tennesseans, whether Democrats or Whigs, overwhelmingly supported the institution of slavery. Thus, they retained a strong devotion to the Union and an acceptance of if not attachment to slavery.

For example, during the Nullification Crisis of 1833, Tennessee joined with her sister Southern states in repudiating South Carolina and the idea of secession. Like most Southerners, Tennesseans believed the tariffs of 1828 and 1832 were unfair to the South, yet they failed to see a link between the tariffs and any potential threat to slavery and abhorred any talk of secession. The strong allegiance of Tennessee to the Union was summed up in the *Nashville Banner*, which declared that "there is a pervading, universal attachment to the Union in Tennessee, which generally revolts at the idea of secession, nullification, and rebellion." When the Nullification Crisis finally ended with the 1833 compromise tariff, the *Banner* rejoiced, declaring, "Nullification is dead and buried—condemned by unequivocal popular sentiment, promptly executed by an indignant and patriotic nation."

Tennesseans remained devoted to both the Union and slavery throughout the antebellum period. However, the Mexican War would begin to chip away at the foundations of Unionism all across the South, including Tennessee. While the war was initially greeted with an outpouring of patriotism across the nation, the question of what to do with the acquisition of any new lands won from Mexico began to enter the political discourse. On January 4, 1847, nearly a year after the outbreak of the Mexican-American War and before its conclusion, native Tennessean President James K. Polk wrote in his diary that "the slavery question is assuming a fearful and most important aspect." Most Americans believed yet another compromise similar to that obtained in 1820 or to the Nullification Crisis would be arranged. Meanwhile, delegates from around the South gathered in Nashville to discuss one such compromise being floated in Washington. The choice of Nashville, Tennessee, as host city demonstrated that the Southern Radicals, or "Fire-Eaters," calling for drastic action and even secession needed support from states in the Upper South such as Tennessee if they hoped to form a strong pro-slavery coalition.

The first meeting took place at the McKendree Methodist Church in June 1850 and was attended by around 175 delegates (one hundred from Tennessee). The Tennessee General Assembly controlled by the Whigs had prevented an "official" Tennessee delegation from attending; therefore, most of the delegates were local Moderate Democrats from Middle Tennessee who supported a compromise measure with the free states. During a recess of the meeting, Congress did pass the multifaceted Compromise of 1850 designed to end any future national discord over slavery. When the group reconvened in November at the Nashville Christian Church, only fifty-nine people attended, and Tennessee sent just fourteen delegates. Despite the congressional compromise, the delegates from the Deep South were Fire-Eaters pushing a pro-slavery, anti-Union agenda. The Tennessee press condemned that rhetoric, and the Tennessee delegation, led by the influential Democratic politician Gideon J. Pillow, refused to sign the measures and supported the compromise reached in Washington. Clearly Tennesseans, even those willing to attend the second Nashville meeting, sought compromise and sectional healing.

Although most Southerners, especially those of the Upper South, were content with the provisions of the Compromise of 1850, many Deep South radicals still believed slavery to be threatened by an ever-growing number of

Northern abolitionists. Overall, while Southern Democrats were gradually becoming radicalized and unified in their defense of slavery, White Tennesseans, irrespective of party, strongly endorsed the institution but generally condemned the Fire-Eating Southern extremists. Yet, cracks developed in Tennessee's solidarity as Whigs took a more conciliatory stance toward the North than did their Democratic neighbors, who sympathized with the Deep South. This pattern would continue throughout the 1850s, gradually wearing away at the state's unity.

The Kansas–Nebraska Act of 1854 shattered not only the Compromise of 1850 but also the Second Party System. The Whig Party was the first to collapse. As Northern and Southern Whigs chose sides, the party disintegrated as a national force, and Tennessee Whigs unexpectedly found themselves without a national affiliation. Like other bewildered party members across the nation, some joined the anti-immigrant American Party. Following its collapse, however, many former Tennessee Whigs organized themselves into what was simply termed the Opposition Party. Others took a more radical course of action. From the mid-1850s onward, as sectional antagonisms over slavery continued to escalate, many former Whigs switched their allegiance to the Democratic Party. Although they may have still disagreed with much of its economic philosophy, they came to believe this party offered the best defense of slavery and Southern rights. Indeed, by the mid-1850s, West Tennessee, a region dominated by plantation agriculture, transitioned its political loyalty from the Whigs toward the Democrats. The emerging Democratic majority in the region, when added to that of Middle Tennessee, was sufficient to enable the party to dominate state politics for the rest of the decade.

Still, while the party system collapsed at the national

level in the 1850s, it lingered in Upper South states such as Virginia, North Carolina, and Tennessee. A surviving two-party system of Democrats and ex-Whigs continued to perform a unifying function within each of these internally diverse states. Both political factions endeavored to link their support for the Union with their support for slavery. Nevertheless, the two-party system in the South dissolved with the tumultuous presidential election of 1860.

As the nation became increasingly polarized over slavery's future, four political factions contended for the presidency. The Republicans, made up of former Northern Whigs and led by Abraham Lincoln of Illinois, found widespread support throughout the North with their free-soil and free-labor ideology. However, Republican opposition to slavery's expansion into the territories and the presence of a strong abolitionist faction in the party meant that Lincoln's name would not even appear on the ballot in most Southern states, including Tennessee. The Democratic Party, having failed to agree on a single candidate, had split in two. A moderate faction nominated Stephen A. Douglas of Illinois, who proposed popular sovereignty in the territories as a panacea for the sectional tension. A radical Southern-rights faction nominated John C. Breckinridge of Kentucky, with the goal of protecting slavery and allowing it to expand into the territories as per the Dred Scott decision. The new Constitutional Union Party nominated John Bell of Tennessee. It opposed extremists on both sides and appealed mainly to Upper South Whigs eager to hold the Union together while protecting slavery.

The Presidential Election of 1860

Like other Upper South states, Tennessee was divided by the election. Five out of the eight major newspapers in Tennessee supported John Bell for president. Two supported John C. Breckinridge and one Stephen Douglas. All ran editorials critical of secession and supportive of compromise and the benefits of the Union. For example, even in the plantation district of West Tennessee, the *Memphis Enquirer* declared, "Let every man put his foot down on disunion; it is no remedy for southern wrongs; or it is only the mad man's remedy." In Middle Tennessee, the *Nashville Republican Banner* even accused secessionists of creating the "vilest, most damnable, deep laid and treacherous conspiracy," while in East Tennessee, Methodist minister and newspaper editor William G. "Parson" Brownlow's widely circulated *Knoxville Whig* unleashed a constant stream of anti-secession rhetoric, condemning secession and all who supported it.

Since the states of the Lower South had pledged to secede in the event of Lincoln's election, Tennessee and the rest of the country waited anxiously for the election returns. On election day, Bell carried Tennessee with 48 percent of the vote, his strongest support coming from the old Whig bastion of East Tennessee. He also won Kentucky and Virginia, demonstrating the conservatism and spirit of compromise that characterized the Upper South. Douglas carried less than 8 percent of Tennessee's total and managed to win the electoral votes of only Missouri and part of New Jersey. Breckinridge made a strong showing in Tennessee, carrying 45 percent of the vote and losing by only 4,600 ballots; he also carried Maryland and the entire Lower South. Despite receiving only 39 percent of the popular vote and almost no votes in the South, Lincoln had carried every free state and won a large majority in the Electoral College. Regardless of the outcome in Tennessee or the rest of the South, Lincoln won the election and was now president.

True to their word, the states of the Lower South departed the Union, beginning with South Carolina in

John Bell. Library of Congress.

William G. "Parson" Brownlow. Library of Congress.

Confederate Governor Isham G. Harris. Library of Congress.

December. Although no hostile action had been taken against slavery, Lincoln's election meant that after his inauguration on March 4, 1861, the presidency would be in the hands of a Northern Free-Soiler. The citizens of the Deep South held that a coercive central government now prevented them from taking slave property into the territories. In the spirit of republicanism, they resolved to depart from a tyrannical and hostile Union and establish a government that was consistent with the principles of the Revolution.

The secession crisis presented Tennesseans with quite a predicament. Although most abhorred abolitionism and championed Southern rights to property, especially slave property, they viewed disunion as a threat to republican government and liberty. Moreover, while Tennesseans sympathized with the Lower South's fears concerning "Black Republican" rule, the vast majority did not support secession. After all, the Republicans had yet to commit a hostile act toward the South, and Lincoln had yet to assume the presidency. Tennesseans believed a wait-and-see attitude to be the most prudent course of action for the South. Indeed, shortly after Lincoln's election, the state leaders of both the Democratic and Constitutional Union Parties urged Governor Isham G. Harris to call the legislature into a January session with the intention that this body would assist in organizing a convention of Southern states to discuss the crisis.

Most Tennesseans were fearful for the Union and for their state. If the Union did dissolve, Tennessee would be torn apart as pro-Union and anti-Union proponents argued to remain or leave. Most hoped that at this critical moment another compromise could be reached and disunion avoided. Unfortunately for Tennessee and the nation, this would not be the case. Long-simmering sectional animosity and resentments would not allow for another compromise. Such animosities were also far too deep-rooted to prevent a split between East Tennessee and the other Grand Divisions. Civil war was coming to the quiet hills and peaceful valleys of Tennessee.

The General Assembly

Once the legislators had assembled in January 1861, Harris, a strong advocate of secession, proposed a state convention to decide whether Tennessee should remain in the Union or join a new Southern republic. The legislature decided to leave the decision in the hands of Tennessee voters, authorizing a February referendum on a convention and the election of delegates. Harris also called on the legislature to adopt resolutions supporting his plan for five constitutional amendments that would forever secure Southern rights. He crushed the hopes of moderates by stating his conviction that disunion could not be thwarted and that Tennessee could not avoid a decision regarding its fate. "The work of alienation and disruption has gone so far," he declared, "that it will be extremely difficult, if not impossible, to arrest it; and before your adjournment, in all human probability, the only practical question for the state to determine, will be whether she will unite her fortunes with a Northern or Southern Confederacy." Harris further expressed his certainty that his fellow Tennesseans would choose the South.

Harris was correct in his assertion that membership in the Union was now the key political question facing the state. Indeed, secession fever had quickly spread from the Deep South to Upper South states such as Tennessee. Loyalty to the Union proved to be the issue that led to the disintegration of the Whig–Democrat party system that had dominated state politics for twenty-five years. The *Knoxville Whig* summed up the political situation when it declared, "Now let our Union people bring out able and true men, irrespective of old party associations. We have no parties but Union men and disunionists."

While protection of slave property proved to be the primary motivation for secession in the Lower South, Upper South disunionists had myriad concerns. Fear of abolition could stir up secessionist support in Tennessee counties with large slave populations such as those in the Middle and West sections. However, the potential loss of the extensive trade links with the Deep South prompted more widespread consternation. Some secessionists argued that the Upper South could experience increased prosperity in a new Southern republic. For example, the *Memphis Appeal* anticipated that Tennessee would become "the chief manufacturer for the South" as a result of its union with the Lower South. Disunionists also contended that the Upper South's secession could avert a war by presenting the North with a united Southern front and that republican liberty could be most effectively preserved in a Southern republic free from abolitionist demagogues.

By late December, secession sentiment had become strong in substantial portions of Tennessee, particularly in counties with large slave populations and Democratic leanings. By mid-January, however, secession fever had dissipated as coalitions of Unionists began to preach the advantages of remaining in the old republic and the perils inherent in joining a new Southern nation. Unionists emphasized that the Lower South's traditional support of free trade would be ruinous to the developing manufacturing interests of the state. Moreover, echoing the traditional republican fear of tyranny, Tennessee Unionists argued that secession was no more than a conspiracy led by a slaveholding elite intent on establishing an aristocracy in a new Southern Confederacy. Finally, many Unionists maintained that secession and the war that would surely follow posed a greater threat to slavery than the Republican administration soon to take office in Washington. While Lincoln had assured slave owners that he did not intend to interfere with the institution where it already existed, the chaos of an armed conflict held the potential to destroy slavery.

Upper South loyalists went on the offensive during the first two months of 1861, creating a source of support for the Union. In East Tennessee, a dedicated group of ex-Whigs and arch-Unionists, including attorneys Oliver P. Temple and John Fleming, William G. Brownlow, and Tennessee Congressman Horace Maynard, along with Democratic senator and former governor Andrew Johnson, provided the leadership for a large Unionist movement that overwhelmed the region's secessionist minority. Loyalists inundated East Tennessee with speakers, leaflets, and editorials urging the region's residents to support the Union of their forefathers and cautioning them against the anti-republican nature of a Southern nation ruled by a "slave aristocracy" determined to "overshadow and dishonor poor white men."

February Referendum

When the ballots of the February referendum were tallied, Tennessee Unionists had scored an overwhelming victory. Despite the fact that the statewide vote on the convention question was relatively close (69,387 to 57,798), votes for Union delegates accounted for over four-fifths of the total (88,803 to 24,749). The delegate vote clearly demonstrated that even if a convention had taken place, it would have been dominated by Unionists. Of the three Grand Divisions, East Tennessee gave the strongest support to the loyalists, with more than 80 percent of the voters rejecting the convention and approximately 85 percent voting for Unionist delegates.

Throughout the eight slaveholding states remaining in the Union that winter, loyalist support remained strong. While voters in Virginia, Arkansas, and Missouri called for conventions, the majority of the delegates were Unionists. Like Tennessee, North Carolina decided against holding a convention. Moreover, voters in Kentucky, Delaware, and Maryland did not even consider holding conventions to discuss secession.

Many loyalists from the North and South soon concluded that most Southerners, at least in the Upper South, opposed secession and that the crisis facing the nation would soon resolve itself peacefully. However, the Unionism of Tennessee and most of the Upper South was highly conditional. The continued loyalty of many Unionists rested on the twin assumptions that Congress could devise an effective long-term solution to the slavery controversy and that the Lincoln administration would refrain from any coercive actions against the seceded states. Moreover, the fragile loyalist coalition was not a true political party in any sense but rather a conglomeration of old Whigs and

Andrew Johnson pictured here as a Senator. Library of Congress.

Unionist Democrats, Conservatives and Moderates, slave owners and yeoman farmers. These disparate groups had only devotion to the Union in common. Indeed, after the February referendum, the loyalist coalition in Tennessee began to disintegrate. Decades of intense party rivalry made it difficult for old Whigs and Democrats to continue to cooperate. In addition, in early March a squabble over the distribution of Federal patronage within Tennessee divided the loyalist coalition along old party lines. Even though former Whigs constituted the majority of loyalists, the Lincoln administration curried the favor of Unionist Democrats by giving Andrew Johnson control of political appointments within the state. In an effort to bolster his own political standing and maintain ties to the Democratic Party, Johnson ignored many Opposition Party office seekers and even supported a known secessionist as district attorney for East Tennessee.

As Tennessee's loyalist coalition dissolved, so too did the foundations upon which conditional Unionism stood. Upper South Unionists had assumed that Congress would soon enact legislation or provide constitutional amendments safeguarding slavery and Southern rights, but this was not to be. Even with the efforts of moderate or conciliatory Republicans led by Secretary of State-designate William H. Seward, President Lincoln, along with the majority of his party, refused to compromise on the issue of slavery in the territories. Upper South Unionists remained optimistic, despite the impasse. Reassured by Seward and the conciliatory Republicans that Lincoln would maintain a "hands-off" approach toward the seceded states, loyalists continued to believe throughout late March and early April 1861 that "peaceful reunion was possible."

The Confederate attack on Fort Sumter in Charleston Harbor on April 12 and Lincoln's subsequent call for seventy-five thousand volunteers to put down the Southern "rebellion" dashed any hope for a compromise. Although a handful of diehard Upper South loyalists continued to look for a peaceful solution, most now realized the only choice left was to fight for the South's independence or the Union's preservation.

The majority of Tennessee's loyalists now supported the Confederate cause as their own because they believed Lincoln and the Republicans had betrayed their trust. Both original and converted secessionists united to defend Southern honor and republican government against the perceived oppression of a tyrannical Federal government determined to subjugate them by force of arms. Secessionist rallies were held throughout Middle and West Tennessee. On the evening of April 17, Governor Harris attended a public meeting in the capitol, where he announced that the United States secretary of war had requested two regiments

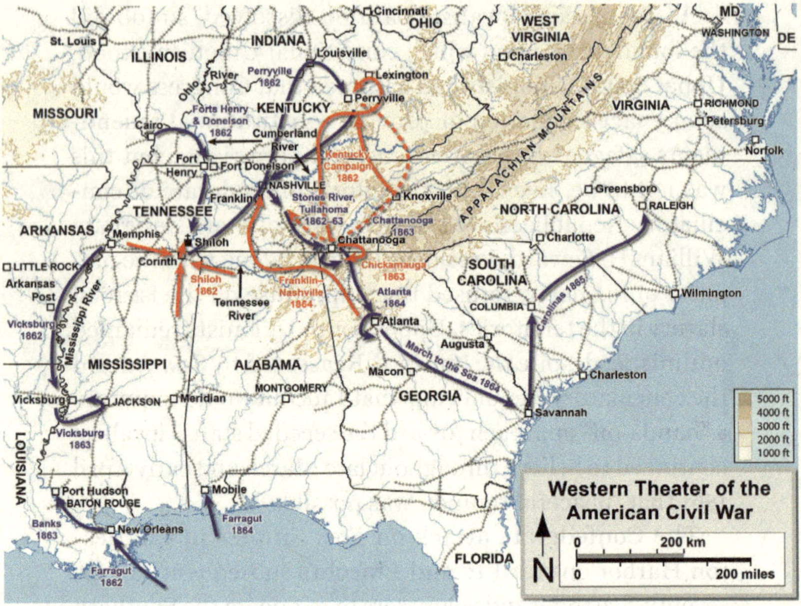

Map by Hal Jespersen, www.cwmaps.com

to help conquer the Rebels. Amid cheers, the governor declared that "rather than sign such an order he would cut his right arm from his body—rather than utter it he would tear his tongue from its root. . . . If . . . this was treason, then before God he was a traitor." The telegram the governor sent in response to the secretary of war's request defiantly asserted that "Tennessee will not furnish a single man for coercion, but fifty thousand, if necessary, for the defense of our rights or those of our Southern brethren."

The following day, the governor called for a special session of the legislature to convene and deliberate Tennessee's future course. On that same day, a group of Unionists led by John Bell published a circular denouncing Lincoln's attempt to coerce the South and declaring the Union dissolved. A few days later, on April 23, Bell delivered a speech in Nashville in which he urged the South to take action "against the unnecessary, aggressive, cruel, unjust wanton war which was being forced upon us."

Governor Harris and secessionist leaders moved quickly to exploit the shift in public opinion caused by Fort Sumter. On April 25, only eleven days after the fort had fallen, the state legislature met in special session to consider taking the Volunteer State out of the Union. Rather than embrace the questionable doctrine of secession, on May 6 the legislature decided to imitate the Revolutionary generation by issuing a declaration announcing Tennessee's independence from the United States. Anxious to demonstrate popular support for their actions, the legislators arranged for the state's Declaration of Independence to be submitted to a referendum scheduled for June 8. Governor Harris and the legislature, however, decided not to wait for the formal public sanction of a vote and immediately began war preparations. On the same day it passed the declaration, the legislature granted Governor Harris authority to create a state army of fifty-five thousand volunteers and authorized bonds and taxes to finance the mobilization. The following day, Tennessee entered into a military alliance with the Confederacy, thereby placing the state's military forces and defense under the control of the Confederate president. Anticipating widespread public support of their actions, the governor and legislature had entered Tennessee into the Confederacy a full month before the people had the opportunity to voice their approval. Tennessee was now, in essence, part of the new Southern republic. But how would the people vote? That question was yet to be answered.

TWO
Confederate Tennessee

★ ★ ★

A State and Nation Divide

In the wake of the attack on Fort Sumter and Lincoln's subsequent call for volunteers to repress the rebellion, citizens in Middle and West Tennessee joined their fellow secessionists across the South. In East Tennessee, however, most refused to participate in what they perceived as an unjust war against the national government. William G. Brownlow spoke for the region when he declared that after having examined the situation, he was for the "Stars and Stripes." Despite the fact that the June referendum was only a month away, East Tennessee loyalists remained confident that the Unionist coalition would keep Tennessee in the Union. Surely, they reasoned, the thoughtful people throughout the state would come to their senses and rise up in support of the Union cause when the time came.

In the meantime, the immediate task of East Tennessee's Unionist leaders was to rally the region's faithful.

While Horace Maynard, Thomas A. R. Nelson, and others canvassed the area, the Unionist press led by Brownlow produced an incessant stream of propaganda. Local leaders organized meetings where hundreds and even thousands gathered to express their support for the Union. The speeches and writings of these men struck a chord with most East Tennesseans. Long accustomed to hearing about the myriad threats to liberty and republican government, East Tennesseans listened while loyalist leaders exposed secession to be an aristocratic plot designed to reduce the common folk to servitude in a great Southern kingdom. In his Senate addresses, Andrew Johnson depicted the national crisis as a contest between democracy and aristocracy and labeled Confederate President Jefferson Davis a tyrant. Likewise, Brownlow declared, "Let Tennessee go into this Empire of Cotton States, and all poor men will at once become the free Negroes of the Empire." He concluded that East Tennesseans "can never live in a southern Confederacy and be made the hewers of wood and drawers of water for a set of aristocrats and overbearing tyrants." Adding weight to the conspiracy theory of the Unionists was the manner in which secession was accomplished in Tennessee. Loyalists charged Governor Harris and the legislature with despotism for taking the state from the Union and allying with the Confederacy without first waiting for public consent.

The perceived threat to republican liberty was not the only argument East Tennessee Unionists used to discourage voters from accepting the state's alliance with the Confederacy. Economic considerations also figured prominently in loyalist rhetoric. Unionists contended that the region had no reason to support Southern independence since only a portion of the state's population was linked to the plantation economy of the Lower South. Indeed, Brownlow's *Whig* declared, "We have no interest in common with the Cotton States. We are a grain growing and stock raising people."

With Unionist leaders crisscrossing the region invoking visions of a tyrannical slave-owning aristocracy, the presence of large numbers of Confederate troops in East Tennessee only added to the growing tension. East Tennessee Unionists viewed the Confederates as an occupation force and proof of Southern tyranny. Likewise, the Rebel soldiers viewed the region's Unionists as traitors to their state and the South. Confederate authorities attempted to avoid an altercation with loyalists prior to the referendum. However, restraining the soldiers proved difficult.

In May, for example, a potentially serious clash between Confederates and loyalists occurred at Strawberry Plains near Knoxville. Several thousand Unionists had gathered on a farm adjacent to the tracks of the East Tennessee and Virginia Railroad. During the rally, a train carrying Confederate soldiers en route to Virginia passed by the crowd. Enraged by the loyalist gathering, a soldier on the train threw a stone at the speaker. Other soldiers seated on the roofs of the passing cars began to fire above the heads of the crowd, creating pandemonium. The Unionists, many of whom were armed, fired back. Miraculously no one was injured or killed, but the incident only increased loyalist animosity toward the secessionist cause.

So great was this animosity that East Tennessee secessionists had a difficult time campaigning for the June vote. Local secessionists invited prominent speakers from throughout the South to their meetings in the hopes of painting a favorable impression of the Confederacy. Influential Tennessee Whigs such as Gustavus A. Henry and John Bell joined with former Mississippi Governor Henry S. Foote and arch-secessionist William Yancey of Alabama to promote the virtues of the new Confederacy and denounce

Lincoln as a tyrant. Despite the stature of these men, they could not counter the influence of East Tennessee Unionists such as Johnson, Nelson, and Maynard. While secessionists found significant support in the Southern counties of East Tennessee and in the towns and villages located along the East Tennessee and Virginia and East Tennessee and Georgia Railways, the rest of the region remained steadfastly loyal.

The East Tennessee Unionists were, however, aware that many in the rest of the state did not share their loyalty to the old Union. Consequently, in late May, a week before the election, loyalists convened in Knoxville to discuss their options in the event that the vote for separation went against them. While they reached no conclusion, the convention did pass several resolutions condemning secession as illegal and declaring Governor Harris and the legislature guilty of conspiracy and extralegal use of power. The body then adjourned, agreeing to reconvene after the election if necessary.

The results of the June referendum stunned Unionists, who did not initially grasp the full implications of the attack on Sumter and Lincoln's call for volunteers to put down the rebellion. Across the state, almost 70 percent of the voters approved the state's secession. Slaveholding Tennesseans of all sections voted overwhelmingly for secession, while non-slaveholders in both West and Middle Tennessee did the same. Overall the vote was strongly in favor of separation, with 108,511 for and 47,238 against. The vote was overwhelming in the plantation district of West Tennessee, with 29,127 votes for and only 6,117 against. Indeed, the Unionists won a majority in only four counties of the division's eighteen counties: Carroll, Decatur, Henderson, and Weakley. The story was much the same in Middle Tennessee, where the votes were 58,265 to 8,198. Again, Unionists managed to win only four counties: Fentress, Hardin, Macon, and Wayne. Only in East Tennessee did a majority reject secession. In fact, only six of the region's twenty-nine counties in East Tennessee voted for separation: Meigs, Monroe, Polk, Rhea, Sequatchie, and Sullivan. Overall, the vote was 32,923 against to 14,780 for. Although the region's Unionist vote had fallen from around 80 percent in February to 69 percent in June, it was nonetheless a forceful affirmation of loyalty; voters had repudiated secession by a better than two-to-one margin. The statewide vote, however, clearly carried Tennessee into the Confederacy.

Convinced by the republican rhetoric of their Unionist leaders that Confederate rule was tantamount to tyranny, the region's loyalists could not reconcile themselves to the election results. Loyalist leaders convened in Greeneville nine days after the June vote to choose a course of action. Following a contentious debate among Radicals such as Nelson and Brownlow, who advocated rebellion against the state, and Conservatives led by Temple, who suggested petitioning the state legislature for separate statehood, the convention decided to follow the conservative approach. The General Assembly politely listened to the convention's request but refused to act on it. East Tennessee would remain part of a state and of a nation that it had rejected.

While the state and Confederate authorities hoped that the loyalists of the eastern counties would support secession, this would not be the case. The region's Unionists would never willingly submit to Confederate authority. Indeed, so intense was the devotion of East Tennessee Unionists that more than thirty thousand would eventually join the ranks of the Federal army during the war.

This willingness to take up arms against fellow Tennesseans and Southerners clearly demonstrates the distinctiveness of East Tennessee. If the northwestern counties of

HARPER'S WEEKLY.

A JOURNAL OF CIVILIZATION.

VOL. VI.—No. 274.] NEW YORK, SATURDAY, MARCH 29, 1862. [SINGLE COPIES SIX CENTS. $2 50 PER YEAR IN ADVANCE.

A THRILLING SCENE IN EAST TENNESSEE—COLONEL FRY AND THE UNION MEN SWEARING BY THE FLAG.—[See Page [illegible]]

East Tennessee Unionists depicted swearing allegiance to the Union in 1861. From *Harpers Weekly,* and courtesy of the Calvin M. McClung Historical Collection.

Virginia can be discounted due to their proximity to the North, then East Tennessee was undoubtedly the Confederacy's great aberration. Several interrelated factors created the uniqueness of the region. First, as previously mentioned, East Tennessee's geography and remoteness had led to a distinctive economy. The area had little in common with the slave-based plantation economy that dominated most of the rest of the South since it was a land of small subsistence farms and few slaves. East Tennessee's distinctiveness also derived from its Whiggish political heritage, which persisted long after the Democratic Party took control of Southern politics. This Whig Party and its leadership would form the core of the region's Unionist dissenters. Finally, and most importantly, East Tennessee's rejection of the Confederacy can be linked to the Unionists' belief that such a government, dominated by large slaveholding aristocrats, threatened republican liberty—the cornerstone of the great American democratic experiment. For East Tennessee loyalists, protecting republicanism required rebelling against the tyranny of Governor Harris and Jefferson Davis. Ironically, the region's small Confederate population agreed that republicanism was under threat. However, they viewed Lincoln, not Harris and Davis, as the tyrant. Interpreting the president's call for volunteers to fight against the South as tantamount to military despotism, many East Tennesseans joined their fellow Southerners in abandoning the old Union in favor of a new Southern republic that would remain true to the principles of the founding fathers. East Tennessee, then, would soon be plunged into a savage internecine civil war of its own with violence and destruction that would devastate the region, leaving physical and psychological scars and bitter animosities long after the war ended.

Tennesseans Brace for War

While Governor Harris had successfully maneuvered Tennessee out of the Union, he now faced the daunting task of preparing his state for war. Manpower for the Provisional Army would not be a problem. Initially, thousands of eager volunteers swarmed county seats and awaited their equipment and drill. Before the end of May, Tennessee had mustered into service twenty-one regiments of infantry, ten companies of artillery, and one regiment of cavalry. Yet while troops were plentiful, weapons were not. Tennessee could not arm the new soldiers, and it would take months to obtain these weapons. During the summer and autumn of 1861, Harris and the army's chief of ordnance, Captain Moses H. Wright, scrambled to develop arsenals and provide the muskets and artillery the recruits needed. Shortages remained, however, well into 1862.

In addition to providing weapons for the army, Harris appointed commanders to each Grand Division and determined initial assignments. He assigned Major General Gideon J. Pillow to West Tennessee, where Pillow established headquarters in Memphis. Major General Samuel Anderson was assigned command of the Department of Middle Tennessee, with headquarters at Nashville, while Brigadier General William Caswell was given charge of East Tennessee, with his headquarters at Knoxville. Other generals took command of forces being organized at induction and training centers across Tennessee, such as Camp Cheatham, Camp Trousdale, and Union City.

Despite these placements, the Provisional Army was not stationed evenly throughout the Volunteer State. Kentucky, which had declared its neutrality initially, acted as a shield for the long Tennessee northern border. Therefore, the defense of West Tennessee along the Mississippi became the primary focus. To comply with this directive, the army began constructing a series of forts along the great river, including Forts Harris, Randolph, Pillow, and Wright. These "forts" were initially little more than entrenched artillery batteries, but they were now expanded and given priority in men and material. Harris stationed nearly half of the state's Provisional Army in West Tennessee to ensure the defense of the region.

Defending East Tennessee

This preoccupation with the defense of West Tennessee and the Mississippi resulted in a dangerous lack of preparation elsewhere in the state. For example, in late June, concern for the defense of East Tennessee against both internal and external threats prompted General Caswell to deploy elements of his only infantry regiment (the Nineteenth Tennessee) throughout the region to guard the railroad bridges against loyalist guerrilla raids and to seal off the major points of access into the region from Kentucky—Big Creek Gap, Cumberland Gap, and Jamestown, Tennessee. Clearly, more troops were needed; a single regiment could hardly be expected to cover the entire 120-mile Kentucky–Tennessee border within the East Tennessee Department. Caswell hoped that by patrolling the critical thoroughfares, the regiment could guard the Kentucky border against an invasion while preventing the smuggling of arms to loyalists. Governor Harris, however, anxious to placate East Tennessee's Unionists and calm their fears about military despotism, urged President Jefferson Davis to limit the number of Confederate troops in the region and to employ Tennessee regiments exclusively. Even though the region's Unionists

Felix K. Zollicoffer.
Library of Congress.

were already organizing and drilling militia companies and attempting to acquire firearms, Harris still hoped to convert them to the Confederate cause.

Part of the governor's conciliatory plan involved appointing Brigadier General Felix K. Zollicoffer as the new commander of the Department of East Tennessee following Caswell's resignation. Citing the general's extensive political background and significant influence among old Whigs, Harris successfully persuaded President Davis to appoint Zollicoffer to this command. Both Harris and Davis hoped that Zollicoffer's past association with many of the Whig leaders of the region would entice them into the Confederate fold and eliminate the threat of a Unionist rebellion. This hope, however, would not be realized.

When Zollicoffer arrived in Knoxville in late July, he attempted to placate the populace by tolerating their Unionist

Hanging of Fry and Hensie near the railroad, by Colonel Leadbetter. (Page 311.)

"Hensie" and "Fry," Union supporters hanged outside Knoxville, Tennessee, in December of 1861. From William "Parson" Brownlow, *Sketches of the Rise, Progress, and Decline of Secession,* 1862.

sentiments as long as they took no overt action against the Confederate government. Unfortunately, Zollicoffer proved to be a poor choice for such an important post. Despite his past political associations and cordial relationships with Knoxville loyalists, the Unionists in East Tennessee viewed his excessive leniency as weakness, and his lack of proper military training proved disastrous to the soldiers under his command.

In fairness to Zollicoffer, it must be noted that he lacked the resources to perform his duties adequately. The Confederate War Department had charged him with protecting the vital East Tennessee railways, suppressing Unionist guerrillas, and defending the Kentucky–Tennessee border—with only the Nineteenth Infantry Regiment and a few independent infantry and cavalry companies. New regiments would eventually arrive to bolster his strength, but all were poorly equipped and trained, and some still unarmed. Such a weak force could do little more than garrison the major towns and mountain passes, guard the railroad, and sporadically patrol the numerous coves of the region. It could not stop determined Unionist activity.

The state's congressional and gubernatorial elections in early August demonstrated that, despite the efforts of Governor Harris and General Zollicoffer, the East Tennessee loyalists desired to remain in the Union. Harris was reelected, but in the eastern counties he lost by a wide margin to his opponent William H. Polk. Moreover, the region's Unionists defiantly elected four representatives to the *United States* Congress. The election results embarrassed and incensed Harris and Zollicoffer, and both thereafter displayed a markedly less conciliatory attitude toward the region's Unionists. Throughout East Tennessee, Confederate troops began to break up loyalist organizations and arrest their leaders. Conciliation had failed.

Middle Tennessee's Defense

The appalling lack of adequate defensive measures in East Tennessee was equally apparent in Middle Tennessee. Amazingly, even Nashville, the state capital, was not properly prepared to withstand attack. Entrenchments and fortifications were largely nonexistent due to the reluctance of planters to release their slaves for such work even if compensated. Worse still, the control of the Tennessee and Cumberland Rivers was also being neglected. In May 1861, Governor Harris had assigned Brigadier General Daniel S. Donelson to construct fortifications on the two rivers, but progress had been slow. Since Kentucky was a neutral state, the forts had to be situated at the best locations available in Tennessee. With the aid of Colonel Bushrod Johnson of the Corps of Engineers, Donelson selected the sites where the two rivers were a mere twelve miles apart, believing both posts could support one another in case of attack. While the fort on the Cumberland would be located on the west bank of the river and be named for Donelson, the Tennessee fort would be located on the east bank of that river and named after Tennessee Senator Gustavus Adolphus Henry Sr. Fort Donelson was constructed on a bluff near the village of Dover, where a bend in the river north of the fort meant that gunners would have a good field of fire as any boats had to slow down to make the turn. Entrenchments and ravines surrounded a large open space that was more of an encampment than a fortification.

Donelson was in much better shape than Fort Henry. The Rebels designed Henry as a large ten-acre, five-sided earthen fort on the river's eastern bank. While Fort Donelson had been built on a bluff, Fort Henry had been built on low ground in a bend of the river. Although the location allowed the guns along the waterfront to fire directly down the river, the fort was placed on low, swampy ground and dominated by hills on the opposite bank. While the position did give cannoneers an unobstructed field of fire, it made the fort vulnerable to seasonal flooding. On the hills above the west bank of the river and across from Fort Henry, the Confederates had also begun work on another set of fortifications called Fort Heiman (in honor of Confederate Colonel Adolphus Heiman, a member of the Fort Henry garrison) that was in a much better position to control the river with artillery fire. However, it was largely unfinished. In short, the forts lacked adequate garrisons and enough labor to finish or enhance their defenses.

The Importance of Tennessee

Throughout his preparations for Tennessee's defense, Governor Harris cooperated with the Confederate government and its military. The Davis administration was well aware of the critical importance of Tennessee to the fledgling nation's survival. Indeed, noted historian Thomas Connelly called the area of Tennessee, north-central Alabama, north-central Georgia, and northeast Mississippi the Confederate "Heartland." For Connelly and later historians, this vast land of 150,000 square miles was not only the Southern republic's geographic heart but also "its logistical and communications heart as well." It was within this area that Connelly believed the Confederacy's war would be lost as Union forces subdued the region and denied the Rebels the resources they could ill afford to lose. The core of this Confederate "Heartland" was Tennessee, and it was vital to the Confederacy's ability to sustain itself in the war for several reasons.

Geographically, Tennessee formed the Confederacy's northern boundary west of the Appalachian Mountains to the Mississippi, which made it a central focus of the conflict for much of the war. Any invading Union army would have to cross Tennessee to enter the rest of the Heartland. Moreover, three major river systems, the Cumberland, Tennessee, and Mississippi, flowed along or through its borders. Control of these rivers would be critical since they offered easy routes for Union armies to penetrate the South. Also, some of the South's main east–west and north–south rail lines ran through Tennessee. The South's limited rail network could not function well without these routes. For example, the East Tennessee and Virginia and the East Tennessee and Georgia Railroads, a crucial link between Virginia and the West, ran the length of the East Tennessee

Valley from Bristol to Chattanooga, an important rail hub and the gateway to Georgia and the Deep South.

In terms of manufacturing, Tennessee was one of the most industrialized of the Confederate states. Indeed, many of the Confederacy's wartime industries, such as iron works, munitions factories, and gunpowder mills, were located in Tennessee. Along with Richmond and New Orleans, Nashville was one of the key Southern cities in the production of

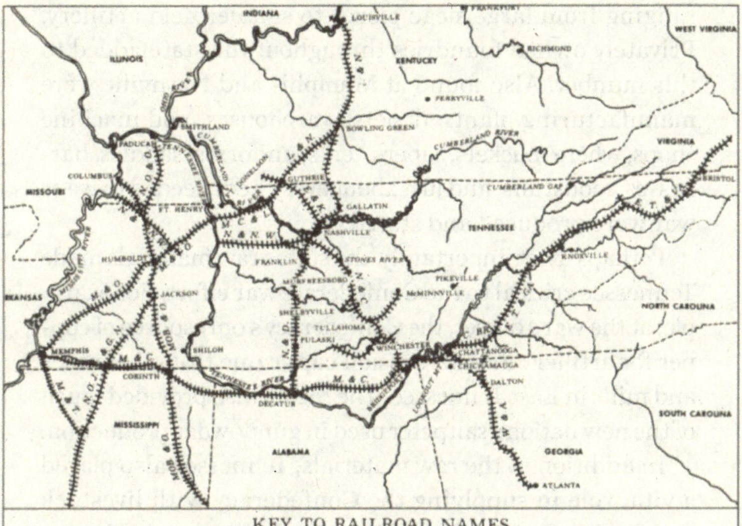

KEY TO RAILROAD NAMES

C. Br. Cleveland Branch, East Tennessee and Georgia
E.&K. Edgefield and Kentucky
E.T.&Ga. East Tennessee and Georgia
E.T.&Va. East Tennessee and Virginia
L.&N. Louisville and Nashville
M.&C. Memphis and Charleston
M.C.&L. Memphis, Clarksville, and Louisville
M.&O. Memphis and Ohio
M.&T. Mississippi and Tennessee
Mob. &O. Mobile and Ohio
N.&C. Nashville and Chattanooga
N.&N.W. Nashville and Northwestern
N.O.J.&G.N. New Orleans, Jackson, and Great Northern
N.O.&O. New Orleans and Ohio
N. & D. Nashville and Decatur
W.&A. Western and Atlantic

Tennessee's railroads in 1861. Tennessee Public Service Commission, Nashville.

artillery, firearms, clothing, and other military equipment. As a result, the Confederacy would depend on the Volunteer State to equip its armies. Additionally, at the war's outset, the Southern republic's largest and most important powder mills as well as numerous munitions factories were located at Nashville. Indeed, together Nashville and Memphis manufactured the cartridges, percussion caps, small arms, and cannon the Confederacy would need to win a modern war. The Ordnance Department's foundries in the two cities produced about two dozen cannon every month in 1861, ranging from large siege pieces to smaller field artillery. Privately owned foundries throughout the state added to this number. Also found at Memphis and Nashville were manufacturing plants, depots, warehouses, and machine shops, where muskets, sabers, tents, uniforms, saddles, harnesses, foodstuffs, and just about every item needed to wage war were produced and stored.

Perhaps most importantly, the state's raw materials made Tennessee critical to the Confederate war effort. For example, at the war's outset, the Confederacy's only source of copper for artillery and percussion caps came from the mines and mills in East Tennessee. The region also provided much of the new nation's saltpeter used in gunpowder production.

In addition to the raw materials, Tennessee also played a vital role in supplying the Confederacy with livestock and foodstuffs. Middle and East Tennessee provided corn, wheat, and vegetables to feed hungry civilians and soldiers alike, and Middle Tennessee farms were known for their cattle and hogs as well as their mules and horses.

The state's manpower from the Provisional Army of Tennessee would form the basis for one of the two largest and most important Confederate armies and ultimately shoulder the responsibility for the defense of the region. Indeed, by the end of the war, Tennessee had provided more than

140,000 soldiers for the Confederacy (more than any other state but North Carolina). In sum, the Confederacy could not hope to win its independence without Tennessee, and no part of the state could fall into Union hands without risking disaster.

The Western Theater: Confederate Perspective

The Confederacy took charge of Tennessee's defense in July 1861. The state was made part of the enormous Military Department No. 2, or the Western Department, stretching from the Appalachians to the Ozarks and covering the Confederate Heartland. Jefferson Davis initially chose his longtime friend Leonidas Polk to command it. A graduate of the United States Military Academy, Polk had quickly resigned his commission to pursue a career in the ministry and then served as the Episcopal bishop of Louisiana. Despite Polk's lack of military experience, Davis commissioned him a major general and gave him command of the Confederacy's largest and most strategically important department. Polk's assignment, however, was meant to be temporary because Davis wanted Albert Sidney Johnston for the position as soon as he arrived from the Pacific coast.

Johnston came with a sterling reputation. He had attended the US Military Academy two classes ahead of Davis, and the two became friends there. He then served eight years in the United States Army before resigning to join the forces in the Texas Revolution. He eventually rose to commanding general of the Republic of Texas's forces and also served as the fledgling nation's secretary of war. Eventually he came back to the US Army when Texas joined the Union in 1845, and in the late antebellum years, he served in the prestigious post as full colonel commanding one of the country's cavalry regiments. Tall, well built,

Confederate soldier Henry Howe Cook, D Company, Tennessee 1st Infantry. Tennessee State Library and Archives.

and handsome, the fifty-eight-year-old Johnston looked the part of a general. Many, including Davis, considered him to be the best general in the old army. Indeed, Davis had him commissioned as the senior field commander of the Confederacy. But Johnston had yet to arrive, and Polk for now commanded the department.

Polk grew concerned that Federal forces would violate Kentucky's declared neutrality and move into the state. Several Union regiments under Brigadier General Ulysses S. Grant were posted just across the Ohio River at Cairo, Illinois. Fearing that these regiments were about to seize the strategic heights above the Mississippi River at Columbus, Kentucky, Polk decided to act. In early September, without consulting the Confederate War Department or the Con-

Albert Sidney Johnston. Library of Congress.

federate president, Polk occupied Columbus. The Federals quickly responded, occupying Paducah and Southland at the mouths of the Tennessee and Cumberland Rivers. Polk's move to occupy Columbus led Kentucky's Unionist-dominated legislature to denounce the Confederate invasion and demand that the Rebels leave. They then invited the US forces to help drive the Rebels from the state. Polk's decision was ill-advised and ill fated. The Confederate invasion had provoked the Kentucky legislature into essentially ending neutrality as Federal troops quickly followed Confederate troops into the state. The result was that Tennessee's long northern border was now exposed to attack. Given that Governor Harris had focused primarily on West Tennessee and not adequately prepared to defend the entire state, this was a disaster. On top of this, less than a week after Polk's advance, Zollicoffer moved troops into Kentucky at Cumberland Gap.

Johnston arrived in West Tennessee just after Polk had placed him and his department in this perilous predicament. Much was expected of Johnston, but he was unprepared for what awaited him. When he took command on September 15, his subordinates were already in Kentucky, and President Davis supported the move. Johnston did not have the resources of men or material to adequately defend an area the size of the Western Department. Moreover, he was indecisive and lacked the leadership skills to cope with the situation he now faced. Clearly, Davis misjudged Johnston's abilities. He was, indeed, a poor choice for a commander.

Johnston had to react quickly to the shifting dynamics of the Western Department. He moved the center of his defensive line and his de facto headquarters some seventy miles north from Nashville to Bowling Green, Kentucky, on the Louisville and Nashville Railroad. This gave Johnston rail contact with both Memphis and Nashville. Hoping to placate the Kentuckians, Johnston secured a brigadier general commission for Simon Bolivar Buckner, the former commander of the Kentucky State Guard, and placed him briefly in command at Bowling Green. Buckner would eventually relinquish command when Major General William J. Hardee arrived with reinforcements.

Western Theater: Union Perspective

Meanwhile, Union forces were also adjusting to the end of Kentucky's neutrality. Following the Union defeat at the Battle of First Manassas, a reshuffling of the Union high command had occurred. Major General George B. McClellan replaced Winfield Scott as general in chief of all armies in November 1861. The thirty-four-year-old McClellan was bright, ambitious, and arrogant. He had schemed for Scott's position, and now he had it. Supremely confident, McClellan would not only serve as general in chief but would also take field command of the Army of the Potomac, the largest Union army in the Eastern Theater.

While McClellan planned to control events in the East, he reorganized the areas west of the Appalachians. Instead of imitating the Confederate model of one giant department, he organized two major ones. The Department of Missouri, including much of the Midwest and stretching east into Kentucky west of the Cumberland River, was now administered by Major General Henry Wager Halleck. Unlike Johnston, Halleck was not an imposing person. He was instead an overweight, balding, and somewhat odd-looking forty-six-year-old who unnerved people when he spoke because he stared at them without blinking. Still, he had been a brilliant student at West Point and before the war had written a number of books on military topics, law, and engineering. His nickname in the army had been "Old Brains." He had also been a professor at West Point and had turned down a full professorship at Harvard. He resigned from the army in the mid-1850s, went into business, and amassed a fortune. Despite his oddities, Halleck had a brilliant mind and was an able administrator. Within a few months of taking command, he brought order to his department, which included around ninety thousand soldiers and naval units. The other major commander McClellan appointed in the West was his close, personal friend, Brigadier General Don Carlos Buell. Buell now oversaw the newly created Department of the Ohio, composed of Ohio, Michigan, Indiana, and Kentucky east of the Cumberland, with headquarters in Louisville, Kentucky. Buell was also a

West Point graduate who had fought in the Seminole War and the Mexican–American War. Introverted, methodical, and stubborn, Buell, though not as brilliant as Halleck, was a competent and thoroughly professional soldier.

Both of these generals were talented, but it would take time to prepare their raw troops for combat, decide on a strategy, and overcome their rivalry. Lincoln was hesitant to give them this time. He was anxious to nip the rebellion in the bud, and he wanted his generals to move—and move quickly. He pushed Halleck, but Halleck parried each request to move. Halleck needed time to formulate his own plan. First, he needed to pacify Missouri and bring it under complete Federal control. Second, he wanted to move into Confederate territory either along the Mississippi or along one of the other rivers. Meanwhile, Buell's objective was to prepare his Army of the Ohio to eventually move down the Louisville and Nashville Railroad and strike the Rebels at Bowling Green. Then they would seize Nashville, all the while using the railroad as their supply line. However, Buell was under considerable pressure from Lincoln to advance into East Tennessee and liberate its Unionist population. Buell felt such a move was impractical given the rugged landscape, the lack of transportation, and the threat of Confederate raids to his tenuous supply line. Thus, with plenty of men and equipment, the most serious problems facing the Union in the West would be a divided command structure, generals reluctant to move, and confusion as to where to strike.

Lincoln Demands an Advance

Lincoln grew increasingly frustrated with his generals as 1861 drew to a close, and as the new year dawned, he had had enough. On January 27, 1862, he issued "General Order No. 1" directing the forward movement of all Union armies by George Washington's Birthday on February 22. However, his efforts were again frustrated by McClellan's lack of action and the increasing rivalry between Halleck and Buell, which made it impossible for them to cooperate. The president had wired both Halleck and Buell urging them to coordinate an advance into Tennessee. Yet both generals stated that they were not prepared to act in coordination and that they were waiting on McClellan's orders. McClellan meanwhile had begun to develop an idea for an advance against the Confederate defensive line in the West. On January 3, he wired Halleck encouraging him to prevent any Confederate forces from shifting to Buell's front. McClellan suggested this could be accomplished with an expedition up the Cumberland River in coordination with Buell. If a demonstration were also made against Columbus, then Confederate forces might not be able to move to add their forces at Henry and Donelson.

This touched off a series of telegrams among Lincoln, McClellan, Halleck, and Buell regarding the possibility of a movement on the Cumberland and Tennessee Rivers. While Halleck and Buell could see the need for an expedition up the rivers, neither man wanted to move first, and neither wanted to take enemy pressure off the other so that their rival could succeed. Both eventually wanted to capture Nashville. Buell also had pressure from Lincoln to move into East Tennessee. Both Halleck and Buell wanted to fight a war with minimum risk to their forces and their reputations. They decided that with thorough preparation and slow and cautious movement, avoiding actual fighting as much as possible, the administration's goals could be achieved.

Meanwhile, Federal reconnaissance revealed that Fort Henry and Fort Heiman (still under construction across the river) were poorly garrisoned and vulnerable to attack. Indeed, since the end of Kentucky's neutrality, the Confederates had made minimal effort to supply or garrison Forts Henry and Donelson. The commander of both posts, Brigadier General Lloyd Tilghman, was aware of the weaknesses and dutifully reported them to Johnston. The Union now had a great opportunity. More telegrams among the Western Department commanders and Washington followed. Halleck was gradually becoming persuaded that Fort Henry was a good target. Aside from the obvious military benefits that could be derived from a campaign up the rivers into Tennessee, outside forces were also at work that helped convince Halleck to finally make a move. A telegram he received from Washington informed him that Confederate General Pierre Gustave Toutant (P. G. T.) Beauregard was heading west to join Johnston with fifteen regiments. The report was partially true; Beauregard would arrive shortly, but he would not be coming with reinforcements. If Halleck were going to act, it would be best to do it before these reinforcements arrived. Before this move could be made, however, events in eastern Kentucky would launch the first blow on Johnston's western line.

Zollicoffer's Campaign in Eastern Kentucky

Since early September 1861, Confederate General Felix Zollicoffer had been engaged in a campaign in the mountains of eastern Kentucky. He had initially gained control of Cumberland Gap before advancing into the Bluegrass State and establishing Camp Buckner on Cumberland Ford (modern-day Pineville, Kentucky). He soon found that the inhabitants of eastern Kentucky were as hostile to the Confederacy as those of East Tennessee, and he feared that home guard units would contest his presence in the state.

On September 18, he ordered a force of some eight hundred men to Barbourville, Kentucky, to destroy Camp Andrew Johnson, a training facility for East Tennessee and Kentucky Unionist militia. Arriving at dawn, the Confederates surprised some three hundred "bushwhackers" (guerrillas), and after a brief exchange of gunfire, the Unionists fled, leaving the Rebels in possession of the camp and its meager supplies.

Still fearful of home guard activity and a Union army offensive, Zollicoffer sent out a constant stream of cavalry patrols and raids against Unionists. Johnston wanted Zollicoffer to avoid further advances into Kentucky, but Zollicoffer let his aggressive nature get the better of him. Disregarding orders, he planned another strike against Union forces. On October 16, he marched his entire available force from Camp Buckner ten miles north to Flat Lick. That night while in camp, he decided to proceed northward along the Wilderness Road the next day and attack Camp Wildcat. Yet his command was in no condition for a fight: supply shortages and sickness had taken a toll on the men, and Zollicoffer's advancing column numbered only about four thousand soldiers.

Nonetheless, Zollicoffer eagerly pressed ahead, force-marching his men along the Wilderness Road. The Rebels reached the ford of the Rockcastle River on October 20, having covered some eighty miles in three days. This was remarkable considering that as they advanced, Zollicoffer's green troops had endured Federal patrols sniping at them and slowing their progress. As the Rebels approached Camp Wildcat, the harassment increased, and heavy skirmishing ensued. Zollicoffer's men pushed the Federal scouts back and discovered felled trees designed to block their advance. After his troops cleared these obstacles, Zollicoffer reconnoitered the Federal position. He discovered that Camp

Wildcat was a fortified hillock at the head of a gorge about a quarter of a mile wide. The position was formidable, with dense forests, rough, broken terrain, and extensive entrenchments. The general, however, was determined to "feel" the Federal position.

The terrain prevented the Confederate assault force from engaging en masse, which led to piecemeal attacks that were easily beaten back by the Federals. After probing the defenses for some three hours, Zollicoffer realized that the position could be taken only with heavy casualties if at all, and he finally abandoned the assault. During the night, Zollicoffer's men, their campfires still burning, left to begin the long retreat to Camp Buckner in the darkness.

The news of the Confederate repulse at Camp Wildcat thrilled East Tennessee's Unionists, who now eagerly anticipated the "liberation" of their region by advancing Federal forces. In fact, East Tennessee's loyalist leadership had been in secret discussions with authorities in Washington about precisely such a move. Plans were underway for a Unionist revolt to coincide with a Federal invasion.

Although unaware of the planned insurrection, Zollicoffer was indeed worried about a potential invasion. By late October, the general received reports that a strong Union force under Brigadier General George Thomas planned to enter East Tennessee somewhere between Cumberland Gap and Bowling Green. In response to this new threat, Zollicoffer began to shift his forces rapidly to Cumberland Gap and to improve the fortifications there. Leaving a large garrison at the Gap, Zollicoffer moved the rest of his command southward into Tennessee. He marched his exhausted men across the Cumberland Plateau, fortifying the mountain passes and deploying small detachments along the way. He gradually became convinced that the turnpike between Albany, Kentucky, and Jamestown, Tennessee, would be

Thomas's invasion route. Endeavoring to beat the Federals to the area, he force-marched most of his command to Jamestown.

The East Tennessee Revolt

News of the impending invasion panicked East Tennessee's Confederates. Many of the region's leading secessionists, predicting the capture or destruction of the railroads, begged Richmond for reinforcements. They had cause to be worried. Early the previous July, William B. Carter, an ardent East Tennessee Unionist, traveled to Washington and held numerous talks with George McClellan and Andrew Johnson. The talks resulted in a daring plan to liberate East Tennessee from Confederate control. In conjunction with an advance by troops under General Thomas from eastern Kentucky into East Tennessee, Unionists would burn nine important bridges between Bridgeport, Alabama, and Bluff City, Virginia, on the night of November 8. Thomas would move on Knoxville, and the region's many Unionists would rise up. The Unionists struck as planned on November 8 and burned the bridges over the Holston River, Lick Creek, Hiawassee River, and two over Chickamauga Creek. The other bridges were too well guarded. However, the effort was for naught; the Federal army did not advance from Kentucky. Instead, the Federals had been preoccupied with Zollicoffer's advance and repulse at Camp Wildcat. Federal forces would follow Zollicoffer's retreat as far as London, Kentucky, but they would advance no farther. There would be no Federal army to help the insurrection.

The Confederate authorities took swift action. A livid Zollicoffer declared that "the leniency shown them [Unionists] has been unavailing." There would be no more mercy given. Two of the bridge burners were hanged, and the region's Unionists suffered a slew of arbitrary arrests. Moreover, many prominent Unionists or their families, such as Mrs. Andrew Johnson, Mrs. William Brownlow, Mrs. Horace Maynard, and Mrs. W. B. Carter, were forced to leave their homes and journey to Union-controlled areas.

Meanwhile, Zollicoffer was more concerned with stopping a Federal advance into East Tennessee. Therefore, he left Colonel William B. Wood, post commander of Knoxville, and Brigadier General William Carroll to handle the situation in East Tennessee. Zollicoffer moved cavalry, artillery, and several regiments of infantry into Kentucky. With the weather deteriorating rapidly, Rebel engineers searched for a suitable location for winter quarters. The site they chose was Mill Springs, a small village on the south bank of the Cumberland River.

Reacting to Zollicoffer's advance, Buell sent a brigade under Brigadier General Albin Francis Schoepf to Somerset, ten miles from Mill Springs, to prevent Zollicoffer from crossing the Cumberland and advancing into central Kentucky. After the two forces skirmished, Zollicoffer made an ill-advised decision to cross the river and occupy the north bank at Beech Grove. With a river prone to flash floods at his back and an enemy to his front, Zollicoffer had endangered his small brigade. Upon crossing most of his men to Beech Grove, he set about fortifying his position.

Frustrated with Zollicoffer, the Davis administration decided to replace the amateur general as commander of the Department of East Tennessee with Major General George Crittenden in mid-December. Once Crittenden discovered that Zollicoffer had placed his army in a vulnerable position on the north bank of the Cumberland, he immediately ordered him to withdraw across the river to Mill Springs. Zollicoffer, however, inexplicably continued to hold his position throughout December.

Battle of Mill Springs

When an exasperated Crittenden arrived at Mill Springs in early January to assume command, the situation was dire. The Cumberland River had reached flood stage due to torrential rains, which made a retreat difficult and increased the danger that the brigade would be trapped if the Union forces attacked—a decision that the Federals had already made. Federal forces under General Thomas left Lebanon, Kentucky, on January 1 and headed for Somerset. Luckily for the Confederates, the same rain hampering them also hampered the Union advance. Thomas reached the settlement of Logan's Crossroads (now Nancy, Kentucky), ten miles north of Beech Grove, on January 17, where he paused to await the arrival of General Schoepf's brigade.

Always prudent, Thomas wanted to unite his forces before engaging the enemy. Although a native Virginian, he had made the hard decision to remain loyal to the old Union. This decision destroyed many of the relationships within his family. He had enjoyed a distinguished antebellum military career following his graduation from the US Military Academy in 1840. Thomas looked the part of a general, with a solid frame, imposing height, and piercing blue eyes. His calm, stern demeanor gave him an air of confidence. Thomas's tactical ability would mark him as arguably the finest Union general to serve the Western Theater—as Crittenden and Zollicoffer were soon to discover.

Meanwhile, Crittenden prepared to move Zollicoffer's brigade to the south bank. However, on January 15, Carroll arrived from Knoxville with another brigade, and Crittenden had a change of heart. This brigade raised Rebel strength to that of a small division, and this increase in numbers convinced Crittenden to engage Thomas. He, therefore, consolidated his men on the north side of the

Cumberland at Beech Grove and prepared to attack Thomas before Schoepf could join him.

As a cold rain fell on the night of January 19, the Rebels moved out for the Federal camp. About 11:30 p.m., with two cavalry companies forming a vanguard, Zollicoffer's brigade filed out of the Beech Grove entrenchments, with Carroll's brigade following. The shivering, thinly clad Rebels trudged along the Mill Springs Road for the next six hours, braving an icy rain and muck a foot deep in places. The artillery caissons frequently became mired, and every step for the infantrymen became a struggle.

Crittenden's battle plan called for a full assault at dawn to surprise the sleeping Federals, but the rain and abysmal roads slowed the Confederate advance to a crawl. As daylight broke, most of the Rebels were still toiling along in a column strung out for nearly three miles. Crittenden would have no time to close up his force and position it for attack, however. Sometime around 6:00 a.m., gunfire shattered the morning stillness: Zollicoffer's cavalry had encountered the enemy's pickets. Crittenden had now lost the element of surprise and would have to commit his regiments piecemeal.

Zollicoffer deployed his lead regiments to drive back the Federal pickets while Carroll's brigade double-timed up the muddy road to join the battle. The opposing forces engaged in a running skirmish for about a quarter of a mile as the pickets slowly gave ground. The Federals attempted to hold at a log house on the west side of the road at the base of a ridge. Rebel numbers, however, forced them out of the house and up the ridge. Zollicoffer halted at the foot of the hill to organize his brigade into a line of battle. Once his men were positioned, he advanced his brigade, driving the Federals slowly backward.

The Confederate assault soon stalled, however. The heavily wooded and broken terrain disrupted Rebel command

and control. Moreover, the unrelenting rain continued to fall, while claps of thunder and streaks of lightning added to the chaos of battle. The dark overcast along with the smoke of battle, and a thin mist filtering through the tall trees and thick undergrowth of dogwood and blackjack, created a murky, surreal atmosphere. In the eerie gloom and haze, the nearsighted Zollicoffer became convinced that his men were firing on one another and rode forward into the Federal line. He did not realize his mistake until one of his aides began firing his revolver at the enemy. Before the general could turn his horse and escape, a fusillade blasted him from the saddle, leaving his lifeless body in the mud. The fire of the enemy, coupled with the shock of Zollicoffer's death, panicked the Rebels, and they began to fall back.

One of Zollicoffer's regimental commanders, Colonel David H. Cummings of the Nineteenth Tennessee, assumed command of Zollicoffer's brigade and tried to hold the line. Attempting to stabilize the situation, Crittenden ordered Carroll to come to Cummings's aid, and together elements of both Confederate brigades exchanged fire with the Federals. Crittenden also deployed some artillery, but the terrain rendered cannon fire ineffective. Increasingly heavy Union fire and an advance on the Confederate left began to weaken Rebel resolve. Sensing an opportunity, Thomas ordered a charge at 9:00 a.m. The Rebels broke and fled in confusion. As the Rebel left crumbled, a simultaneous flanking attack on the right forced back the Confederates, and panic ensued. Tired, frightened Rebels ran from the field in the face of a renewed Federal advance all along the front.

Confederate cavalry screened the routed troops, but fortunately for them, General Thomas did not launch an immediate, all-out pursuit. Around 3:00 p.m., the weary and demoralized Confederates trudged into the Beech Grove defenses soaked to the skin. Federal artillery arrived within an hour and began an exchange of fire with Confederate batteries that lasted well into the night. As darkness descended, a small stern-wheel steamboat, the *Noble Ellis*, with two flatboats lashed to its sides, ferried the disheartened little army across the river throughout the long night.

At dawn, Crittenden had the *Noble Ellis* burned and initiated the long retreat southward along the Cumberland River to Gainesboro, Tennessee, where his army could be supplied. The Rebels had little to eat during the retreat because Crittenden had had to abandon most of his commissary stores and camp equipment, along with almost all of his artillery, many small arms and much ammunition, more than one hundred wagons, and around one thousand horses and mules. The shattered force began the dismal eighty-mile trek toward Gainesboro. The extreme right flank of Johnston's western defensive line had been broken, yet he faced a much more pressing crisis.

As Crittenden's men were being driven from the field at Mill Springs, a serious situation had developed elsewhere along Johnston's defensive line. Since January, McClellan, Halleck, and Buell had been contemplating a strike on the forts guarding the Tennessee and Cumberland Rivers. Halleck had chosen Fort Henry as the logical point for the attack. He was approached by one of his subordinates, General Ulysses S. Grant, for an opportunity to lead an assault on the fort. Grant was joined by Flag Officer (senior captain) Andrew H. Foote commanding the Western Gunboat Flotilla.

Grant welcomed the opportunity for action. Although a graduate of the US Military Academy and a Mexican War veteran, little in his military career had demonstrated any great ability. Indeed, he had resigned his commission in

1854 because of homesickness and rumored alcohol abuse. Between that time and the coming of the war, Grant had supported himself and his family through aid given by his father and father-in-law. The war offered him the chance to redeem himself and achieve the success that had thus far eluded him.

While Halleck, Buell, and McClellan had all discussed a strike at Fort Henry, Grant's and Foote's urging, combined with reports of General Beauregard's movement from Virginia with thousands of reinforcements, finally convinced Halleck to allow the river campaign to proceed. On January 30, Halleck telegraphed Grant, "Make your preparations to take and hold Fort Henry. I will send you written instructions by mail." That same day, Halleck wired McClellan acknowledging the information about Beauregard and stating that he was ordering Grant and Foote to seize Henry and cut the railroad between Columbus and Bowling Green.

On January 31, Grant received Halleck's full message of instructions for the campaign. He was to gather all the troops he could from the various garrisons under his command, leaving sufficient force behind to guard the garrisons against enemy raids. The roads were almost impassable, so the troops and supplies would travel by steamers, escorted by Foote's gunboats. The objective: "Fort Henry should be taken and held at all hazards." Halleck wanted the road to Donelson, and the nearby village of Dover, cut so that reinforcements could not reach Fort Henry. Cavalry would then be sent to destroy the railroad. Halleck also informed Grant of Beauregard's approach, stating that "it is therefore of the greatest importance that we cut that line before he arrives. You will move with the least delay possible."

Halleck informed Buell of the expedition on January 31. Buell responded with an offer of assistance—an offer that

Halleck declined since he only planned to seize and occupy Fort Henry and Fort Donelson and cut the railroad from Columbus to Bowling Green. It appears that Halleck hoped that by concentrating a large force at Henry and Donelson, the Rebels would be forced to withdraw from either Bowling Green or Columbus to protect the railroads. If it were the former, Halleck hoped Buell would advance to Nashville; if the latter, Halleck planned to move on Columbus. Halleck was clearly looking to shatter the entire Rebel defensive line in the West. If successful, such a move would not only bring large portions of Kentucky and Tennessee under Union control; it might also win Halleck recognition and overall command in the West. It had been far too long in coming, but a Federal advance against Johnston's defensive line was finally happening. After months of Lincoln cajoling and threatening his generals to take action and months of those generals arguing among themselves as their tempers, their egos, and their fears overwhelmed them, there was finally movement toward the heart of the Rebel defenses.

THREE

1862 Tennessee

The Struggle for the Rivers

★ ★ ★

Battle of Fort Henry

On February 5, Ulysses S. Grant landed the first of his seventeen thousand troops a short distance down river from Fort Henry on the eastern shore of the Tennessee River. Grant's transports were escorted by the Western Gunboat Flotilla, a riverine force commanded by Commodore (senior captain) Andrew H. Foote. The gunboats of the flotilla included the ironclads *Cincinnati*, *Carondelet*, *Essex*, and *St. Louis*, as well as the wooden gunboats *Conestoga*, *Lexington*, and *Tyler*. Foote was confident that his imposing fleet could handle anything the Confederates could offer, even the torpedoes (mines) found bobbing in the muddy waters of the Tennessee. The recent hard rains had increased the force and speed of the river, and this, along with the poor construction of the devices, allowed Foote's sailors to easily dispose of the mines and proceed. Accompanied by Grant, Foote took the ironclads up the river to inspect Fort Henry

Ulysses S. Grant. Library of Congress.

Andrew Foote. Library of Congress.

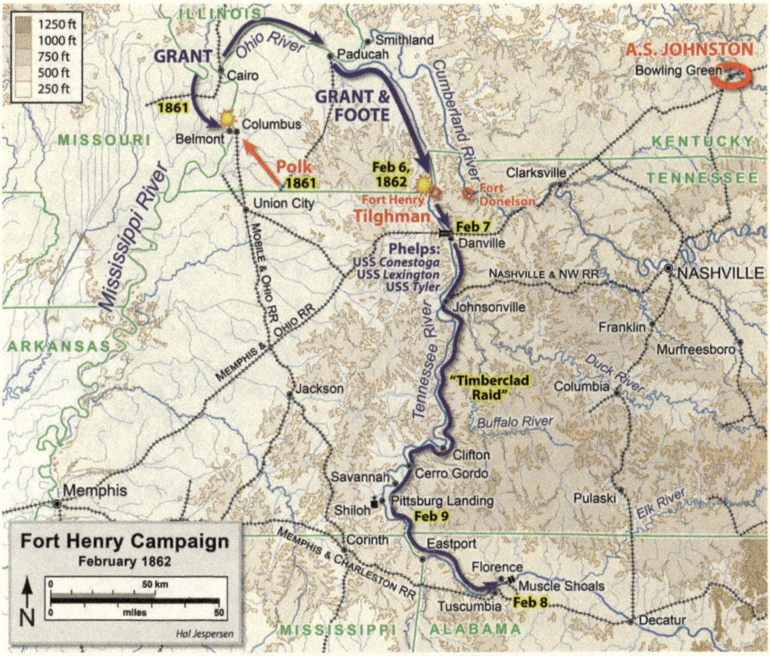

Map by Hal Jespersen, www.cwmaps.com.

closely and to test the range of the fort's guns with an exchange of cannon fire.

Grant's battle plan was simple but sound. He would land most of his two divisions, commanded by Brigadier Generals John A. McClernand and Charles F. Smith, on the eastern shore to secure the landward approaches to Henry. However, two brigades of Smith's division would storm Fort Heiman on the opposite shore. From there, they could rain shells down upon Henry while Foote's gunboats engaged the fort as well. Surrounded and under attack, the Rebels would have no choice but to surrender. The rapidly rising river that threatened to inundate the fort would add to the

Bombardment of Fort Henry. Tennessee State Library and Archives.

Confederate worries, but those same heavy rains had also turned the trails into quagmires, and it was going to be slow going for Grant's men. In fact, Foote reckoned that he could pound the fort into submission long before Grant's men could get into position.

The Confederates knew Federal troops and gunboats had arrived, and they were ill-prepared to engage them. Not only were they outgunned by the flotilla, but the river was also now spilling into the fort. This deluge left only nine of the fort's seventeen gun emplacements tenable and threatened to inundate the powder magazine. Realizing that the situation was hopeless, the fort's commander, General Tilghman, abandoned Fort Heiman and sent most of

Capture of Fort Henry by US gunboats under the command of Flag Officer Andrew Foote. Library of Congress.

his 2,500-man garrison at Henry on the twelve-mile march to nearby Fort Donelson on the Cumberland River. He remained behind with one artillery company at Fort Henry to fight a delaying action against the Federal troops and gunboats.

The next day, February 6, at around 12:30 p.m., the Federal ironclads approached the fort four abreast with the wooden gunboats following closely behind. At about 1,700 yards from the fort, the flotilla opened fire and continued firing as they steamed to within 600 yards. For nearly two hours, the Rebel cannoneers and Foote's fleet pounded one another. The depleted Rebel force scored numerous hits on the Federal flotilla and inflicted some damage, but most shots simply bounced off the plates of the ironclads. One vessel, the *Essex*, did sustain serious damage when a thirty-two-pound shot tore through the armor and into the boilers, killing or wounding thirty-two men, including the gunboat's captain, William D. Porter. The crippled gunboat then drifted powerless downriver. With half his men dead or wounded, with only one cannon capable of firing, and with the powder magazine underwater, Tilghman finally lowered the Confederate flag and surrendered the fort around 2:00 p.m. Foote sent a small boat through the sally port and into the badly flooded fort to bring Tilghman aboard the *Cincinnati* for the formal surrender, all while Grant's men continued to slog through mud trying to surround the fort. When Grant's troops finally arrived around 3:00 p.m., Foote's flotilla and the flood waters of the Tennessee had already forced a capitulation. Indeed, the flooding of Fort Henry was so severe that one Federal naval officer declared that "if the attack had been delayed forty-eight hours, there would hardly have been a hostile shot fired; the Tennessee would have accomplished the work by drowning the magazine."

Following the capture of Fort Henry, Foote was anxious to exploit the situation and immediately sent three wooden gunboats under the command of Lieutenant Commander S. L. Phelps on a reconnaissance in force up the Tennessee River. Per General Halleck's orders, they damaged the railroad bridge of the Memphis and Ohio and tore up a portion of track. Proceeding another 150 miles further upriver, they captured several vessels (including a half-finished Rebel gunboat), forced the Confederates to burn another half dozen steamboats to avoid their capture, and shelled the Confederate camp near Savannah, Tennessee, before returning downriver.

Battle of Fort Donelson

Grant messaged Halleck on February 6, declaring, "Fort Henry is ours; I shall take and destroy Fort Donelson on the 8th." As would often prove the case, Grant was overly optimistic. The rainy weather delayed needed supplies and slowed his troop's advance overland. Furthermore, Foote's wooden gunboats were just beginning to launch their raid up the Tennessee, and while the Federal flotilla had bested Henry's cannoneers, the *Essex* had been put out of action and several other ironclads had sustained superficial damage and would need repairs at Cairo and St. Louis. Moreover, while Donelson was a mere twelve-mile march

Henry W. Halleck. Library of Congress.

P. G. T. Beauregard. Library of Congress.

overland for Grant's men, Foote's scattered fleet would have to steam down the Tennessee, up the Ohio, and then up the Cumberland to Fort Donelson. The move on the next Confederate river bastion would take time.

And time was exactly what the Confederates needed. The news of Fort Henry's fall and the attack on the Memphis and Ohio Railroad stunned Johnston. On February 7, he called a council of war at the Covington Hotel in Bowling Green. Grant's small army (eventually called the Army of the Tennessee) was now between Johnston's two main forces at Bowling Green and Columbus. The Rebel high command feared that the Federals might attack Columbus or perhaps move against the small garrison (five thousand men) at Fort Donelson. There was even concern that

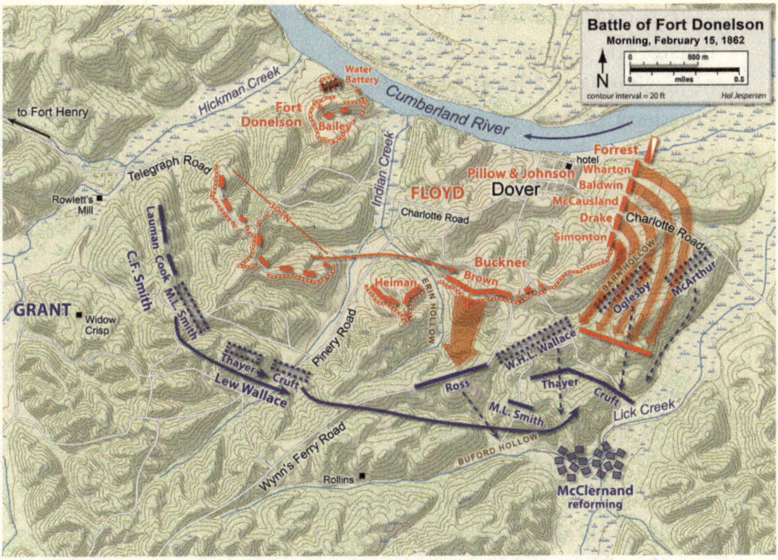

Map by Hal Jespersen, www.cwmaps.com.

Grant might advance northward toward Bowling Green while Buell's nearly fifty thousand men of the Army of the Ohio would move south from Louisville. If this happened, Johnston's twenty-five thousand troops at Bowling Green would be pinned between them.

The meeting and the mood were somber. The only hint of aggression came from General Beauregard, who had just arrived from Virginia. He advocated seizing the initiative and striking at Grant while he was isolated. Johnston, however, rejected the idea and instead focused his efforts on holding Nashville. He decided to abandon Bowling Green and divide his army. Hardee would take approximately thirteen thousand men to Nashville and prepare the city for imminent attack. Brigadier General John B. Floyd would take the other twelve thousand or so to Fort Donelson to bolster the garrison against Grant's expected attack. Floyd's objective would be to slow the Federal advance and buy Hardee time to prepare Nashville's defenses before he retreated and reunited the army at the Tennessee capital. Johnston had originally wanted Beauregard to take command of the forces at Donelson, but the Creole demurred because of a persistent throat ailment. Johnston's decision to assign General Floyd command at Donelson ranks as one of his worst decisions as an army commander. Floyd owed his rank to his political connections and not to military experience or knowledge. He had held various prestigious offices, including governor of Virginia and secretary of war in President James Buchanan's cabinet. During the secession crisis, many Northerners singled him out as a traitor for allegedly shipping weapons south in preparation for the conflict. One would have to look hard to find an officer with worse qualifications for such an important assignment.

As the Rebels prepared for the defense of Nashville, Halleck pleaded with McClellan for reinforcements and continued to send all available troops to Grant. On February 11, Grant finally issued orders for his troops to begin their movement toward Donelson the next day along two roads leading to the fort. As Grant's army marched toward Fort Donelson on the morning of February 12, they ran into Confederate cavalry under Colonel Nathan Bedford Forrest. Forrest, a West Tennessee planter and slave trader, was another Confederate commander without prior military experience. A wealthy, self-made man, Forrest had enlisted as a private in June 1861 and rose to lieutenant colonel of a cavalry battalion he raised and equipped at his own expense. Despite his lack of military training, he possessed a native military intelligence and determination that eventually propelled him to high command and made him one of the greatest cavalry commanders of the war. As the Federals skirmished with the Rebel horsemen, they began to discard their overcoats and blankets in the unseasonably warm weather—a move that would come back to haunt them later.

Grant's plan of attack for Donelson was essentially the same as for Henry. While the Federal infantry covered the Confederate outer works to prevent troops from getting in or out, land artillery and Foote's gunboats would pound the fort into submission. However, Donelson was a much stronger position and was well garrisoned. Its river batteries were located on a high hill overlooking a bend in the river. As vessels slowed to take the curve in the river, they would be exposed to plunging fire from the fort. Moreover, the land approaches to the fort were well protected. On the far northern side lay a swampy area that was impassable. This meant the only points open to attack were the west and south. However, the terrain there was a maze of steep ravines and copses of trees that opened onto a large, cleared killing zone that the Rebels had fortified with abatis (a barricade of felled trees with sharpened branches). Any attacker would have to cover the open ground quickly while enduring heavy fire from the rifle pits and batteries of the Rebels.

While the garrison and the fortifications at Donelson were strong, the Achilles' heel of the post would prove to be the leadership. Floyd was undeniably an abominable commander, and his second-in-command, Brigadier General Gideon J. Pillow, was equally inept. Pillow had fought in the Mexican War, but his current position was largely due to his political connections and not his ability as a military leader. The only competent general officer at Donelson was General Simon Bolivar Buckner, who had served briefly as commander at Bowling Green.

The Rebels were strengthening the earthworks when Grant's army appeared on a rainy February 13. Three probing attacks occurred that day as Grant waited for Foote's fleet and the rest of his troops to arrive, but these attacks did nothing but generate unnecessary casualties. Frustrated, Grant turned to the navy and a test of the river batteries. The only gunboat currently on station, the *Carondelet* under Commander Henry Walke, suffered a massive hit from the Rebel cannon that tore through the ship's armor and wounded twelve men. Clearly, Donelson was no Henry.

That night freezing temperatures turned the rain into snow, and three inches of ice and snow fell. The Union soldiers shivered without the coats and blankets they had cast off earlier. Worse still, campfires were forbidden because of the danger of Rebel sharpshooters. The next morning, transports brought another ten thousand Union soldiers. Foote also appeared with four of his ironclads and two of his wooden gunboats. Grant organized the new regiments into a third division commanded by Brigadier General Lew Wallace, placing Wallace's men between Smith's and McClernand's divisions. This pushed McClernand to move his command farther to the right to cover the road that led from Donelson and Dover to Nashville.

With the arrival of the reinforcements and the gunboats, Grant felt ready to begin the assault. He planned for his artillery to join the gunboats in the afternoon to bombard the fort. Around 3:00 p.m., the attack began. The *Louisville, St. Louis, Pittsburgh*, and *Carondelet* again formed a line with the wooden gunboats *Tyler* and *Conestoga* behind the ironclads. Unlike the assault at Henry, this attack was a disaster for the Union navy. The Confederate batteries on the high bluff plunged fire onto Foote's flotilla, tearing into the lightly defended upper decks of the vessels. Confederate shot riddled the smokestacks, tore away the tiller ropes, cracked the armor plates, and ripped through the pilot houses and decks into the holds of the gunboats. The Rebels inflicted fifty-four casualties on the flotilla as they pummeled the vessels with hit after hit. The *Pittsburgh* was so badly damaged it had trouble staying afloat. Foote himself was wounded, ironically in the foot, as a Rebel shell ripped through his flagship. Yet after exchanging fire for nearly two hours, the Federals failed to inflict a single casualty or destroy a single Confederate cannon during the engagement. The ironclads had been bested and would now need extensive repairs before they would be fit for any further service. The Confederates cheered as the flotilla broke contact and steamed away. Fort Henry had been avenged.

A disappointed Grant accepted that a siege would be inevitable, yet he would need more men to completely isolate the fort. Meanwhile, Floyd sent a message to Johnston relaying news of the great victory over the gunboats. Still, Floyd and his officers knew that they could not hold Donelson for long in the face of growing Federal numbers. Grant's army would eventually be strong enough to surround the fortifications, cutting off supply and preventing any escape. The nearly besieged defenders had accomplished all they could, and they were determined to escape to Nashville.

That afternoon, Floyd held a council of war in his headquarters at the small hotel in the hamlet of Dover. The Rebel generals planned for Pillow to lead an assault with part of his division against McClernand's division at dawn, push McClernand's men out of the way, and allow the Rebels to escape down the road to Nashville. However, as the Rebels began preparing for the coming assault, a Federal sharpshooter killed one of Pillow's aides, who was standing near him. The gruesome scene, coupled with the realization that the Federals were too numerous for a partial attack, apparently unnerved Pillow. He called off the morning assault without notifying Floyd, which mystified and angered the commander.

Later that afternoon and evening, as temperatures plummeted to freezing and snow fell on the shivering soldiers once more, Floyd met again with his senior officers concerning the breakout. His division commanders, Pillow and Buckner, planned for a stronger assault on the Federal lines to commence the next morning. The most logical place to launch the attack was still on the Federal right against McClernand's men where the road to Nashville lay. The plan was for Pillow to hit McClernand's right flank with about ten thousand men and push the Federal line back and left toward the center. Buckner would then attack Wallace's troops in the center and leave just enough troops to man the trenches on the Confederate right. The combined attacks would push the Federal right backward like a gate swinging on a hinge. Buckner would then position his men to hold the breach while Pillow and the rest of the Confederate garrison fled down the Clarksville Road toward Nashville. That night they shifted troops to Pillow's sector on the left. The noise of the preparations was masked by the falling snow and howling winds.

The next morning when the Rebels launched their attack, Grant was downstream conferring with Foote aboard his flagship. He had left his army with no second-in-command and no instructions other than to avoid action with the enemy. This would not be the last time Grant's neglect would lead to near disaster in the face of an enemy surprise attack.

On this occasion, Grant's orders to simply hold their position prevented the two division commanders on the left (Smith) and center (Wallace) from doing much to help McClernand's division on the right, which bore the brunt of the Confederate assault. After hours of fighting, McClernand's men ran out of ammunition. Demoralized, they fell back, all the while holding up their empty cartridge boxes as a sign that they had held out as long as possible. The Rebels now had their gap in the Federal line and a clear road to Nashville. Inexplicably, however, at this point the Rebel plan collapsed. Pillow had observed the horrendous casualties from the day's fighting and believed his men were exhausted. He, therefore, lost his nerve again, reasoning that the garrison could not possibly march cross-country and fight off a pursuit by the Union forces. He persuaded Floyd, over Buckner's desperate pleading, to call off the movement toward Nashville and return to the field works.

It was during this lull in the fighting that Grant returned from his meeting with Foote. He immediately ordered his officers to reorganize their units and counterattack in an attempt to regain the initiative and lost ground. Grant correctly reasoned that in order to strengthen their left flank for the breakout attempt, the Rebels had weakened their own right flank. He had General Smith hit that area hard with great success. The counterattacks drove the Rebels back to their original positions and in some cases beyond. As night fell on the snow-covered landscape, nearly four thousand dead or wounded Federals and Confederates lay scattered across a bloody frozen field.

That night at Floyd's headquarters, recriminations flew as the Rebel generals argued and blamed one another for the day's disaster. Pillow still wanted the garrison to fight its way out. However, an angry and dejected Buckner believed that escape was now impossible. His men had fought hard to open the road to Nashville, and now they were exhausted and disheartened. Moreover, he did not feel they could stand up to a determined Federal assault even for an hour. Reluctantly, all agreed that surrender was now the only alternative. What transpired next was one of the most cowardly and bizarre events in American military history. Floyd, fearing his previous stint as US secretary of war might lead to his being hanged as a traitor, decided he would not allow himself to be taken. He turned command of Donelson over to Pillow and, commandeering two steamboats docked near Donelson, he and fifteen hundred of his Virginia troops fled down the river to Nashville. In an equal show of cowardice, Pillow also felt himself too important to be captured, so he and his staff took a small boat and escaped into the night. This left Buckner in command. He chose not to abandon either his responsibility or his men. He would remain and ask Grant for terms.

That night as rumors spread of a surrender, some Rebels refused to give up and opted instead to escape through the thinly manned Yankee lines. One such Rebel was Forrest, who before daybreak led seven hundred troopers and any others who wanted to ride double with his men out of Fort Donelson, across an icy stream too deep for infantry to ford, and through the Federal lines to Nashville.

In the early hours of February 16, Buckner sent a proposal to Grant for discussion of surrender terms. Grant's blunt reply stunned Buckner: "No terms except an unconditional and immediate surrender can be accepted. I propose to move immediately on your works." Buckner expected much better considering that he and Grant had been friends in the prewar army. He had even given Grant money to help him get home after his resignation from the army in 1854. Buckner felt humiliated but had little choice other than to accept Grant's "ungenerous and unchivalrous" terms.

As dawn broke, news of the surrender spread among the soldiers of both armies. While Federal troops took control of the fort and disarmed the Rebels, Grant sent a telegram to Halleck announcing the capture of Donelson and "from 12,000 to 15,000 prisoners, including Generals Buckner and Bushrod [R.] Johnson; also about 20,000 stand of arms,

48 pieces of artillery, 17 heavy guns, from 2,000 to 4,000 horses, and large quantities of commissary stores."

Word of Donelson's fall soon reached the North. Church bells rang and cannons fired salutes to celebrate the triumph. An overjoyed Lincoln promoted Grant to major general and considered an even greater reward for Halleck. The capture of the forts on the Tennessee and Cumberland Rivers were the first great victories for the United States during the Civil War. Beyond boosting morale, the opening of the Tennessee and Cumberland Rivers immediately changed the entire military dynamic in the West. Suddenly, most of Tennessee and much of the Confederate Heartland were opened to Federal invasion. Johnston's defensive line was in shambles, and his army was in a precarious situation; he had lost nearly a third of his available forces at the forts. The remainder were now split between Nashville and Columbus, nearly two hundred miles apart, with a Federal army and the gunboats in between controlling the rivers and railroads. Worse still, larger Federal armies threatened to defeat the scattered Rebels. Buell's Army of the Ohio was poised to move toward Bowling Green, while Major General John Pope's Army of the Mississippi now threatened Polk at Columbus.

Johnston had to face the reality that Nashville could not be defended either against the Federal land forces or the gunboats since there were few fortifications in place. Even if he chose to fight for the city, the railroad bridge over the Cumberland was the only feasible escape route for the Confederate army, and if Foote's gunboats destroyed it, the Rebels could not flee the city easily. He, therefore, believed he had no choice but to evacuate the city, which he did on February 23. This threw the citizens of Nashville into a panic. Those with the means attempted to escape the advancing Yankees. The roads heading south were filled with carriages, wagons, and open carts that carried women, children, and valuables. Meanwhile inside the city, looting and general lawlessness occurred. Forrest and his troopers attempted to restore order by attacking mobs, but they could not secure the city. Soldiers tried to transport as much foodstuffs, armaments, and supplies as possible, although much of it had to be abandoned or destroyed. Nashville quite simply was in chaos.

Johnston's army moved southward to Murfreesboro, abandoning much of Middle Tennessee, in what would become a long, grueling march. Meanwhile, Beauregard arrived at Columbus, Kentucky, to assume command of Polk's garrison and prepare them to evacuate the fortress. A few days after Nashville was evacuated, Beauregard led the Rebels in retreat from Columbus to Corinth, Mississippi, opening all of West Tennessee to the Yankee forces. The Confederate forts along the Mississippi were now isolated from the rest of the Rebel army, which was fleeing southward.

The Shiloh Campaign

Gone were the cheering crowds and confidant smiles that had greeted Johnston on his arrival in Tennessee. Praise was replaced with savage condemnation. Indeed, newspapers charged him with incompetence, drunkenness, and even treason. Tennessee congressmen petitioned Davis for his removal from command, but Davis stood by his old friend, declaring, "Gentlemen, I know Sidney Johnston well. If he is not a general we had better give up the war, for we have no general." Johnston stoically refused to reply to his critics. He understood that "the test of merit, in my profession . . . is success," noting that "it is a hard rule, but I think it right. . . . What the people want is a battle and a victory."

Johnston briefly halted his men at Murfreesboro to rest and refit them before continuing southward. Meanwhile, in West Tennessee and northern Mississippi, Beauregard was organizing a new army, and he requested that Johnston join him. Johnston and Beauregard continued to correspond and evaluate options as Johnston marched his men southward from Murfreesboro. Over the next two weeks, his troops plodded along the muddy roads of Middle Tennessee and northern Alabama to the town of Decatur. The march was largely uneventful except for the terrible weather. The men were buffeted by heavy rains, occasional snow, and high winds.

Johnston at last decided that he should join Beauregard at Corinth, a strategic junction of the main north–south and east–west railroads in the Mississippi Valley. On March 15, Johnston's weary troops left Decatur, arriving at Corinth on March 20. The commander's morale had collapsed when his defensive line shattered, and Beauregard, acting as his chief of staff, stepped into the breach and helped Johnston concentrate on Corinth. There, Johnston reunited the remnants of his army. President Davis understood how critical it was to hold as much of Tennessee as possible and end the Rebel collapse in the West. He transferred troops from around the Confederacy, including five thousand men from New Orleans and another ten thousand from Florida and the Gulf Coast garrisons under the command of Major General Braxton Bragg. Johnston's army had grown to around forty-four thousand men by March, but the majority were raw recruits. He turned once more to Beauregard and gave him the responsibility of organizing this new army. Bragg, an ill-tempered, irascible disciplinarian, commanded the Mobile troops. He was not liked by his men, but he was feared. A West Point graduate and Mexican War hero, Bragg had a reputation for being difficult to get along with, and he eventually left the army to become a successful sugar planter in Louisiana. Although an eccentric martinet, Bragg was an able organizer, and he had the best drilled force in Johnston's growing command.

At Corinth, Beauregard and Johnston created the Army of Mississippi out of the hodgepodge of units and organized it into four corps under generals Hardee, Polk, Bragg, and John C. Breckinridge. Breckinridge, a native Kentucky politician, a former vice president of the United States, and the Southern Democratic candidate in the 1860 election, had replaced Crittenden when he was arrested for drunkenness.

Meanwhile, the capture of Forts Henry and Donelson had so impressed Washington that Lincoln and McClellan had Halleck promoted to the command of all Union troops west of the Appalachians. Halleck now had the command he had long desired, and he intended to follow up on his earlier success. Grant had also been promoted to major general and Halleck's second-in-command. However, the two argued over Grant's apparent refusal to obey Halleck's orders and follow proper military protocol. This was resolved in Grant's favor, and Halleck eventually sent Grant's Army of the Tennessee (consisting of the three divisions that had seen action at Fort Donelson, commanded by McClernand, Lew Wallace, and Brigadier General W. H. L. Wallace—who replaced the injured Charles F. Smith—and three new divisions commanded by Brigadier Generals William Tecumseh Sherman, Stephen A. Hurlbut, and Benjamin M. Prentiss) to a small riverboat stop called Pittsburg Landing on the Tennessee River, twenty miles north of Corinth. Halleck also ordered Buell to march from Nashville with his thirty-five thousand men in the Army of the Cumberland and rendezvous with Grant. Once the two armies were linked, Halleck planned to join them and lead the army against the Rebels at Corinth.

The Confederates were aware of the Federal plan, but they had to prepare the newly christened Army of Mississippi before they could act. This new force had impressive numbers, but it lacked any real experience. Bragg's troops had been well trained, but few of the other new recruits or their officers had much if any training or combat experience. Nonetheless, after organizing the army, Johnston and Beauregard meant to strike Grant's Army of the Tennessee, now positioned near Pittsburg Landing, before Buell could join him. If this were accomplished, the Confederates might defeat the two Federal forces in detail and perhaps liberate West and Middle Tennessee.

Johnston left the formulation of all plans to his second-in-command, Beauregard. Given the condition of the Confederate troops and the logistical issues that the Rebels faced, Beauregard drew up an unrealistic timetable. He allowed only one day for the corps commanders to assemble their scattered units, march some twenty miles, and get into position for an attack the next morning. The combination of poor roads, bad directions, and inexperienced troops made a one-day march impossible.

To make matters worse, on the morning of April 4 (the time designated for the attack), a torrential rain began to fall, which turned the roads into thick mud. By that time, the operation was twelve hours behind schedule, and Johnston was forced to postpone the attack until the following morning. However, that night, the rain continued, and the already sodden roads became quagmires with muck a foot deep. By late afternoon on April 5, Polk's and Bragg's corps were still not properly deployed, and Breckinridge's tired, mud-splattered troops (designated as the army's reserve) were still far to the rear. The attack had to be postponed yet again.

Johnston finally gathered his army less than two miles

from the Federal camps and began preparations to launch the attack the next morning. That evening, the Confederate commanders held their last council before the coming assault at dawn. Beauregard argued that the attack should be canceled. The element of surprise had surely been lost since the untrained soldiers, curious if their rifles would fire in the wet weather, had test fired them during the day, essentially alerting the enemy. Johnston, however, overruled his objections, determined to strike. He sent a message to be read to all regiments, promising "a decisive victory over agrarian mercenaries, sent to subjugate and despoil you of your liberties, property, and honor. . . . Remember the dependence of your mothers, your wives, your sisters, and your children on the result. . . . With such incentives to brave deeds . . . your generals will lead you confidently to the combat." Johnston ordered his corps commanders to finish their preparations and declared resolutely: "Gentlemen, we shall attack at daylight tomorrow." No amount of persuasion would change his mind. Johnston's blood was up, and as he grimly stated to his officers, "I would fight them if they were a million."

Beauregard's warnings about having lost the element of surprise were sound, yet miraculously, they were wrong. Neither Grant nor Buell felt a sense of urgency. Five of Grant's six divisions were camped haphazardly west of Pittsburg Landing. The sixth, under Lew Wallace, was stationed five miles to the north guarding the army's supply depots at another river landing. Grant had forgotten the lesson of Fort Donelson, and he once again focused his mind so intently on his own plans that he did not conceive that the Rebels had plans of their own.

Worse still, Grant had ignored Halleck's orders to entrench his men. The Union divisions let their brigades and regiments lay out their camps without structure or defen-

William Tecumseh Sherman. Library of Congress.

sive preparations. Union picket patrols were inadequate to detect enemy movements more than a few hundred yards away, and even worse, the two divisions nearest Corinth, which would receive the first thrust of any attack, were composed of raw recruits. William T. Sherman commanded

Don Carlos Buell.
Library of Congress.

one of these divisions. With a tall, slim physique and plain looks, Sherman was not an imposing military figure. Although a West Point graduate, his military career prior to the Civil War was unremarkable. Resigning his commission in 1853, Sherman embarked on a career in banking and law with limited success. In 1859, he moved his family to Louisiana to become the superintendent of a military college. When the war came, Sherman, much like Grant, saw it as an opportunity to remake himself. After suffering a possible nervous breakdown in Kentucky in 1861, he was determined to rebuild his reputation while serving under Grant in Tennessee.

Like Grant, Sherman was overconfident and eager to demonstrate bravado. To one nervous colonel reporting

Rebel movement nearby, Sherman allegedly said, "Take your damned regiment back to Ohio. Beauregard is not such a fool as to leave his base of operations and attack us in ours." Likewise, Grant interpreted any reports of nearby Confederate activity as only a possible threat to Lew Wallace's isolated division downriver and not to the army as a whole. Indeed, Grant arrogantly wired Halleck on April 5 that he had "scarcely the faintest idea of an attack (general one) being made upon us, but will be prepared should such a thing take place."

Grant was sorely mistaken, and he was in no way prepared for what was about to happen. Early on the morning of April 6, Union pickets began to exchange fire with advancing Rebel skirmishers. Soon thousands of Rebels burst from the woods and slammed into the two green divisions of Sherman and Prentiss, an Illinois political general with Mexican War experience. Against all odds, Johnston had surprised them. Sherman's and Prentiss's men left their breakfasts and hastily grabbed their muskets. As Sherman rode forward to see what was happening, a volley rang out, and his orderly fell dead at his side. In shock, Sherman exclaimed, "My God, we're attacked!" He was finally convinced that the Rebels were there and in force.

The Confederates hit Prentiss's and Sherman's divisions hard, but there was a fatal flaw in the Confederate plan of attack that would ultimately save the Federal cause that day. Johnston had approximately forty thousand men, which gave him a slight numerical advantage over Grant; however, given the narrow confines and terrain of the battlefield, not all Rebel forces could engage at once. To make matters worse for the Confederates, Beauregard had devised a poorly conceived battle plan in which the Confederate army would advance to the attack in four long, parallel lines of battle, each wave consisting of a corps. These successive

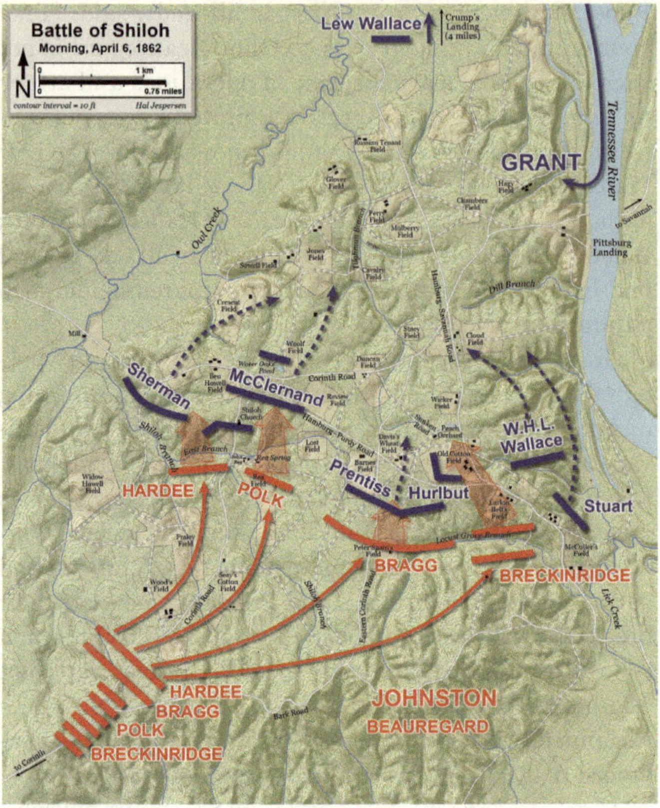

Map by Hal Jespersen, www.cwmaps.com.

waves were designed to sweep the enemy from the field. General Hardee's corps (the largest) was in front, spread out nearly three miles between Owl Creek on the left and Lick Creek on the right. Bragg's divisions brought up the second line, which was about five hundred yards behind Hardee's men. About eight hundred yards behind Bragg came Polk's smaller corps of around nine thousand men. Finally, behind

Bragg and to his right came Breckinridge's reserve corps of approximately seven thousand troops. Beauregard thought Hardee's and Bragg's men might be enough to sweep the Federals back, and he considered both Polk and Breckinridge to be support and reserve elements to move forward only in the face of stubborn Federal resistance. Confederate cavalry guarded the flanks of the infantry as it surged forward. What Beauregard inexplicably failed to consider was that upon contact with the enemy, the four corps could become hopelessly stalled, stacked, and intermingled as the waves crashed into one another. This would destroy any semblance of command and control and turn the Confederate army into a mob of virtually independent division, brigade, and even regimental units.

Moreover, Johnston had originally indicated that he wanted to strike the Federal left with a massive blow and push them back and away from Pittsburg Landing, preventing retreat and thereby forcing Grant to either surrender or face the annihilation of his army. However, this was not in any way the plan Beauregard devised since the successive waves were to push forward, overwhelming the Federal army and pinning it against Pittsburg Landing. Complicating the poor planning further, Johnston insisted on leading the army from the front, meaning that Beauregard, the architect of the plan, would be assigned to the rear of the army to funnel men and supplies as required. With Johnston, the army's titular commander, isolated on the battlefield with particular units, Beauregard would be the only one with an overall picture of the developing battle, and thus he would essentially be in command of the field.

As at Fort Donelson, Grant was again absent from the field during the Confederate surprise attack. When the muffled sound of cannon fire coming from Pittsburg Landing announced the assault, he and his staff were sitting down to breakfast at his headquarters ten miles downriver in Savannah. Luckily for the Federals, advanced elements of Buell's army had arrived, and Grant ordered Brigadier General William "Bull" Nelson's division to move upriver to Pittsburg Landing where it could be ferried across to join his men. Grant and his staff then quickly boarded the small steamboat *Tigress* and headed upriver. Grant arrived on the battlefield between 8:30 and 9:00 a.m. and quickly realized that he faced a full-fledged assault by Johnston. He communicated with his division commanders on the field and attempted to organize the Union lines. He also sent a courier to summon Lew Wallace's division to the battlefield. However, a miscommunication between Grant and Wallace meant that the latter took the wrong road and had to countermarch, arriving too late to participate in the battle on April 6. Meanwhile, Grant's five green divisions were not prepared for what hit them, and the Rebel assaults had caused many soldiers to flee to the rear and cower under the bluffs at the landing. Sensing the potential for disaster, Grant established a line of reorganized stragglers and artillery along the ridge west of Pittsburg Landing to make a last-ditch stand should the Rebels get that far. It appeared they would.

On the Federal left along the road from Corinth, Prentiss's men were buckling under the Confederate onslaught. A gap developed between Prentiss and Sherman that allowed the Rebels to attack both the front and flanks of the two Union divisions. Sherman's division had borne the brunt of the assault and was slowly losing ground and being driven past Shiloh Church.

By around 9:00 a.m., just as Grant was arriving on the battlefield, Prentiss ordered the remainder of his division to fall back about a half mile to a sunken road, where troops from Hurlbut's and Wallace's divisions joined them and where Prentiss established a new defensive line. This position, called the "Hornet's Nest," along the "Sunken Road" became the center of the Union line.

Meanwhile, Johnston spent the early morning in the thick of battle, riding around the front lines and encouraging the Rebels forward. Unfortunately, while he attempted to rally Rebel troops in an area known as the "Peach Orchard," he was shot in his right leg. His staff officers saw his horse reel and then saw the general slump in his saddle. Isham Harris, serving as one of Johnston's aides, approached and found him wounded. The staff guided the general's horse into a nearby wood and lifted Johnston gently to the ground. No one noticed that a bullet had pierced Johnston below the back of the knee and just above his high riding boot, which obscured the wound from sight. Moreover, the round had actually cut his popliteal artery in the back of the knee, and he was quickly bleeding to death. The blood was flowing into his boot and could not be seen. He needed a tourniquet quickly, but no one knew what to do. Unfortunately, earlier in the morning, Johnston had sent his personal surgeon to tend wounded Confederate soldiers and Union prisoners. As Johnston faded from consciousness, his officers, including his brother-in-law Colonel William Preston, attempted unsuccessfully to revive him. His pulse faded, and he stopped breathing. The stunned staff wrapped the general's body in a blanket and took him to the rear, informing Beauregard that he was now in command. Conscious of the effect Johnston's death could have on the army's morale, Beauregard attempted to conceal it from the troops until the action had been settled. Nonetheless, news of Johnston's demise spread to both sides.

By this time, the Rebels had driven back the Union right and left flanks two miles from their starting point and were nearing Pittsburg Landing. In the center, though, Prentiss,

with the remaining fragments of his division and parts of two others, continued to put up resistance. Grant had ordered Prentiss to "maintain that position at all hazards," and that was what he intended to do. Although the heaviest fighting of the day had occurred on the Federal flanks, the Union center would now become the focus of Rebel assaults.

Instead of containing and bypassing Prentiss's position, Beauregard and his generals now launched attack after attack. Although 18,000 Confederates closed in on some 4,500

Battle of Shiloh. Library of Congress.

Federals from W. H. L. Wallace's division and the remnants of Prentiss's division, the uncoordinated nature of Southern attacks enabled the Federals to repel each of them in turn. Eventually, the Rebels assembled a mass of more than sixty artillery pieces and pounded the "Hornet's Nest" area while Confederate infantry began to close in on all sides. By 5:00 p.m., with the sun low in the sky, Wallace badly wounded, and the exhausted Federals almost surrounded, Prentiss realized that "further resistance must result in the slaughter of every man in the command." He surrendered himself and about 2,200 men. After the surrender, a brief lull in the fighting occurred as the Rebels attempted to reorganize themselves for a final assault on Pittsburg Landing. The stubborn Federal resistance on the flanks, which bent but did not break, along with the late afternoon struggle at the "Hornet's Nest" had given Grant more than enough time to build a strong line of defense along the Pittsburg Landing ridge. There, he placed all available cannon wheel to wheel and ordered Hurlbut to form a defensive line from the landing around to the right and connect with the remnants of McClernand's and Sherman's troops in an arc. On the river, the gunboats *Tyler* and *Lexington* moved closer to shore to add their guns to the massed Union artillery. The Federals were preparing for what would almost certainly be the last fight of the day. By then, Nelson's men were finally crossing the river and joining Grant's mangled army.

As Nelson's men marched off the steamers at Pittsburg Landing, they were appalled to see thousands of shirkers hiding under the cover of the river bluff. Nelson estimated that seven to ten thousand men cowered with fright along the riverbank. Buell, too, was stunned to see that "the face of the bluff was crowded with stragglers from the battle.... At the top of the bluff all was confusion. Men mounted and on foot, and wagons with their teams and excited drivers, all struggling to force their way closer to the river." Buell's men pushed their way through this mob to reach the battlefield, with Buell "berating them and trying to shame them into joining their regiments. He even threatened them with shells from the gunboats nearby. But it was all to no effect."

Meanwhile, the Rebel assaults on Grant's rally point were badly organized and piecemeal, and the Confederates charging this line found the rifle and cannon fire unbearable and retreated in disorder. By 6:00 p.m., with dusk

Nathan Bedford Forrest. Library of Congress.

approaching, Bragg hastily organized various brigades for one final assault on the Federal left. General Breckinridge prepared to support the charge. Unexpectedly, Beauregard sent word to call off the assault. Believing the Yankees to be in retreat and his own men in need of rest, he saw no value in a frontal attack against the strong Federal position. The tired, hungry, and bloodied foot soldiers facing the wall of cannon undoubtedly agreed.

Beauregard wired Richmond, declaring that "after a severe battle of ten hours, thanks be to the Almighty, [we] gained a complete victory, driving the enemy from every position." He realized that he needed to reorder his disorganized men, rest them, and prepare to finish driving Grant's army from the field; however, the Rebels did not realize that their worst fear had already happened. As Beauregard prepared for bed in Sherman's captured tent, Buell's army was arriving. Nathan Bedford Forrest's scouts watched boats ferry Buell's brigades across the river all through the night, and Forrest attempted to find Beauregard and warn him. Unable to do so, he warned other Rebel commanders, who simply ignored him. His prediction that "we'll be whipped like Hell" in the morning was crude but prophetic.

As darkness fell, the Union gunboats *Lexington* and *Tyler* lobbed eight-inch shells over the heads of the Federal troops and into what they thought were the Confederate lines. However, the Rebels had fallen back to regroup and to plunder the overrun Federal camps; therefore, the shelling only churned the earth, dismembered the dead, frightened the living, and prevented anyone Federal or Confederate from sleeping soundly. Adding to their misery, the soldiers were treated to mother nature's wrath with the appearance of a massive thunderstorm that drenched the living and dead while loud, peeling thunder and jagged lightning lit up the macabre scene. It was truly a horrific night for the men of both armies, especially the thousands of wounded still littering the cold, soggy ground awaiting help. After filling their stomachs, the men looked for a place to rest, whether in the captured tents or at the roots of trees. Lying in the pouring rain, the Rebel soldiers could hear the cries of the wounded and the boom of Federal cannon all through the night. Most thought they had won a great victory. Little did they expect what the next morning would bring.

During the night, the Federals were reinforced by General Buell's army and the fresh division of Lew Wallace, giving them a substantial numerical advantage. Far from retreating, Grant and Buell planned to sweep Beauregard's army from the field the next morning. Around 3:00 a.m., the thunderstorm subsided. The Federals organized the remnants of Grant's and Buell's armies into a united front. Grant's men formed the right wing with Lew Wallace's division on the far right. Positioned to Wallace's left were the remnants of Sherman's division, McClernand's division, the remainder of W. H. L. Wallace's division (now under Colonel James Tuttle), and Hurlbut's division. Buell's Army of the Ohio formed the left wing on the left of Hurlbut, with Brigadier Generals Alexander M. McCook, then Thomas L. Crittenden, and finally William Nelson on the far left near the river. Just before the cold, wet dawn of April 7, the combined Federal armies, forty-five thousand strong, advanced cautiously toward the Confederate camps.

The previous night, Sherman had found Grant standing under a tree smoking a cigar as the rain poured down. Sherman commented on the army's close call, to which the ever-confident Grant replied, "lick'em tomorrow, though."

Grant's prediction was sound. His own army had been mangled, but Buell's fresh divisions would give him the advantage. Perhaps he would have been even more confident if he had realized how disordered the Rebels were. In truth, the Confederate army was exhausted and completely disorganized. Beauregard's poor plan of attack on April 6 had led to the hopeless commingling of the corps. Worse, many men just stopped where they were when the fighting ceased and made no attempt to rejoin their units. Others spent most of the night wandering around trying to find their commands, while still others prowled the Federal camps to plunder whatever food or clothing they could find and to seek protection from the weather. Confederate staff officers rode through the night desperately trying to organize the scattered army.

The commingled Confederate corps could not possibly be separated out during the night, so Beauregard and his generals decided to let their men rest and have the Rebel corps commanders take charge of separate sectors of the battlefront in order to restore some semblance of command and control. Staff officers located the corps commanders and assigned them sections of the Rebel line. On the far right, General Hardee was in control. Breckinridge was to Hardee's left in the center of the Rebel line, and Bragg took command of the far left. Between Breckinridge and Bragg was an area eventually filled by Polk and remnants of his corps. It was not an ideal arrangement, but it did bring some semblance of order, and at this point, it would have to do. Since Buell's arrival was not yet generally known, all were confident that they simply had to finish off Grant's army at their leisure.

As the Federals advanced at dawn on April 7, the Rebels were the ones who were now caught by surprise. The Confederates were slowly pushed back by the weight of Federal numbers and the greater firepower. Initially, the attack confused the Rebels. They could not understand from where all of the Union units were coming.

Grant and Buell had, indeed, surprised Beauregard, and his inability to mount an organized defense early had allowed the Federals to move across yesterday's battlefield; however, Beauregard soon established a battle line that slowed the Federal advance. He had Hardee and Breckinridge launch counterassaults at the Federals, hoping to reverse the momentum. The Rebels fought tenaciously for every foot of ground, but the men were exhausted from the day before. Buell's fresh troops continued to push the Rebel line on the right, and that line teetered.

Breckinridge's corps, which had maintained its cohesion throughout the fighting on the sixth, was the most organized of the Rebel units, and Beauregard needed it to launch attacks at the Federals. Although Breckinridge's men managed to push back the Yankees, they could not

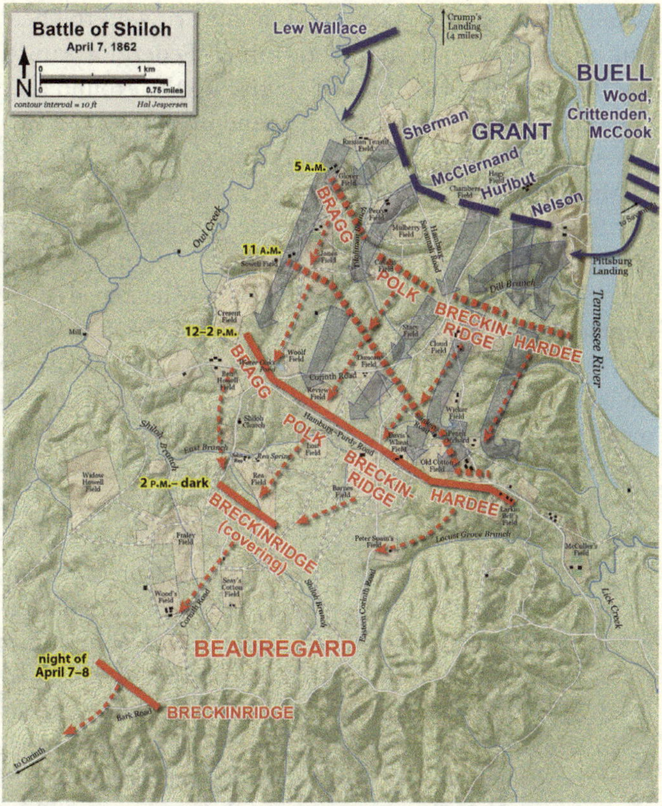

Map by Hal Jespersen, www.cwmaps.com.

maintain a sustained attack. They simply did not have the numbers. Even so, the Federals could not break the Rebel line despite the use of Buell's fresh troops. Soon, reminiscent of the previous day, the struggle in that sector of the battlefield dissolved into small but intense firefights between smaller units. Buell's divisions continued to test the

Rebel line, and by 11:30 a.m., all of his army on the field was engaged. Yet, despite determined Federal assaults, the Rebels stubbornly refused to give up the ground they had taken the day before. Hardee's and Breckinridge's men somehow managed to hold Buell's army.

Meanwhile, the situation was essentially the same on the Confederate left as the initial attacks by Grant's divisions of Sherman, McClernand, and Hurlbut met heavy Rebel resistance and stalled. Also, the Rebels here launched counterattacks in the hope of breaking up the Union assaults and reversing the momentum. Around noon, Lew Wallace's division, which had avoided earlier contact, managed to outflank the Confederate battle line on the left and force the Rebels into a fighting retreat as they attempted to assemble a new line.

Despite their poor organization and fatigue, the Confederates had not only stymied most Federal attacks during the morning but had also managed to launch local counterattacks. Beauregard grew optimistic that his weary units could form a stable battle line, but that optimism was short-lived. As the afternoon progressed, renewed Union attacks by Buell's divisions began to wear down Confederate resistance. Likewise, Grant's divisions, especially those of Sherman and McClernand, pressured the other end of the new Rebel line. By 1:00 p.m., Beauregard withdrew to yet another defensive line south of the Hamburg-Purdy Road near the edge of the original battlefield. The Rebels were wearing down.

Indeed, by 2:00 p.m., it was becoming obvious to Beauregard and his officers that the exhausted and outnumbered Rebels could no longer hold the Union divisions at bay. Isham Harris, still serving as a volunteer staff officer, declared that it seemed as if the fighting was going badly and questioned "whether there was not danger in tarrying so long in the field as to be unable to withdraw in good order." One member of Beauregard's staff even compared the army's condition to that of a lump of sugar, thoroughly soaked with water and ready to dissolve. Realizing that his army could take no more, Beauregard ordered a retreat.

The Creole general skillfully pulled his army back while launching localized assaults or spoiling attacks to prevent the Federals from interfering with the withdrawal as the army was in motion. Breckinridge moved first, setting up a rearguard position. After Breckinridge was safely away, Polk's corps fell back, then Hardee, and finally Bragg. The retreat was accomplished with little loss, and Beauregard claimed, "There was no flurry, no useless haste, among the men or officers; and even the stragglers dropped into line and rejoined their command as they passed." By 3:00 p.m., Beauregard had positioned a five-thousand-man rearguard on a ridge south of Shiloh Church along Corinth Road. Breckinridge's brigades made up the bulk of the force. This line held the Federals at bay until about 5:00 p.m., allowing the battered Southern army to withdraw. Breckinridge then moved his command to the intersection of Corinth and Bark Roads and camped there for the night. The next day, the corps moved to Mickie's (sometimes spelled Micky's) farm, eight miles from Corinth. Breckinridge would continue to hold this position, allowing Beauregard to make good his army's escape and organize a defense at Corinth. Sherman mounted a reconnaissance in force with two brigades on April 8 and advanced four miles down Corinth Road, but he soon retreated after a brief skirmish with Colonel Forrest's cavalry. There would be no real pursuit of the Rebels as they moved southward to Corinth.

The battle of Shiloh was over, and the officers on both sides had reason to be proud of the performance of their men. Despite the fact that most of the troops in the battle had never been in combat or "seen the elephant" as they would have termed it, most gave a good account of themselves. The effects of this bloodbath on the men who fought there and the populace of both nations were far reaching. This was the costliest battle in the conflict to date (twenty-three thousand combined casualties); moreover, more Americans died in this single battle than in all of America's previous wars considered together. Beauregard placed Southern casualties at approximately 25 percent of his total force. Shiloh thus erased any notion of a quick war from the minds of those both North and South. The battle had cost Johnston his life and nearly cost Grant his career. Buell and the Army of the Ohio had saved Grant and his army from the Rebels, but they could not save Grant from his legion of critics.

For years after the battle, Grant and Buell (and their respective supporters) would disagree over how much Buell's troops contributed to the eventual Federal victory. By any reasonable measure, Grant's army had been beaten. More than half his men had been killed, wounded, captured, or had simply run away. They had lost their camps, been forced back several miles, and barely hung on to a narrow strip of land along the river. Of Grant's original force, only about half were ready to continue the fight, and even with Lew Wallace's men, they would be up against more than twenty thousand troops that Beauregard still had available. It is possible that Grant's army could have successfully remained on the defensive, but without Buell, it was impossible for them to go on the attack.

While the Federal soldiers had performed well, Grant's leadership had been lacking. He had been surprised and unprepared for the Rebel assault, yet Halleck and Lincoln decided to save his career. Indeed, when a prominent Republican visited Lincoln complaining that Grant was incompetent, a drunkard, and a political liability to the administration, the president heard him out and replied: "I can't spare this man; he fights." Grant would have a chance to redeem his reputation on the battlefields of Tennessee.

Island No. 10

Meanwhile, on April 7, as Beauregard's battered army began its retreat to Corinth, a Union army–navy team scored another triumph, this time on the Mississippi River at Island No. 10. Around two months earlier, when the Confederates evacuated Columbus in February, they left a garrison of seven thousand men and fifty-two big guns at Island No. 10, fifty miles downriver. This strong point, so named because it was the tenth island south of the Ohio River, blocked Northern shipping at a sharp bend in the river. The Confederates had also fortified New Madrid, Missouri, a few miles downstream at another bend.

Halleck ordered another army–navy combined operation against the position. He sent Andrew Foote's river fleet of seven ironclads and ten mortar boats, in conjunction with Major General John Pope's newly formed Army of the Mississippi consisting of about twelve thousand men, to take the position. The Confederate defenses were formidable. The island stretched nearly a mile long with nineteen heavy cannon. Additionally, the Rebels had a floating battery and more guns on the Tennessee shore for a total of fifty-two guns. Foote's vessels bombarded the Rebel defenses at long range without much effect. Meanwhile, Pope took New Madrid and gained control of the Missouri bank below the island. He then put his troops and runaway slaves to work digging a shallow canal that accommodated the passage of several draft transports during the season's high water. The New Madrid Canal allowed Pope to get troops south

Bombardment of Island No. 10 in the Mississippi River. Courtesy of the Missouri History Museum and the Missouri Historical Society.

of Island No. 10, but he now needed to get them across the river in order to cut the Confederate's tenuous supply line through the swamps on the Tennessee side of the Mississippi. He pleaded with Foote for a gunboat to run the gauntlet of guns on the island and protect a downriver troop crossing. Foote was reluctant to risk running his vessels by the Rebel batteries, but he finally relented. In a thunderstorm on the night of April 4, *Carondelet* ran the batteries and was followed by the *Pittsburgh* two nights later during yet another storm. Protected by the gunboats, Pope's army crossed the Mississippi and surrounded the garrison on April 7, which surrendered some 4,500 men in addition to the other supplies and the heavy guns. Halleck considered

Pope's victory an even more brilliant success than Grant's at Donelson, and Pope's achievement gained the attention of Washington.

Siege of Corinth

Following the Union victories at Island No. 10 and Shiloh, General Halleck arrived at Pittsburg Landing on April 11 and immediately assumed command of all the Federal forces, leaving Grant and Buell in command of their respective armies. On April 21, the victorious General Pope arrived at the landing with thirty thousand men. Halleck was now in command of an army group consisting of three separate armies: the Army of the Ohio, commanded by General Buell; the Army of the Tennessee, commanded by Grant; and Pope's Army of the Mississippi. Although few recognized the significance, Halleck had assembled perhaps the greatest military force the United States had fielded up to that point. In addition to the thousands of infantrymen, cavalrymen, and artillerymen, Halleck's officer corps was equally impressive. It included a number of future Civil War army notables: himself, Buell, Pope, and Brigadier Generals William Rosecrans, George H. Thomas, and James B. McPherson. Even more impressive, Halleck, Grant, Sherman, and Philip Sheridan (then a captain) would all eventually rise to the rank of general in chief of the United States Army. The Confederacy would struggle throughout the war to match the quality of these Western Theater commanders.

By late April, it was time for the great Federal force to advance. Halleck had changed the organization of his force into four parts: right, center, left, and a reserve. General Thomas was put in command of the right wing consisting of his own division and the Army of the Tennessee (minus the divisions of McClernand and Lew Wallace). General Buell commanded the remainder of the Army of the Ohio in the center, and General Pope led his Army of the Mississippi on the left wing. McClernand was named commander of the reserve with his and Wallace's divisions. Grant was originally supposed to command the right wing and reserve and act as second-in-command of the entire army, but after Grant's near disaster at Shiloh, Halleck decided to make him his second-in-command only and to watch his movements carefully. Grant sulked and requested a transfer, but Halleck would hear none of it. Instead, he spent his energy on the campaign at hand.

Determined not to be surprised by a sudden Rebel strike as Grant had been, Halleck inched his giant army group toward Corinth. Each day the force moved a few miles only to stop and entrench, daring the Confederates to strike. If Halleck's precautions made sure that Beauregard could not attack him, they made equally sure that he could not effectively attack Beauregard. Halleck was executing the campaign in strict adherence to the eighteenth-century ideas of maneuver warfare. Corinth was a key strategic transportation point—the city, and not Beauregard's army, was Halleck's focus. He hoped to either force Beauregard out of Corinth without a fight or destroy his army if the latter was foolish enough to engage them.

Jefferson Davis and Beauregard also considered Corinth a crucial strategic point. Indeed, Beauregard suggested that "if defeated here [Corinth], we lose the whole Mississippi Valley and probably our cause." Davis concurred, and again the Confederacy brought together reinforcements from across the South. Some came from East Tennessee and others from coastal garrisons. The biggest addition was from Brigadier General Earl Van Dorn, who arrived from the Trans-Mississippi with his fifteen thousand men.

However, these combined forces could muster only some fifty thousand troops—half the number of the Union forces slowly advancing toward Corinth.

The Confederates also faced another problem at Corinth. Yellow flags belonging to the Confederate hospital corps decorated the town's hotels, public buildings, schools, churches, and larger homes. These makeshift hospitals overflowed with more than twenty thousand sick and wounded soldiers. Men smeared in filth and blood lay on the sidewalks, porches, and railroad platforms groaning in agony and awaiting care or death. The horrific situation was exacerbated further by a scarcity of physicians and medical supplies.

In addition to these horrors, epidemics of typhoid fever, erysipelas, dysentery, malaria, and measles raged through the army camps, and a severe shortage of food, especially fresh vegetables, led to widespread malnutrition and scurvy. For example, the men of the Nineteenth Tennessee subsisted on flour, sugar, molasses, a little beef, and rye for coffee. Water was also scarce, and the limited supply was contaminated. One veteran in the regiment remembered the men having to dig holes in the ground to allow "seep water" to fill a pit, where it was drunk eagerly by the thirsty soldiers. With latrines nearby, it is little wonder that dysentery and typhoid plagued the men. After a day or two, "wiggletails" would infest the water hole, and new sources would have to be dug out of the swampy ground. Indeed, as camp conditions deteriorated, Beauregard lost almost as many men from disease at Corinth as were killed in battle at Shiloh.

By early May, Beauregard, faced with this devastation and the prospect of being surrounded by a siege, changed his mind about the need to hold Corinth at all costs. As Halleck was extending his lines around the city and hauling forward his siege guns, Beauregard on May 25 decided to pull out, moving his army about fifty miles south to Tupelo. He did so with great skill and stealth, leaving behind only a few stragglers and a pestilential town as spoils for Halleck. Beauregard believed that the successful evacuation of Corinth and preservation of his army was as good as a victory.

Davis, however, did not agree. The Confederate president was shocked and angered by the news. He lamented that another such "victory" would sink the Confederacy. Although Beauregard talked of resuming the offensive, Davis had heard enough of his grandiose plans. When Beauregard took an unauthorized leave of absence to recuperate due to his persistent throat ailment, Davis seized the opportunity and replaced him with Braxton Bragg.

Memphis Falls

Meanwhile, the last Confederate bastions along the Upper Mississippi were falling into Union hands. The capture of Island No. 10 opened the Mississippi to Fort Pillow about fifty miles north of Memphis. There, on April 14, Foote's gunboats opened fire on the fort while Pope's army in thirty transports waited to disembark. However, Pope received a message from Halleck ordering him to take his army to Pittsburg Landing. Pope left two regiments to cooperate with Foote as his fleet continued to pound the fort. The fort with its forty guns stubbornly held on for weeks. On May 10, a small makeshift Rebel fleet launched a surprise attack on the Federal gunboats. The Union flotilla, now commanded by Flag Officer Charles Henry Davis who had relieved Foote the day before, engaged the Rebel ships commanded by Captain James E. Montgomery near the mouth of Plum Run Creek. The eight Confederate gunboats that comprised the River Defense Fleet were poorly armored civilian ships. However, they amazingly sank two of the Federal ironclads by ramming them. The ironclads would be raised and put back into action, but it was a stunning victory for the Rebels. The overconfident Montgomery assured Beauregard that the Yankees "will never penetrate farther down the Mississippi." His victory, however, was short-lived. Beauregard ordered the evacuation of the fort on June 3, when his withdrawal from Corinth made it vulnerable to land attack. The Federal fleet then prepared to re-engage the Confederate River Defense Fleet downriver at Memphis. On June 6, as crowds gathered on the river bluff to watch, the two fleets collided.

This time Flag Officer Davis was prepared for the Rebel rams, and, indeed, brought rams of his own. Charles Ellet Jr., a civil engineer, had converted seven fast civilian steamers into rams for Davis's fleet. Ellet commanded the flagship of the ramming fleet himself while seven other members of his family served in one capacity or another, some as captains. In a hard-fought, two-hour struggle, Ellet's rams and the Federal gunboats won a great victory—sinking, burning, or capturing seven of the eight Rebel vessels. Although Ellet died of a leg wound received during the battle, his sacrifice was not in vain. The Federals landed troops and quickly secured the city. The Union now controlled the Mississippi along the entire Tennessee shore.

A Season of Federal Triumph

On July 11, General Halleck received orders to report to Washington. An exasperated Lincoln had finally tired of General McClellan's delays, and he now promoted Halleck general in chief with the hope that he could bring the war to a quick and successful conclusion. Halleck appeared to be the best man for the job; his armies in the West had produced a nearly unbroken string of victories in 1862 that had laid the Confederate Heartland open to Federal advance and occupation.

While Halleck prepared to leave for Washington, he divided his army group and assigned each force to different parts of the conquered territories. Meanwhile, in Tupelo, Bragg was reorganizing and refitting his battered army. He knew that Davis expected him to take the offensive. Whether that would be against Corinth or beyond was not yet clear, although regaining Tennessee was not far from his or Jefferson Davis's mind.

Overall, the first five months of 1862 had brought great Federal victories and crushing Confederate defeats in the Western Theater. The Federals had control of the Cumberland and Tennessee Rivers. Most of the Mississippi River was now in Union hands, and key manufacturing centers such as New Orleans, Memphis, and Nashville had been taken from the Rebels. Much of the Confederate Heartland had been overrun by Union forces. Yet, the loss of Tennessee represented perhaps the greatest logistical and geographic Federal achievement. The Volunteer State's manufacturing, her farmlands, and her key geographic location were crucial to the Confederacy's survival. Retrieving Tennessee, then, would be the Rebels' key focus in the West for the second half of 1862.

FOUR

The Fight for Middle Tennessee

★ ★ ★

The Kentucky Campaign

In late summer 1862, authorities in Washington expected to see renewed action in the Western Theater. In Tennessee, Major General Don Carlos Buell was under tremendous pressure from his former commander Halleck and President Lincoln to advance his forty-thousand-man Army of the Ohio on the vital rail hub of Chattanooga and begin liberating Unionist East Tennessee. Buell, however, tried in vain to explain the myriad problems he faced. First, he needed to consolidate his divisions from across Middle Tennessee. Second, his logistics were shaky at best, and his army needed to stockpile food, fodder, ammunition, and other supplies for the advance. The vulnerability of his supply lines exacerbated his problems. The Tennessee and Cumberland Rivers were too shallow this time of year for boats to move upriver. Moreover, the more reliable rail lines stretched either to Memphis or through Nashville and on to Louisville, Kentucky, and were under constant threat of Rebel cavalry raids. In July 1862, for example, Brigadier General Nathan Bedford Forrest's cavalry struck Murfreesboro south of the main Union base at Nashville, capturing the garrison, burning the bridges on the Nashville and Chattanooga Railroad, and looting or destroying badly needed supplies. A couple of weeks later, guerrillas cut the Memphis and Charleston Railroad east of Corinth, and in mid-August, Rebel troopers under Colonel John Hunt Morgan rode out of Knoxville on a lightning raid that seized Gallatin, Tennessee, and wrecked the nearby Big South Tunnel. The damage was so severe that it would require extensive repair work, which would take months and prevent supplies from moving from Louisville to Nashville. Still, Buell's superiors offered little sympathy, and Halleck even warned the general that he would be replaced if he could not speed up his advance.

Meanwhile, on the Confederate side, Buell's plodding but steady advance on Chattanooga concerned the new commander of the Department of East Tennessee, Major General Edmund Kirby Smith. Smith also worried that a Union division under Brigadier General George Morgan at Cumberland Gap might enter his department as Buell approached. Smith appealed to Braxton Bragg for reinforcements, and Bragg sent what men he could spare. What Smith really wanted, however, was for Bragg to bring his army to Chattanooga to counter Buell's advance. Smith's pleas and letters, visits from prominent Kentuckians, and reports of the enthusiastic welcome Kentuckians had given Morgan's men began to influence Bragg's thinking. He decided that he would transport the thirty thousand infantry in his Army of Mississippi via the ramshackle Southern rail system in a circuitous route from Tupelo to Mobile to Montgomery to Chattanooga. The army's wagons, cavalry,

Braxton Bragg.
Library of Congress.

and artillery would move overland by road. Then, Kirby Smith would join him, and with their combined force, they would march northwest into Middle Tennessee and draw Buell into battle at a time and place of their choosing. After defeating Buell, Bragg and Smith could then advance into Kentucky and regain the territory lost to the Federals over the past six months. Bragg was convinced that the citizens of the Bluegrass State would rise en masse against the Yankee occupiers if a Confederate army entered the state in support. Indeed, he was so confident of this that he had his baggage train loaded with an extra fifteen thousand small arms to give to the Kentuckians he expected to flock to his banner.

For Bragg's advance against Buell to succeed, he had to make sure Buell did not receive reinforcements from

Ulysses S. Grant in West Tennessee. Therefore, the general wanted two small detachments in northern Mississippi to support his endeavor. While sixteen thousand men under Major General Sterling Price shadowed Grant, another sixteen thousand under Major General Earl Van Dorn (currently guarding Vicksburg) could aid Price as long as Vicksburg was secure. Once Buell was defeated, Bragg even envisioned Price and Van Dorn moving into West Tennessee and perhaps eventually joining him in Kentucky if the opportunity presented itself.

When Bragg arrived in Chattanooga, he met with Smith to develop a detailed plan for dealing with Buell. Although Bragg outranked Smith, he could not issue orders to him since both men were department commanders unless the forces of the two generals were combined in the field. Well aware of the limits of Bragg's authority, Smith remained reluctant to join forces with him throughout the coming campaign. He did, however, agree to operate with Bragg against Buell. While Bragg continued to wait for his artillery and wagon trains to arrive, Smith would take two of Bragg's best divisions along with his own command and move north to cover any possible Union advance from Cumberland Gap. Unfortunately for Bragg, Smith began to alter their arrangement on his own initiative. Against Bragg's protests, he took his army of about twenty thousand, including Bragg's reinforcements, northward, bypassing the Federals at Cumberland Gap and moving directly into Kentucky. This left Bragg in an awkward position. He could not face Buell with his force alone, but because of the illogical nature of the Confederate Department system, he could not order Smith to comply with their original plan. Exasperated with the situation, Bragg had to now protect Smith from any attack Buell might launch against his small army. Therefore, as soon as all of Bragg's forces were consolidated in Chattanooga, he followed Smith carefully, keeping his army between Buell and Smith while attempting to cajole Smith into honoring their agreement.

On August 30, Smith's army defeated and captured most of the green Union garrison at Richmond just south of Lexington, Kentucky. He then pushed forward and occupied Lexington on September 2 and the state capital at Frankfort the next day. He wrote to Bragg, informing him that he expected thousands of Kentuckians to join the Rebels soon. Bragg's army, meanwhile, had moved quickly across Tennessee in August and entered the Bluegrass State in September on a parallel route to Smith about one hundred miles farther west. Realizing that the Rebels were north of Nashville and threatening his supply lines, Buell had abandoned his campaign against Chattanooga and raced northward.

From Glasgow, Kentucky, on September 14, Bragg issued a proclamation to the citizens of the Bluegrass State explaining that his army had come to liberate them from "the tyranny of despotic rule." Three days later, Bragg's troops captured Munfordville, Kentucky, which put them astride Buell's supply and communication lines out of Louisville. However, Bragg was not ready to force Buell into a battle. He wanted to combine his army with Smith's at Bardstown, Kentucky, some thirty miles southeast of Louisville, and then block Buell's path to the city. He chose, therefore, to move toward Smith, thus temporarily leaving a route to Louisville open to Buell. Buell took advantage of the Rebel misstep and hastily pushed his weary Army of the Ohio through Bowling Green and past Bragg to secure the Union rail and supply hub of Louisville.

By late September, Bragg became frustrated with the campaign. Buell's army was in Kentucky, and the local populace had shown no signs of flocking to Bragg's banner. He wrote Richmond of his deep concerns about the success of the campaign and attempted to spur Van Dorn to action in northern Mississippi. Bragg needed reinforcements and supplies to turn his situation around. Desperate for some success, he even issued a proclamation attempting to convince the citizens in the northwestern states to make a separate peace with the Confederacy and end the bloody and useless war. The general was clearly growing more anxious by the day.

Frustration was mounting with the Union as well. Neither Halleck nor Lincoln had been happy with Buell's performance for a long time, and they decided to replace him as commander of the Army of the Ohio with Major General George Thomas. Thomas, however, refused to accept the command until the current campaign had been decided. Although the authorities in Washington concurred, Buell's days as an army commander were numbered.

On October 1, Buell's army left Louisville to confront Bragg. He had organized the reinforced army into three corps under Major Generals Alexander M. McCook, Thomas L. Crittenden, and Charles Champion Gilbert Creating an awkward situation, Thomas accompanied Buell as his second-in-command. Buell divided his army into separate columns and sent them along separate roads searching for the Rebel army. Meanwhile, Bragg tried to rally Kentuckians to the Confederate cause by installing Kentucky politician Richard Hawes as the new Confederate governor of the state. However, on October 4, 1862, while Bragg and Smith attended Hawes's inauguration, the sound of Union artillery in the west forced the cancellation of the celebration that evening. Establishing a Confederate Kentucky would not come that easily.

Realizing Buell was on the move, Bragg departed Bardstown and ordered his forces east to link up with Smith's small army. He was convinced that Buell's army was approaching Frankfort and Lexington. In fact, the opposite was true. As the Federals advanced on the rear of Bragg's column, the Rebels turned on their pursuers near the small town of Perryville on October 8. There, a confusing engagement ensued in which neither army commander fully realized what was happening until the end. In the initial action, Bragg's army struck an isolated Federal division in the early morning. However, the single division was soon reinforced by Alexander McCook's corps. By the afternoon, Bragg had brought three divisions against McCook and was pounding the Federals. In reality, the Federal army was actually in a good position to crush Bragg while he was engaged with McCook. However, due to an acoustic shadow caused by atmospheric conditions, most of the other Federal corps and Buell were unaware that a fight was taking place and never united their forces.

With the Federals dispersed and unaware, it was an excellent chance for the Rebels to overwhelm one corps of Buell's army. However, poor Confederate coordination and stubborn Yankee resistance combined to help McCook's men hold on until nightfall. That night, scouting reports revealed the situation to both Buell and Bragg. While Buell planned to unite his army and crush Bragg, Bragg wisely slipped away to join Smith. The Battle of Perryville ended with an inconclusive Confederate tactical victory of sorts.

Once Bragg united with Smith, his army was nearly the same size as Buell's. However, he decided not to re-engage Buell's men or even continue the struggle for Kentucky. His army lacked supplies, especially food and fodder, and winter was fast approaching. More importantly, he was annoyed by the lack of local support for his "liberation" of the Bluegrass State. His entire campaign had depended on new Kentucky recruits. Moreover, Bragg had recently received distressing news from northern Mississippi. Van

William S. Rosecrans.
Library of Congress.

Dorn and Price were supposed to keep Grant from reinforcing Buell and, if possible, strike northward in conjunction with Bragg's invasion. But Grant and Major General William S. Rosecrans had frustrated both objectives. Grant had sent several thousand soldiers to Buell, and in two battles at Iuka and Corinth, Rosecrans blocked Price and Van Dorn's plans to move into West Tennessee.

In mid-September, Price had occupied Iuka in northeast Mississippi. Grant planned to trap him between two Union forces. While nine thousand men under Rosecrans advanced northward, another force of eight thousand men from the Army of the Mississippi under Major General Edward Ord would approach from the west. However, the two armies failed to converge. Price struck Rosecrans on September 19, but an acoustic shadow similar to that in Perryville prevented Ord from hearing the battle. Unable to drive Rosecrans from the field and realizing that Ord was nearby, Price moved to join Van Dorn some forty miles to the west. The Federal forces then united and moved toward Corinth. There on October 3, the forces of Van Dorn and Price struck at the Federals. After driving the Yankees back two miles, the Rebels halted for the night. When they renewed their attack the next morning, the Federals inflicted a brutal defeat. The battered Confederates retreated southward, but Rosecrans considered his force too exhausted to pursue. The Battles of Iuka and Corinth had cost the Union three thousand casualties to nearly twice that number for the Rebels. Yet, most importantly, the engagements had prevented Van Dorn and Price from moving into Tennessee and perhaps advancing on Memphis or Nashville.

A despondent Bragg decided to withdraw toward Cumberland Gap on October 13. The Confederate retreat into Tennessee was rapid, and Buell pursued cautiously but did not molest the Rebels. Although pressured by Lincoln to enter and liberate East Tennessee, the Union commander stopped at the Tennessee mountains because he was unwilling to pursue into barren country and risk his men and animals. He believed that he needed supplies and time to launch such a campaign, so he returned to Nashville. This was enough for Halleck and Lincoln; Buell was finally replaced—not by Thomas, however, but by Rosecrans, who would now command the army.

The Confederate invasion of Kentucky failed in its goals of shifting the strategic balance in the Western Theater and convincing most Kentuckians to join the Confederacy. However, it did succeed in forcing Union troops out of northern Alabama and much of Middle Tennessee, albeit temporarily, and it would take the Union forces a year to regain the lost ground. During the campaign, neither Buell nor Bragg had performed particularly well, and this would cost Buell his command. Davis, however, supported Bragg under an avalanche of criticism from the Southern press and even Bragg's chief subordinates, Polk and Hardee. While Bragg's decisions in the campaign were questionable, his subordinates carry a larger share of blame for the poor showing. Kirby Smith resisted any attempt to unite with Bragg, and his lack of a unified command forced Bragg into decisions he would not otherwise have had to make and took away a good bit of his freedom of action. Hardee and Polk had never demonstrated great generalship and were often insubordinate, ignoring Bragg's instructions. Bragg was even forced to direct Polk's forces at Perryville at one point due to the general's lack of basic tactical skill. Price and Van Dorn had not exhibited great leadership either. In the end, Jefferson Davis kept Bragg in command of his army, although General Joseph E. Johnston would soon assume theater command for the Rebels. The Kentucky adventure was over, and Bragg was back where he started. He would now have to hold what was left of Middle Tennessee and protect the strategic rail hub of Chattanooga.

Battle of Murfreesboro

The Union victory at Corinth propelled Rosecrans to national attention and secured him a promotion to commander of the Army of the Ohio. On assuming command of the army, Rosecrans changed the name to the Army of the Cumberland to fit with his assigned Department of the Cumberland. Rosecrans was a tall and imposing figure with a deep devotion to his Catholic faith. He possessed great energy and determination, and he was liked and respected by his soldiers, who called him "Old Rosey." Gradually, Rosecrans concentrated his forces at Nashville, where he set to work preparing the army for its next campaign. He reorganized the army into three "grand divisions" or "wings" (essentially corps), with the right commanded by Major General Alexander McCook, the center by Major General George Thomas, and the left by Major General Thomas L. Crittenden. Brigadier General D. S. Stanley commanded an independent cavalry division. Rosecrans had to address serious problems with sickness, training, and supply before any advance could take place. Since the army's rail supply line was still exposed to Rebel cavalry raids, Rosecrans began to build a huge reserve of provisions in anticipation of possible disruptions. Like his predecessor Buell, Rosecrans faced intense pressure from Lincoln and Halleck to advance and push Bragg's nearby army from Middle Tennessee. However, also like Buell, Rosecrans refused to be unduly pressured and would not launch his campaign until his preparations were completed.

While Rosecrans prepared for a new offensive, Bragg was about thirty miles southeast of Nashville, near Murfreesboro, watching and waiting. He expected Rosecrans to spend the winter in Nashville, which would allow the Rebels time to rebuild, rest, and refit. Bragg used this time to reorganize his army and was even able to get authority from Davis to merge Kirby Smith's units into his own forces for the creation of a new army, which Bragg named the Army of Tennessee.

In mid-December, Jefferson Davis came to inspect the army, consult with Bragg about future movements, and attempt to alleviate the mounting dissension in the army's high command. Since replacing Beauregard, Bragg had been forced to keep incompetent and insubordinate officers in the army. Also, many Kentucky officers were now angry with Bragg over the outcome of the foray into the Bluegrass State. These men were deeply affecting morale and, therefore, the fighting ability of the army. Bragg was having an especially difficult time with his chief subordinates, Hardee and Polk. Hardee was arrogant and willful, while Polk added utter incompetence to those same traits. Davis was not inclined to do more than attempt to keep the peace at this point. He did rearrange the command structure of the West, however, by placing Major General John C. Pemberton in Mississippi to protect Vicksburg and, most importantly, placing General Joseph E. Johnston as theater commander of the West. Johnston's promotion to theater command was surprising. He and Davis never got along. Part of the reason for the enmity stemmed from the fact that both were arrogant and viewed the other as lacking strategic vision. Johnston resented his new position. Even though he assumed a great deal of responsibility, he had little real power because Davis constantly intervened. For example, anxious to protect Vicksburg from Union assault, Davis had Bragg send a division of more than eight thousand men to the river bastion. Johnston objected. He vehemently opposed any weakening of Bragg's small, thirty-six-thousand-man force in the face of Rosecrans.

Bragg, meanwhile, spread out the infantry around Murfreesboro to enjoy the rich bounty of the Middle Tennessee farms. To prevent the Rebels from being surprised by any sudden Federal movements, Major General Joseph Wheeler's cavalry kept an eye on Nashville. Believing himself secure, Bragg unleashed the bulk of his cavalry to raid Rosecrans's supply lines. Forrest again took his men west to disrupt the Federals by attacking the railroads near Nashville while Morgan's cavalry raided the railroads in Kentucky between Nashville and Louisville. Bragg, thus, settled in for what he thought would be a quiet winter. In this he was terribly mistaken. Rosecrans was aware that a division had been sent to Vicksburg and that most of Bragg's cavalry was out raiding in West Tennessee and

Kentucky. He reasoned that this was an opportune time to strike Bragg an unexpected blow. On Christmas night, Rosecrans met with his officers and informed them that they would launch the long-awaited campaign the following day. So at dawn on December 26, the advancing Federal columns set out southward in a bone-chilling icy rain. The struggle for Middle Tennessee had begun.

Rosecrans had developed an excellent plan of attack. He reasoned that with the Rebel corps spread out and without adequate cavalry to screen their army, he could bewilder the enemy with multiple thrusts. He sent McCook's corps consisting of three divisions down the Nolensville Pike toward Triune and into contact with Hardee's corps. Thomas, meanwhile, would advance on McCook's right down the Franklin and Wilson Pikes and threaten Hardee's right flank before shifting toward Nolensville. Crittenden would advance down the Murfreesboro Pike toward La Vergne. McCook was to attack Hardee, with Thomas to support him if needed. If Hardee were beaten or withdrew south to join the rest of Bragg's forces, Crittenden was to advance past La Vergne while Thomas attacked the enemy's left and McCook moved around to the rear. The result would be a crushing blow to Hardee.

The Union advance was slowed by the inclement weather and muddy roads as well as by Wheeler's troopers, who harassed the Yankee columns. Indeed, Wheeler's cavalry performed superbly. In two days, they not only slowed the Federals' march, but they also managed to ride completely around Rosecrans's army and overtake McCook's wagon train of three hundred vehicles near La Vergne. There, the Rebels plundered or destroyed immense quantities of supplies and captured eight hundred prisoners. But as spectacular as Wheeler's achievements were, he could not stop the Federal advance. For the next couple of days, the

Yankees deftly maneuvered the Rebels back upon Stones River north of Murfreesboro.

By December 28, Bragg began to consolidate his army and establish a defensive position at Murfreesboro. He positioned Polk on the left flank about two miles from town and west of Stones River. Hardee's corps would form on the right, east of the river, and Rebel cavalry would guard both flanks. Serious problems, however, plagued the Rebel deployment, the most obvious of which was Stones River itself. Although the river was currently passable, if the heavy rains continued, it could rise rapidly and split the army. In addition, higher ground in front of the Rebel line would offer Federal artillery excellent positions from which to batter the Rebel army. Over the next couple of days, the Federals continued to shift their forces and bring them into position opposite the Rebels. By the morning of the thirtieth, the Federal line was complete, with the left at Stones River and moving mostly south across the Nashville Pike and the Wilkinson Pike to a wooded area just south of Wilkinson's Cross Roads and near the Franklin Pike. The opposing lines were close enough that each commander knew what the other was doing, at least along the front lines.

Rosecrans planned to strike the Rebel right at dawn the next day. On the Federal left, Crittenden was to send two divisions across the river to overwhelm Breckinridge. With a nearly two-to-one advantage, the Federals should have been able to smash the Confederate right and swing in behind the rest of their line. Meanwhile, Thomas would hit the Rebel center along the Nashville Pike, and McCook would feint on the Confederate left to prevent Rebel reinforcements coming to Breckinridge's aid. Ironically, Bragg had also decided to attack the Federal right at first light on the thirty-first. He summoned his corps commanders and outlined a simple yet daring battle plan. At dawn, his strong left wing would attack en echelon, executing a giant wheeling movement designed to push the Federals back past the Nashville Pike and against Stones River. Confederate cavalry would then cut off Rosecrans's army from its supply base at Nashville, leading either to its surrender or its destruction.

Bragg planned to send Hardee's divisions led by Major General John P. McCown and Major General Patrick Cleburne against the right flank of the Federal army. An Irish-born immigrant, Cleburne would prove to be one of the Army of Tennessee's most capable officers. Although serving for a time in the British army as a corporal before coming to the United States, Cleburne would advance from private to major general in service to the Confederacy. Tall and well built with gray-blue eyes, Cleburne cut an imposing military figure. More importantly, he possessed the traits of a keen tactical mind and personal bravery that would make him an inspiration to his men and a determined foe to his enemies.

Polk's corps was to begin its attack after the left had swept past the Federal flank and gotten into their rear. Bragg allocated nearly thirty thousand men for the assault on the Federal right and center. Meanwhile, Breckinridge would hold his position on the far right to protect the approach to Murfreesboro.

The plan was simple in theory, but a wheeling movement of that size and complexity over heavily wooded and broken terrain in the face of enemy resistance would be a difficult challenge. Another potential problem for the Confederates concerned General Polk's rearrangement of his command structure on the eve of battle. Originally, Major General Jones Withers's division, which formed the front line of Polk's corps, was to move forward as a solid line, while Major General Benjamin Cheatham's division followed in support. However, the rough, broken terrain in front of

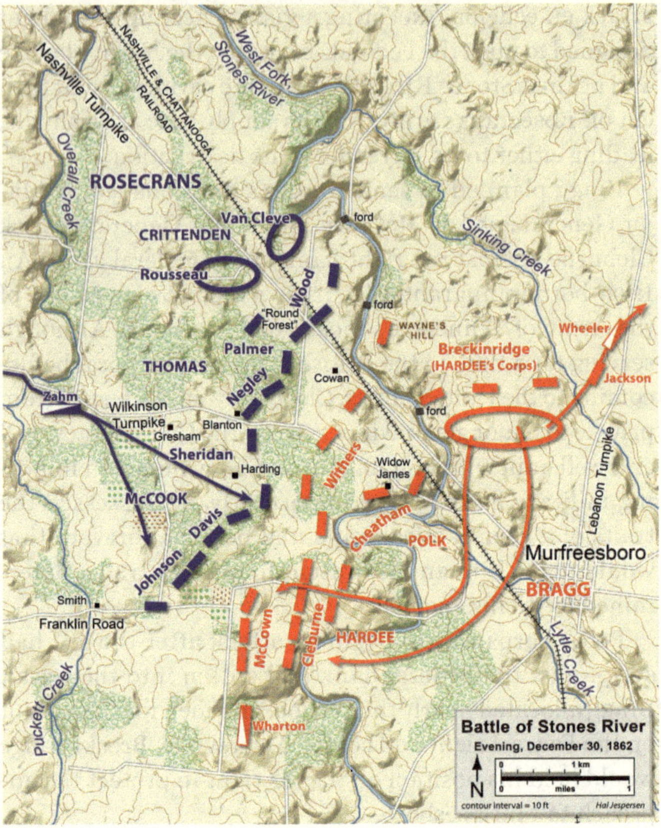

Map by Hal Jespersen, www.cwmaps.com.

Withers and Cheatham prevented the generals from being able to adequately supervise their long battle lines.

Polk ordered the two generals to divide their commands. In addition to his own two left brigades, Cheatham was now to command the two left brigades in Withers's front line. Similarly, Withers would be responsible for the two right brigades of his own division as well as the two right brigades of Cheatham's command. This arrangement provided each general a two-brigade front with an additional two brigades in reserve. It was sound structuring, but it could prove confusing for the brigade and regimental officers who had never served together yet now must cooperate closely.

The icy rain that had fallen throughout the day persisted into the night, and a northerly wind rose and whistled through the dense cedar thickets and across the barren cotton and corn fields where tomorrow's battle would be fought. As the soldiers bedded down to get what rest they could, the military bands of both armies began to play their favorite tunes. The music carried through the wintery night to both sides of the line, and a contest of sorts developed. The challenge of "Yankee Doodle" was answered by "Dixie," and "The Bonnie Blue Flag" was followed by "Hail Columbia." Finally, one by one, the Confederate bands joined the Federal musicians in the playing of the familiar and heart-touching "Home Sweet Home." Soldiers on both sides joined in singing, and Private William J. Worsham of the Nineteenth recalled many years later how deeply the moment affected him and his comrades: "During the stillness of the night, each soldier of both armies, was holding communion with his own soul, his mind occupied with the thought of what tomorrow would bring, whether wounds or death, and would he ever see home again, when the notes of this inspiring tune came floating on the stillness of the night."

Soon the music faded away, the chorus stopped, and the opposing forces who had just joined voices to sing of home and family lay down to await the dawn, when they would raise their voices together once again—this time in the shouts and curses of battle.

Fog blanketed the fields and forests as dawn broke, and a cold drizzle continued to fall. At about 6:00 a.m., while

General McCook's troops were up and preparing their breakfasts, McCown's division advanced through the mist toward the Federal right. Cleburne's men followed about five hundred yards behind. Only when contact was made with the Union pickets did the forest echo with the haunting sound of the Rebel yell. Bragg had attacked first.

Panic filled the Union ranks as the two Confederate divisions overran everything in their path. McCown and Cleburne drove the Yankees back for nearly two miles through the cedar brakes toward the Nashville Pike. Maneuvering through the terrain of limestone outcroppings and cedar stands while engaged in combat, however, was extraordinarily difficult, even for Bragg's veterans. The battle gradually devolved into a series of smaller struggles as unit cohesion broke down while brigade- and division-level officers frantically attempted to retain order. Still, the Rebel surge drove the enemy before them, and the Federals were unable to halt the tide as their lines were repeatedly outflanked and broken.

By 9:00 a.m. the Federal right and center had gradually given way and was forming a right angle. Although meeting stiff resistance, Hardee had driven the Union troops back to the Nashville Pike by 10:00 a.m. Here the Federals attempted to rally. Meanwhile, Rosecrans had canceled Crittenden's attack on the Confederate right and rushed reinforcements to his right flank. He had initially thought that McCook would be capable of turning back Hardee's assault. Rosecrans had been on the Federal left preparing for his own planned attack when the Confederates hit the other end of his line. He now raced across the battlefield directing his units and attempting to establish order out of the chaos around him. He was a ghastly sight as he hastily rode about covered in the blood of his chief of staff, Colonel Julius Garesché, who had been decapitated by artillery while next to Rosecrans.

The second Confederate wave to hit the buckling Federal line came from Polk's corps. Fortunately for the Federals, Major General Philip Sheridan's division realigned to absorb the Rebel attack. Sheridan frantically organized a solid line supported by artillery along the road. The Rebel brigades advanced piecemeal and suffered heavy losses until they were forced back. Sheridan's men continued to hold "The Slaughter Pen" until eventually they ran low on ammunition and had to pull back. Sheridan had bought the Federals precious time to regroup, but as he retreated, the Rebels surged forward into the gap in the Union line.

Meanwhile, a new line was taking shape along the Nashville Pike, where the Federals were amassing brigades and batteries for a final stand. Both Confederate attacks on the new Federal line along the pike had been repulsed, and it seemed that Rosecrans's right, although almost doubled back on the Federal left, was finally going to hold. Bragg realized that the key to winning the battle was breaking the Union right flank and occupying the Nashville Pike. This would cut Rosecrans's line of communication, supply, and retreat. The pike simply had to be taken.

As the Confederate attacks against the Federal right ebbed, the battle reached its culminating point. With the Nashville Pike and a complete victory within their grasp, Rebel momentum was fading. The battle's outcome now hinged on the pivot point of the Union line in a four-acre copse of cedars later known as the "Round Forest." There, a brigade under Brigadier General William B. Hazen held against repeated savage attacks. However, all of Hardee's and Polk's men were exhausted. Bragg's only reserve, the division of John Breckinridge, was still east of Stone's River.

Charge of the First Brigade at the Battle of Stones River. Library of Congress.

He called for the division, desperate to launch one final attack as the sun began to sink in the afternoon sky. However, Breckinridge's men arrived one brigade at a time, and Polk, who commanded this final assault, sent the brigades forward as soon as they arrived instead of amassing them for an attack. These piecemeal assaults were easily rebuffed by the Federals and achieved nothing. As the sky darkened, the fighting subsided. Mercifully, the long bloody day ended.

Except for isolated skirmishing, the battlefield fell silent as darkness descended. Both armies had fought themselves out. The sound of music and singing would not fill the air

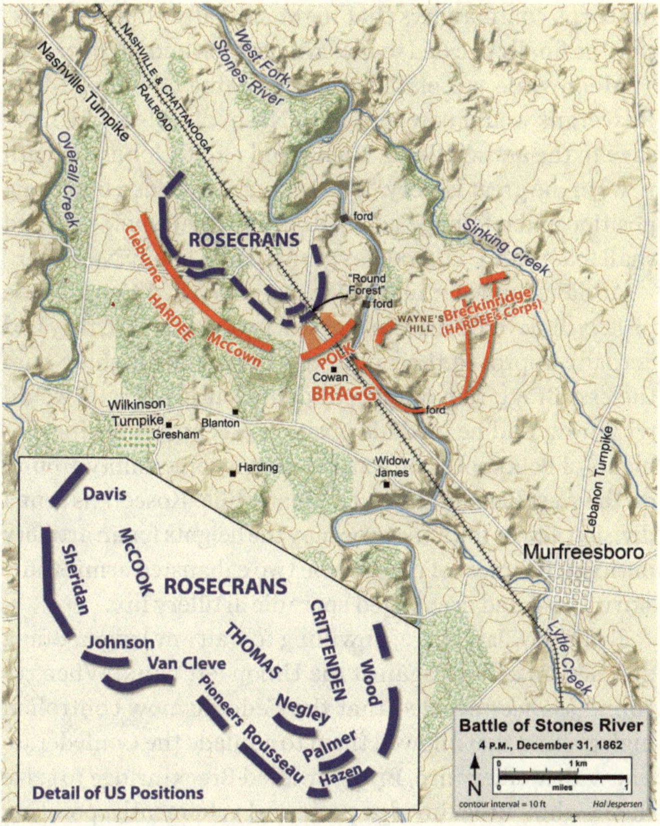

Map by Hal Jespersen, www.cwmaps.com.

that night—only the screams of the wounded and the sound of soldiers entrenching. Bragg's men had nearly routed Rosecrans, but the Army of the Cumberland, although battered, had survived the Rebel onslaught and now held a strong defensive line. And during the night, two brigades arrived to reinforce the Federal army. Rosecrans met with his corps commanders that night, and after much discussion, he finally decided to hold his position and "fight or die."

Meanwhile, an elated Bragg became convinced that Rosecrans would now retreat to Nashville. He sent a message to the authorities in Richmond and to Johnston with news of the great victory. "The enemy has yielded his strong position and is falling back. We occupy [the] whole field and shall follow him. . . . God has granted us a happy New Year."

At dawn on New Year's Day, 1863, shocked Confederate pickets discovered the Yankees still in place. In fact, they had actually improved their positions during the night. Nonetheless, Bragg remained confident that Rosecrans would withdraw, and he held his position except for moving elements of Polk's corps forward to occupy some empty ground on the west bank of the river. Meanwhile, Rosecrans sent a division across the river to occupy the heights for an artillery position. For most of the day, the two exhausted armies only skirmished and exchanged sporadic artillery fire.

By Friday, January 2, unwilling to wait any longer, Bragg planned an assault against the Union left flank. When reconnaissance revealed that the Federals now controlled high ground that allowed them to enfilade the Confederate line with artillery fire, Bragg ordered Breckinridge to seize the heights. Breckinridge protested vehemently, pointing out that Federal positions on both sides of the river could pour fire down on his men. Bragg, however, insisted that his orders be carried out. The late afternoon assault was a disaster. Breckinridge's division was decimated and forced to retreat with appalling losses. That night, Bragg moved two divisions to the right to prevent Rosecrans from counterattacking Breckinridge's battered division.

Another miserable night of sleet and freezing temperatures followed. Wet clothes froze to the skin of the shivering soldiers. Early on the morning of January 3, Bragg received erroneous scouting reports that reinforcements had joined Rosecrans. After spending several hours considering the options, Bragg finally decided the Federals would not retreat, and around 10:00 a.m., he reluctantly decided to withdraw.

During the afternoon, baggage and ordnance trains headed south toward Shelbyville, carrying with them most of the wounded. Some in the worst condition, however, had to be left behind. Sleet continued to fall throughout the night as the Army of Tennessee abandoned Murfreesboro and plodded southward. Bragg continued to ponder his options and his destination while sending Polk's corps to Shelbyville. After days of indecision and countermarching, Bragg decided to establish a defensive line on the ridges of the Duck River Valley.

Throughout the grueling march southward, the Rebels endured bitter cold and incessant rain with barely any food. The majority of the soldiers believed that they had won a great victory, yet they had abandoned the field. Morale plummeted, and the men grew sullen. Most blamed Bragg's incompetence for their suffering and the retreat, and their confidence in his ability began to ebb.

The Federals were unaware that the Rebels had withdrawn until the afternoon of the fourth. Heavy casualties, coupled with the poor condition of the roads, convinced Rosecrans that the battered army could not pursue the fleeing Confederates. On the fifth, he received a wire from an exuberant President Lincoln, declaring, "God bless you, and all with you! Please tender to all, and accept for yourself, the nation's gratitude for your and their skill, endurance, and dauntless courage." The winter of 1862 had been a dismal one for the Union, and Rosecrans's victory provided a crucial boost to Lincoln and the Union cause. While often chided by Halleck and Lincoln for his deliberate preparations, Rosecrans's star was at its zenith now. This, however, would not last. Both armies had fought themselves into exhaustion at Stones River, each suffering about thirteen thousand casualties (close to one-third of the men engaged). As a result, neither Rosecrans nor Bragg would be able to launch another campaign for months, during which time Rosecrans's good will in Washington would gradually wither.

The Tullahoma–Shelbyville Line

After prematurely proclaiming a great victory, the Army of Tennessee and even Braxton Bragg were stunned by the retreat from Murfreesboro, and the Confederate press now savaged the general. They even hinted that Bragg's officers had tried to stop him from retreating both in Kentucky and at Murfreesboro. On January 11 from his new headquarters at Tullahoma, Bragg attempted to stop the avalanche of criticism and regain his good name. He started by writing to several of his top subordinates, asking them to confirm that they were the ones who first suggested the army retreat from Murfreesboro. He wrote, "Finding myself assailed in private and public by the press, in private circles by officers and citizens, for the movement from Murfreesboro, which was resisted by me for some time after advised by my corps and division commanders, and only adopted after hearing of the enemy's re-enforcements by large numbers from Kentucky, it becomes necessary for me to save my fair name, if I cannot stop the deluge of abuse, which will destroy my usefulness and demoralize this army."

Bragg did not stop there. He went on to write, "I shall retire without regret if I find I have lost the good opinion of my generals." Most of the officers reading the circular admitted that they had supported the retreat. However, Bragg also received frank replies as to his ability to continue to lead the army. Both Breckinridge and Cleburne suggested that while they and their officers thought highly of Bragg's patriotism, they did not believe he held the confidence of the army. Hardee's reply was especially harsh, stating that even though the officers respected Bragg's dedication and character, "Frankness compels me to say that the general officers, whose judgment you have invoked, are unanimous in the opinion that a change in the command of this army is necessary." After the other generals informed Bragg of their lack of confidence in his ability to command the army, General Polk wrote to his friend President Davis on February 4, suggesting that Bragg be removed and given a position where his organizational skills might be beneficial.

While many of Bragg's generals (especially those from Kentucky and Tennessee as well as his two corps commanders, Polk and Hardee) were greatly dissatisfied with Bragg and his performance at Perryville and Murfreesboro and wanted his removal, Davis responded to the complaints by dispatching the theater commander to investigate the condition of the army. Johnston, still chafed in his position as commander of the Western Theater, greatly desired to lead an army in the field. However, removing Bragg and assuming command of the Army of Tennessee did not appeal to him. It would appear calculated and unseemly. In late January, he arrived in Tullahoma and quickly discovered the dysfunction prevalent in the Army of Tennessee's higher command. However, he also observed Bragg's skills as an administrator. His men appeared to be well supplied and prepared for future operations. Moreover, Johnston agreed with Bragg's decisions regarding the campaign around Murfreesboro. In the end, he supported Bragg's retention.

In reality, even if Johnston or Davis had removed Bragg, Davis had limited options when it came to a replacement. His choices essentially were either Johnston, who would be demoted from theater command, or Beauregard. Davis had a contentious relationship with both, but it was much worse with Beauregard. With the situation still unsettled, Davis ordered Bragg to Richmond for consultation in March and instructed Johnston to temporarily take command of the Army of Tennessee. However, Bragg's wife, who was traveling with the army, could not be left alone, so Bragg remained in Tullahoma. With another Federal push for Vicksburg occupying Johnston's time, no more serious effort was put into alleviating the tense situation in the Army of Tennessee. In the end, Davis decided to leave things as they were. This tacit support of Bragg allowed the general to consolidate his hold on the army and remove or punish many of his detractors. This only served to fuel more animosity against Bragg, especially among Tennessee and Kentucky soldiers and their officers.

In the meantime, Bragg established a defensive line to the south near Tullahoma with the main goal of blocking a Federal advance on Chattanooga. The terrain between the Union forces in Murfreesboro and the Confederate forces near Tullahoma was part of the Highland Rim region of Middle Tennessee that consisted of rugged and steep ridges and narrow ravines. Four gaps provided the primary routes through the ridges, and Bragg deployed his army to cover them. Polk's corps on the left flank occupied well-fortified positions around Shelbyville and would protect Guy's Gap, where Bragg thought the Federals might advance. Meanwhile, Hardee occupied the Rebel center and right around the village of Wartrace. From there, Hardee's soldiers covered the gaps of Bell Buckle, Liberty, and Hoover's. In addition to protecting the gaps, Bragg's cavalry, nearly a third of his entire army, was situated on his flanks to defend against a Federal sweep around the gaps and to forage for the army. Wheeler's cavalry occupied the far right near

Men repair a single-track railroad after the Battle of Stones River. Library of Congress.

McMinnville, while Forrest's troopers covered the far left around Columbia.

In Murfreesboro, Rosecrans continued to ponder how best to advance on the Rebels. Indeed, he spent six months preparing for the next confrontation with Bragg's army, during which time he lost the goodwill he had attained after Stones River. Lincoln, Secretary of War Edwin M. Stanton, and General in Chief Halleck continually pressed

Rosecrans to advance on Bragg. Part of the reason for Washington's relentless pressure on Rosecrans stemmed from strategic necessity. The main Union objective in the Western Theater in 1863 was to capture Vicksburg, and Washington feared that if not pressured, Bragg's army would send reinforcements to aid Pemberton. Rosecrans, however, objected and used this time to issue new weapons, gather reinforcements, provide instruction and drill, and reorganize his army. By now, the army consisted of three infantry corps commanded by Thomas, McCook, and Crittenden; a small reserve corps under Major General Gordon Granger; and a cavalry corps commanded by Major General David S. Stanley.

Halleck eventually telegraphed Rosecrans that if he were unwilling to move, some of his troops would be sent to Mississippi to reinforce Grant. Grant was currently besieging Vicksburg but was threatened by an impromptu force quickly assembled by Joseph E. Johnston, who was dealing with yet another problem in his theater of command. Finally, on June 24, after months of preparation, Rosecrans sent a long-anticipated telegram to Washington, proudly announcing that "the army begins to move at 3 o'clock this morning." The campaign to drive the Rebels from southern Middle Tennessee was underway at last.

The Tullahoma Campaign

The start of the campaign had actually begun hours before when, on June 23, elements of the reserve corps under Granger had advanced with a cavalry division due west from Murfreesboro toward Triune to begin part of an elaborate feint. This maneuver was designed to fool Bragg into believing that the main attack would come on his left flank in the direction of Shelbyville. At the same time, another

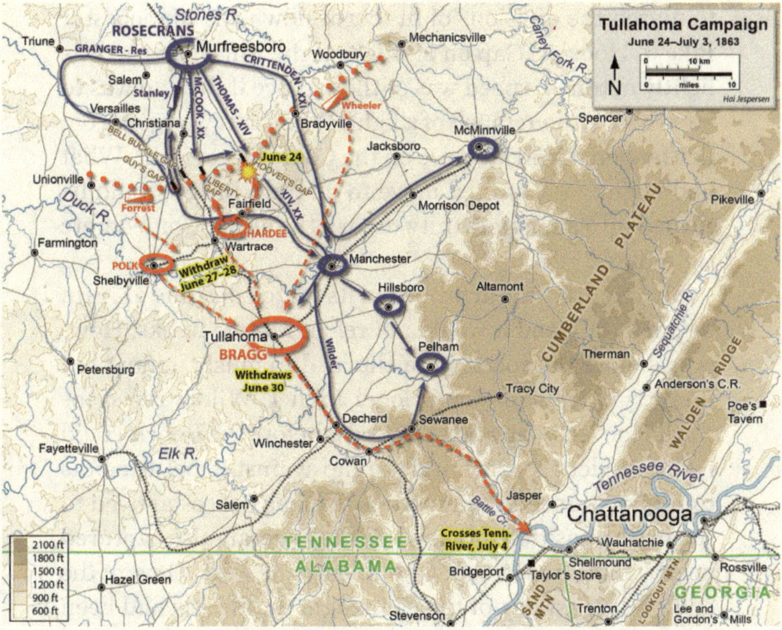

Map by Hal Jespersen, www.cwmaps.com.

Federal infantry division moved to Bradyville, well beyond the Confederate right flank, where it could drive back Confederate cavalry and move in the direction of Manchester, advancing on the Confederate rear. It was only after these movements were underway that Rosecrans assembled his corps commanders to hear his detailed orders for the upcoming campaign.

Rosecrans informed his generals that McCook's troops were to come up behind Granger, then move east through Liberty Gap, and advance on Hardee in the Rebel center. Granger would continue to threaten Shelbyville and take control of the roads in the area. Thomas, meanwhile, was to march the divisions of his corps down the Manchester Pike to Hoover's Gap on Hardee's right. Since the gap was lightly manned, speed was of the essence if the gap was to be seized without much of a fight. While this was going on, Crittenden would advance on the Confederate right. What had begun as a limited move to distract Bragg would be turned into an opportunity to turn the entire Confederate right flank.

Shortly after the army began its march on June 24, rain began to fall, and it would not relent for two weeks. However, before the roads were churned to mush, a mounted infantry brigade under Colonel John T. Wilder raced toward Hoover's Gap and captured it before the Rebels could react. Wilder's brigade held the gap against Rebel attempts to retake it until infantry from Thomas's corps arrived to secure the position. Meanwhile the Federals also captured nearby Liberty Gap about six miles to the west. Thus, at the end of the first day of the campaign, the Rebels had been taken by surprise, and the Federals possessed two of the four key gaps. Rosecrans's plan was working.

On June 25, the Rebels launched local attacks to retake Hoover's and Liberty Gap, but to no avail. Because of Rosecrans's seizure of two of the gaps and the accompanying feints to the Rebel flanks, Bragg was still unsure of Federal intentions, and his cavalry could not ascertain the main Union objective. The next day, Bragg met with Polk at Shelbyville. Believing now that Granger's force was a decoy, Bragg ordered Polk to march his corps through Guy's Gap that night and attack the Union force at Liberty Gap from the rear while Hardee pressed them in front. However, Polk argued that the maneuver was too difficult for his men to execute, and Hardee apparently did not fully understand his role in the plan. It did not matter, because once Hardee became aware of the presence of the bulk of Thomas's corps near Hoover's Gap, he ordered his men to retreat toward Wartrace, thus breaking the rest of Bragg's defensive line.

By the twenty-seventh, Bragg had no choice but to pull his army back safely within the works around Tullahoma. He planned to make a stand there, but Polk and Hardee disagreed, believing the Federals could outflank the position too easily. The next day, Federal mounted infantry launched a raid into the Rebel rear to cut Bragg's supply line on the Nashville and Chattanooga Railroad. The raid did little damage, and it was repaired quickly. Polk and Hardee continued to advocate for a retreat, and by the afternoon of June 30, Bragg agreed and issued orders for a nighttime withdrawal across the Elk River. The next morning, the Army of the Cumberland formed in line of battle and advanced on the Tullahoma works, only to find them empty.

As Bragg moved southeastward toward Chattanooga, he continued to look for a place to make a stand. At first he issued orders to set up a position behind the Elk River, but on the evening of July 1, he changed his mind and continued heading toward Chattanooga. Passing one position after another, Bragg could not decide where or even if he should stop to face the enemy. Rosecrans was pursuing the Rebels at a distance, and cavalry skirmishes were common. By July 4, the lead units of the Army of Tennessee were crossing the Tennessee River, and by the evening of the seventh, the exhausted troops ended their march and camped around Chattanooga.

Tullahoma was a brilliant campaign of maneuver, executed almost flawlessly by the Army of the Cumberland. Rosecrans's men had driven the Confederates out of Middle Tennessee with minimal losses of around six hundred. Yet Rosecrans's remarkable campaign did not receive the acclaim it deserved because it coincided with the defeat of Robert E. Lee's army at Gettysburg and the capture of Vicksburg by Grant. Rosecrans felt slighted that while his army forced the Rebels out of Middle Tennessee at little loss of life, Washington overlooked them. In nine days, his army had driven the Rebels from two fortified positions and captured the southern portion of Middle Tennessee. The campaign was a masterpiece of planning and execution. In contrast, Bragg and his dysfunctional high command had proven themselves unworthy of the soldiers they led. As a result, morale plummeted even further as the army retreated, and many men simply deserted.

Rosecrans did not immediately pursue Bragg toward Chattanooga. Instead, he followed his pattern of pausing to regroup and deal with significant logistical problems. The Cumberland Plateau separating the two armies was a rugged, barren country with roads more akin to tracks. As usual, Rosecrans was under intense pressure from Washington to move toward Chattanooga while another Federal army under Major General Ambrose E. Burnside advanced into East Tennessee. Rosecrans, however, knew that he would have difficulty receiving supplies from his base with any advance across the Tennessee River. He, therefore, took the time to accumulate enough supplies and transport wagons to operate away from his supply lines and carefully planned his next steps. Rosecrans again devised a plan of maneuver designed to capture Chattanooga without fighting Bragg for the town. The Federals would march across the Cumberland Plateau and cross the Tennessee River south of Chattanooga. Bragg had to believe the Federals were moving directly on Chattanooga and thus position his men to protect the town. Then the army would advance on a wide front through the mountains. Crittenden's corps would drive toward Chattanooga from the west, while Thomas's corps would cross Lookout Mountain about twenty miles south of the city. Meanwhile, General McCook's corps and Stanley's cavalry corps would drive even farther to the southeast toward Bragg's supply line, the Western and Atlantic Railroad. If all went according to plan, Bragg would have to abandon Chattanooga or attempt to hold the town without a supply line.

Rosecrans ordered his army to move on August 16. The abysmal roads slowed their progress, and the engineers needed time to bridge the Tennessee River. Meanwhile, Rosecrans's plan of deception was underway. Wilder's mounted infantry brigade moved to the north of Chattanooga, where his men were deceiving the Confederates into thinking that they were part of a large Federal force north of the town that was attempting to link with Burnside's army. Bragg, now also in command of the forces in East Tennessee under Major General Simon B. Buckner, sent reinforcements to the general, who had already abandoned Knoxville and was stationed about thirty-five miles northeast of Chattanooga. Bragg soon had the Rebel army concentrated above the city waiting for the Federal attack that would never come.

The first Federal crossing of the Tennessee River was accomplished near Stevenson, Alabama, on August 29. That was soon followed by crossings at other locations, and by September 4, most of the Army of the Cumberland had safely crossed the river unmolested. They still faced an arduous journey, however, with mountainous terrain and narrow roads, and they would have to maneuver around the formidable barriers of Sand Mountain, Lookout Mountain, and Missionary Ridge. This meant that the corps would have to advance by separate routes. On the right flank,

McCook's corps moved southwest toward Valley Head, Alabama; in the center, Thomas's corps moved just across the Alabama border to Trenton, Georgia; and on the left, Crittenden's corps moved directly toward Chattanooga around Lookout Mountain. On September 8, after learning that Rosecrans's army was below the town and threatening his line of supply, a frustrated Bragg ordered the evacuation of Chattanooga. The Rebel general had been badly deceived and outmaneuvered by Rosecrans yet again. The Rebels trudged southward along the road toward LaFayette, Georgia, about twenty miles from Chattanooga. Union forces occupied Chattanooga on September 9, and a jubilant Rosecrans telegraphed Halleck, declaring that "Chattanooga is ours without a struggle and East Tennessee is free."

In truth, Rosecrans had every reason to celebrate. He had again used deception and rapid maneuver to force Bragg out of prepared defenses and into retreat. He had outwitted and outmaneuvered him repeatedly, first by refusing to abandon his position at Murfreesboro, then by capturing Middle Tennessee, and now by seizing the great prize of Chattanooga. Rosecrans was not finished, however. Instead of his usual period of consolidation and careful preparation after a victory, this time he planned to keep the pressure on Bragg. Sensing that Bragg and his army were totally broken and fleeing southward, he planned to pursue him and catch the Rebels unaware. Unfortunately for Rosecrans, the one time he did not consolidate and carefully prepare plans for his next move was the one time he should have.

Bragg, encamped at LaFayette, learned that the Union corps were spread out over forty miles and too far apart to support each other. The Rebel general soon developed a plan of his own. Confederate soldiers posing as deserters fed Rosecrans's belief that the Rebels were unable and unwilling to fight and would not stop retreating. Although Thomas cautioned Rosecrans that pursuing Bragg with the Army of the Cumberland's corps dispersed and its supply lines unsecured and tenuous was dangerous, Rosecrans ignored him. "Old Rosey" would continue the advance—an advance that would bring him straight into Bragg's trap. Rosecrans would soon learn that the struggle for East Tennessee was not over. It was just beginning.

FIVE

The Liberation of East Tennessee

★ ★ ★

IN THE AUTUMN OF 1863, it appeared to most that Federal forces had finally liberated East Tennessee and driven the Rebels not only from the region but from the whole of the Volunteer State as well. Yet appearances were deceiving: the Confederate government and the Army of Tennessee had no intention of giving up East Tennessee so easily.

Throughout 1862 and 1863, Lincoln had pressured his Western Theater commanders to liberate the Unionist population of East Tennessee. Along with the advantage of reuniting the region's loyalists with the rest of the nation, occupation would cut a vital Rebel rail link from the Deep South to Virginia. When Major General Ambrose Burnside was appointed to command the Department of the Ohio and its army in March 1863, Lincoln admonished him to move into East Tennessee. Pressure from the president and a desire to resurrect his tarnished reputation after the humiliating defeat at the hands of Robert E. Lee at

Fredericksburg convinced Burnside to push forward with this plan. Just like his predecessors, however, he faced serious obstacles launching a campaign in the rugged terrain of the region.

Lincoln and the War Department had hoped that Burnside could enter East Tennessee while Rosecrans was maneuvering against Bragg at Tullahoma in the spring of 1863, but Burnside's advance was initially delayed by the need to shift some of his forces to reinforce General Grant's campaign against Vicksburg. While awaiting the return of his men in June 1863, Burnside launched a raid under Brigadier General William P. Sanders, whose mixed brigade of horsemen and infantry destroyed railroad track and disrupted communications around Knoxville.

Sensing that a new Union effort to take the region was imminent, Major General Simon B. Buckner, the Confederacy's new department commander for East Tennessee, pressed Richmond for reinforcements. Buckner's intuition was correct. On August 16, as Rosecrans maneuvered Bragg out of southern Middle Tennessee and toward Chattanooga, Burnside initiated his campaign for Knoxville, leading a force of around eighteen thousand. Rather than attempting to storm the Confederate defenses at Cumberland Gap on the Tennessee–Kentucky border, Burnside feinted toward the gap while he flanked the position to the south. Marching rapidly across the rough ground, Burnside's men then moved toward Knoxville.

Meanwhile, as Bragg fell back to Chattanooga, authorities in Richmond ordered Buckner to support the defense of the vital rail hub. Buckner left only a small force at Cumberland Gap and an infantry brigade east of Knoxville and moved the bulk of his men southward to operate with Bragg. With no opposition, then, a Union cavalry brigade simply rode into Knoxville on September 2, and the next day, the city's loyalist population cheered as Burnside's infantry marched into the city. Knoxville had at last been liberated, and the surrender of Confederate forces at Cumberland Gap on September 9 quickly followed. The same day the Federals entered the gap, Rosecrans moved elements of his army into Chattanooga. Although the War Department ordered Burnside to march his command southward to link up with Rosecrans, Burnside believed the lack of adequate food and fodder and unreliable supply lines prevented such a movement with winter coming, and he therefore remained in the Knoxville area.

Following the loss of Knoxville, the Rebel forces in the East Tennessee Department were incorporated into Bragg's army, which was also receiving reinforcements from elsewhere in the Confederacy as Jefferson Davis frantically tried to bolster Bragg's position. Although Bragg was forced to abandon Chattanooga to counter Rosecrans's advances south of the town, he was not prepared to retreat any farther than LaFayette, Georgia.

Chickamauga

Bragg was not fleeing in panic as Rosecrans believed. In fact, he was actually concentrating his army behind Pigeon Mountain at LaFayette. He reasoned that with the three Federal corps pursuing him spread out at least twenty miles from each other in mountainous terrain, they could not possibly support each other if attacked. From his army's position, Bragg could strike at any of them with overwhelming force. He soon decided on his target: Thomas's corps.

Meanwhile, as elements of Thomas's corps continued to advance through the gaps in Missionary Ridge and Pigeon Mountain, they moved into McLemore's Cove. The lead division was commanded by Major General James S.

Negley, and it was followed by Brigadier General Absalom Baird's division. The unsuspecting Federal divisions were in a vulnerable position. As they moved across the mouth of McLemore's Cove on the Dug Gap road, they were enclosed on three sides by Lookout and Pigeon Mountains. This left only one opening to the northeast, where Bragg could position elements of his army. If the Rebels advanced into McLemore's Cove from that position while more Rebels moved over Pigeon Mountain through nearby Dug Gap, they could strike the Yankees in the front and flank. The Federals would then panic and be forced to retreat the way they had come, clogging up the small mountain road, only to be overwhelmed by the enemy. This was the opportunity Bragg had been waiting for.

Essentially, Bragg planned to destroy Thomas's corps in detail one division at a time. Since Thomas's corps was eighteen miles from McCook's corps and twenty-four miles from Crittenden's men, help could not possibly arrive in time. It was an excellent plan, yet it began to unravel almost immediately. On the night/early morning of September 9–10, Bragg ordered Major General Thomas C. Hindman to move his division to McLemore's Cove to be supported by Major General Patrick Cleburne's division. Once hit from front and flank by the superior numbers of these Rebel units, Negley's division should be routed or destroyed.

Much to Bragg's consternation, however, his subordinates balked at his orders. Cleburne failed to move his division, and although Hindman managed to position his division for the attack, he would not launch the assault without reinforcements. On the morning of September 10, then, an exasperated Bragg ordered Buckner to move his division to the cove in support of Hindman. However, by the time Buckner arrived, Hindman had decided that it was now too late in the day to attack and asked Bragg to revise his orders. While the Rebels argued, Negley's men had skirmished with Rebel cavalry, and he now realized that Confederates were nearby. Negley withdrew to Davis's Cross Roads on the evening of September 10 to await Baird's division. Anxious not to lose this opportunity, Bragg sent several messages to Hindman during the evening emphasizing the need for immediate action the next day at dawn. Yet Hindman once again refused to attack. He remained convinced that unseen Federal forces were preparing to strike him.

An incensed Bragg was now determined to force his officers to obey his commands. He again directed Cleburne to move his division toward Negley, and he ordered reinforcements to join Cleburne's division for the assault. Bragg also admonished Hindman to attack at the earliest hour possible the next morning. Early on September 11, Bragg rode out to Dug Gap to check on Cleburne's progress. Although Cleburne's men were passing through the gap and awaiting an indication of Hindman's assault, morning soon passed into early afternoon with still no sound of fighting. Despite having twice the number of troops as Negley (plus support), Hindman stubbornly refused to attack, still convinced that Federals were lurking in his rear.

While Bragg was trying desperately but in vain to get his generals to carry out his orders, the Federals eventually realized their precarious position. That same morning, Baird's division came forward to support Negley, and together the two Federal generals began a cautious and slow retreat from McLemore's Cove to Stevens Gap. They faced only skirmishing, however, and not a massed assault as they escaped Bragg's well-planned trap. With the fiasco at McLemore's Cove, Bragg lost his best opportunity of the campaign to batter a portion of the Federal army. The Army of Tennessee's dysfunction was becoming palpable. Furious and bewildered, Bragg could only watch as insubordination and incompetence cost the Rebels a golden opportunity.

Realizing the Rebels were in the area and in strength, Thomas ordered consolidation of the four divisions of his corps near Stevens Gap on the morning of September 12 and was prepared for a Rebel assault that never came. Bragg still struggled to get his subordinates to move quickly enough to mount an attack. Initially, Rosecrans was unconcerned about Thomas's warnings of Confederate forces in strength. He was still not convinced that his army faced any real danger and, therefore, wanted to continue to pursue the "retreating" Confederates. Union cavalry, however, soon brought reports of large Confederate forces near LaFayette as well as on the east bank of the Chickamauga Creek near Lee and Gordon's Mill. Rosecrans now understood the urgency and was determined to unite his army to prevent a Rebel strike at any of his isolated corps.

That same day, Rosecrans ordered McCook and the army's cavalry to move northeast to Stevens Gap to join with Thomas's corps. Together, they would then continue northeast to rendezvous with Crittenden's corps at Lee and Gordon's Mill. Major General Nathan Bedford Forrest's scouts reported these Federal movements to Bragg, who now believed he had another opportunity to strike an isolated Federal corps (this time Crittenden's) as it marched toward Lee and Gordon's Mill. He ordered Lieutenant General Leonidas Polk to attack Crittenden's lead division, under Brigadier General Thomas J. Wood, at dawn on September 13 with his entire corps. Polk, however, blatantly refused, believing he was facing the entirety of Crittenden's corps. He summoned his subordinates to support his decision and demanded reinforcements before considering such an assault. Bragg, though frustrated, acquiesced and sent him another seven brigades. Polk now had a two-to-one advantage, yet, inexplicably, he still would not move. Bragg rode to Polk's headquarters to find that the bishop had made no preparations for an attack. Infuriated at Polk's incompetence and insubordination, Bragg immediately began making the preparations for the assault himself. By then, however, it was too late: Crittenden's corps had passed the Rebel front and concentrated at Lee and Gordon's Mill. Another priceless chance to strike a blow at the Federals had been squandered by willfulness.

For the next four days, both armies maneuvered and coalesced while seeking to locate the other. Rosecrans continued to consolidate his forces near Lee and Gordon's Mill, intending to withdraw northeastward to Chattanooga. Meanwhile, Bragg still sought an opportunity to strike the Yankees a blow before they could reach their destination. By the evening of September 17, Bragg's scouts reported that the Federal left flank rested at Lee and Gordon's Mill, which placed the Rebel army farther north than Rosecrans but on the opposite bank (east) of Chickamauga Creek. Moreover, Bragg had been reinforced by Brigadier General Bushrod R. Johnson's division from Mississippi and expected another two divisions from the Army of Northern Virginia under Lieutenant General James Longstreet to soon arrive. He felt that he had the numbers and the opportunity to execute a new plan. He intended for his army to cross Chickamauga Creek the next day at four points—Reed's Bridge, Alexander's Bridge, Thedford's Ford, and Dalton's Ford—while cavalry covered the army's flanks. This plan involved two key provisions. The Rebels had to gain control of two roads (the LaFayette Road and the Dry Valley Road—the LaFayette being the more important) from LaFayette to Chattanooga, both passing in the vicinity of Lee and Gordon's Mill. Once the Rebels had cut the roads, they would strike and shatter the Federal left flank (closest to Chattanooga) and drive the entire Army of the Cumberland westward into McLemore's Cove and away from their supply base at Chattanooga.

The next morning, September 18, around 7:00 a.m., fighting began. Rebel infantry and cavalry ran into dismounted Federal cavalry that were protecting the crossing points. Stubborn resistance at Reed's and Alexander's Bridges delayed the Confederates, but the few Yankee defenders could not hold indefinitely. By nightfall, Bragg controlled all the Chickamauga crossings and was moving his men to the west bank. Moreover, elements of the Army of Northern Virginia had arrived to reinforce his command. Bragg assumed he was now above Rosecrans's left flank and had to simply cut the roads and hit that flank and push the Federals away from Chattanooga to their doom.

Despite his optimism, things would go terribly wrong for Bragg and the Rebels on September 19, largely due to the general's misjudgment of the battlefield. When his scouts had reported that the Union left flank was at Lee and Gordon's Mill on the eighteenth, they had been correct. However, while Crittenden's corps was, indeed, still concentrated around the mill, this was not now the left flank. Thomas's corps had marched from McLemore's Cove undetected by the Rebels, and Rosecrans had positioned it north of Lee and Gordon's Mill, extending his left flank. Additionally, Thomas had spread his divisions in a wide, protective front that stretched from Crawfish Springs to the Widow Glenn's house, to Kelly Field, and around the McDonald farm, which gave him a broad front. Major General Gordon Granger's reserve corps was also spread along the northern end of the battlefield from Rossville to McAfee's Church. Rosecrans had no intention of losing control of his line of supply and retreat to Chattanooga and had taken measures to secure his left flank. Yet Bragg's entire battle plan was based on an attack against the Federal left

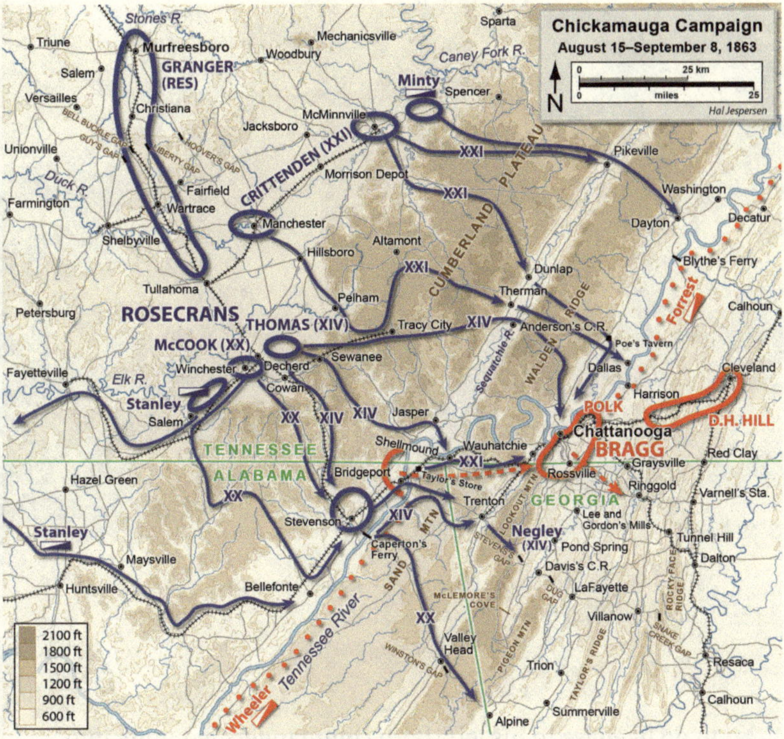

Map by Hal Jespersen, www.cwmaps.com.

utilizing the bulk of his divisions while other Rebel units were either in reserve or pinning Federal units in place on the Union right.

On the morning of the nineteenth, Forrest's cavalry probed Thomas's position, initiating the start of the battle along the LaFayette Road and Chickamauga Creek. Assuming that Rosecrans was attempting to move the center of the battle farther north, Bragg rushed reinforcements from all parts of his line to his right, which prompted Rosecrans

Alfred Waud sketch of the Battle of Chickamauga.
Library of Congress.

to do likewise to his left. Both commanders fed units into the fight throughout the day. Because the thick woods prevented division or brigade commanders from adequately surveying the battlefield, the fighting devolved into small unit actions. The battle lines surged back and forth in savage clashes. By nightfall, the two armies had fought each other to a standstill and occupied positions that roughly paralleled the LaFayette Road. The line stretched from Kelly Farm in the north to Viniard Farm about a mile north of Lee and Gordon's Mill. Although much blood had been spilt, Bragg had failed in his objective to turn Rosecrans's flank, and the Federals still held both the LaFayette and Dry Valley Roads and thus a line of retreat to Chattanooga.

That night Longstreet and the rest of his force from the Army of Northern Virginia arrived. Bragg inexplicably decided to reorganize his army on the spot into two "wings" consisting of a corps and a division each, placing Longstreet on the left and Polk on the right. However, allowing the stubborn and incompetent Polk to command the right, where the main Confederate action was supposed to begin the next day, was a poor decision. Bragg expected Polk to attack at dawn and continue the plan of turning Rosecrans's left flank.

Not surprisingly, the next morning on the twentieth, Polk yet again failed to strike. When Bragg arrived to investigate, he found that Polk had never properly informed his subordinate commanders about the attack. No plans had been discussed, so now it would take precious time to position the units. Bragg and his staff began preparations for the assault—preparations that Polk should have made the previous night. Finally, three hours behind schedule at around 9:30 a.m., their attack on the Union left began. Unfortunately for the Rebels, the Federal units—having wisely used the morning hours to construct breastworks—would now take a terrible toll on the advancing Confederates. As Thomas felt the pressure of the heavy assault, he asked Rosecrans for reinforcements, which arrived in a steady stream. The Rebels also fed units into the attack but could not break Thomas's solid line.

To pressure the other end of the Union line, Longstreet was to launch an attack by 11:00 a.m. Instead of simply sending his divisions forward in a line of battle, the general decided to hit the Federals to his front with a column of attack or a stack of divisions designed to break an enemy line with overwhelming numbers and then exploit any breakthrough. The point on the Union line that faced this assault would have to absorb the impact of eight veteran brigades from the Confederacy's premier army. Around 11:00 a.m., just as Longstreet was preparing to send the gray-clad wave forward, the Federals committed a staggering blunder.

Throughout the day, Rosecrans had continued to send units to Thomas's sector of the battlefield. Eventually, a call came for Brigadier General John M. Brannan's division in reserve to move to Thomas's aid. However, Brannan's unit was not actually in reserve but in the center of the Union line. Brannan immediately realized that the order was a mistake, and he ignored it. However, word got back to Rosecrans that Brannan's division had moved to aid Thomas, which now created a gap. Rosecrans did not check the report but instead ordered the division next to Brannan to "close up" the gap. Since in reality no gap existed, the division of General Thomas Wood interpreted the order to mean he needed to pull his division out of line and position it to the rear of Brannan's in support. Just as Wood's men vacated the Union battle line, Longstreet's divisions surged forward and straight through the gap into the Federal rear. Although the Union divisions on either side of the gap tried frantically to close the hole, their efforts proved futile. The Rebels spilled through and overran the Army of the Cumberland's reserve artillery and wagon park. The entire Union line soon began to splinter.

While many Union units initially stood firm, the Confederate wave and the collapsing Federal line created chaos, ending effective command and control, and the army dissolved into a mob. Rosecrans, McCook, and Crittenden were caught up in the ensuing rout that caused most of the army to flee toward Chattanooga while they still had access to the roads. Other units moved toward Thomas's position, where the Union line remained solid. When Thomas learned of the collapse on his right, he hastily assembled a line facing the Rebels coming from the south. Throughout the afternoon, the Rebels launched attack after attack against Thomas and the last viable Union position. Despite pressure from both Longstreet's and Polk's men, Thomas's units that were anchored on Horseshoe Ridge and around Kelly Farm repulsed successive waves of Rebel assaults. Although Thomas wanted to remain on the field until nightfall, Rosecrans, now in Chattanooga, ordered him to withdraw in order to save his portion of the army. Reluctantly, Thomas complied. As the long day ended and the haphazard Rebel pursuit faded, the weary Federal soldiers retreated northward through Rossville Gap.

When night came, the Rebels remained in possession of the battlefield, and while many believed they had won a hard-fought victory, a dejected Bragg knew all too well that his plan to trap and destroy Rosecrans had failed. Despite routing more than half of the Federal army, Rosecrans had escaped his clutches and succeeded in getting his army back to Chattanooga. Although many of his officers urged Bragg to mount a rapid pursuit of the Yankees, he demurred, realizing that his army was exhausted and badly disorganized. He would, indeed, advance toward Chattanooga—but not until he rested and regrouped his forces. Chickamauga had been a bloodbath for both armies. The Federals lost about sixteen thousand casualties out of approximately sixty thousand engaged, while the Confederates suffered eighteen thousand casualties out of about sixty-five thousand engaged. Few men of either side could fully contemplate such a bloodletting. This would be the costliest battle in the Western Theater and second only to Gettysburg as the bloodiest of the war.

Chattanooga Under Siege

When the Army of Tennessee finally arrived outside the Chattanooga defenses, Bragg faced limited options. He

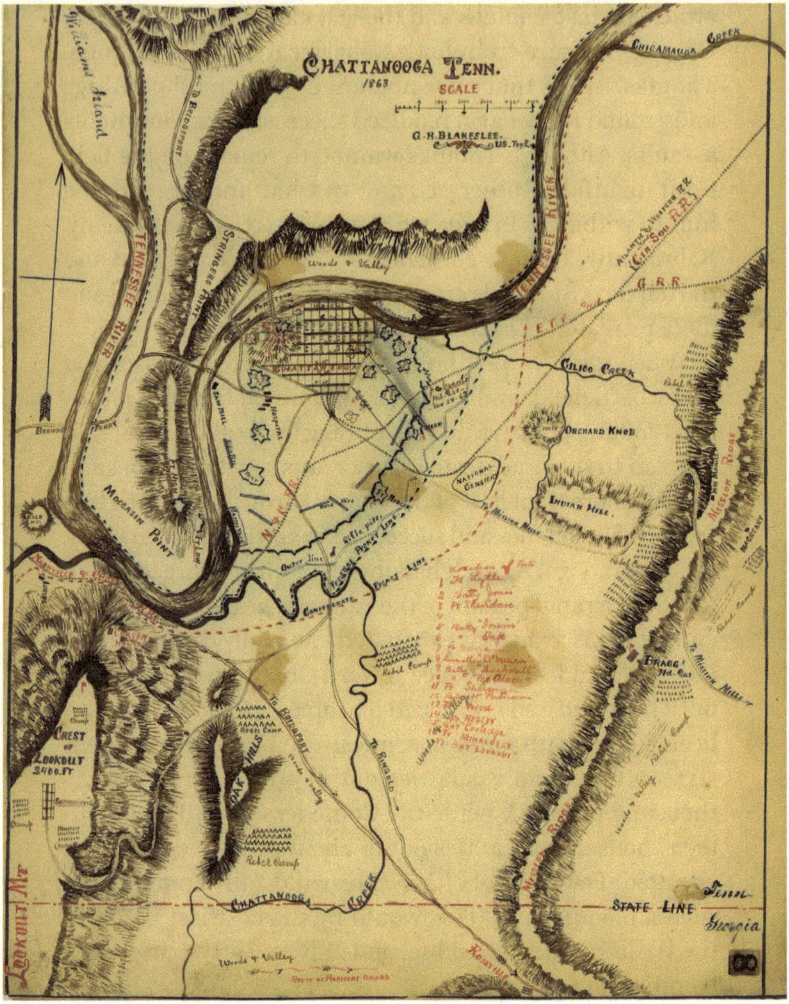

Sketch of Chattanooga in 1863 showing fortifications, Union/Confederate picket lines, rifle pits, "Rebel camp[s]," roads, railroads, and streams. Library of Congress.

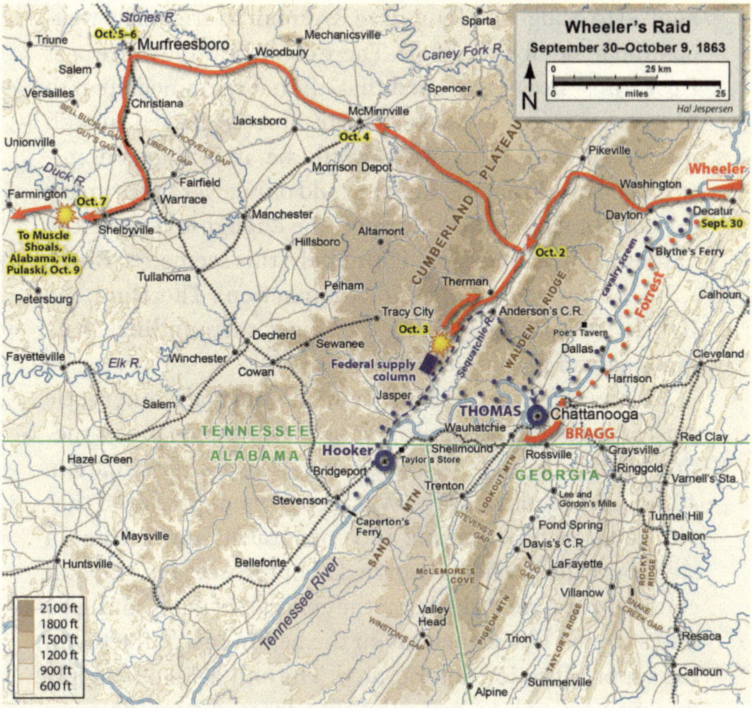

Map by Hal Jespersen, www.cwmaps.com.

could attempt to storm the town's defenses hoping that the Federals were demoralized. However, the Union forces had enhanced the old Rebel fortifications to create a strong three-mile-long semicircle of works around Chattanooga, and Bragg rightly did not believe his men could overwhelm those defenses. Another option would be to attempt to bypass Rosecrans by crossing the Tennessee River and moving deeper into Tennessee to cut the Federal line of supply and perhaps threaten Nashville. This option, however, was impossible, because the Rebels had neither the pontoons needed to bridge the Tennessee River nor the requisite wagons and mules for transport. There could be no advance past Rosecrans. Bragg reasoned that all that remained open to him was to attempt a siege of sorts. Since he lacked enough men to surround the city, it would be, in reality, a demi-siege, meaning that the Rebels could only cover the primary avenues of supply. Still, it might be enough to starve the Yankees into submission. Ultimately, this seemed to Bragg to be the best course of action (or inaction). Therefore, the Rebels took positions along the ridges surrounding Chattanooga and prepared to wait.

Meanwhile, in Chattanooga, the normally energetic Rosecrans had lapsed into a stupor over the near destruction of his army and the seriousness of the present situation. Although Lincoln and the War Department promised that aid would be forthcoming and encouraged him to remain steadfast, the president worried about Rosecrans's mental condition and remarked that the general seemed "confused and stunned like a duck hit on the head." Inside the town, the supply situation deteriorated. The only available supply line was a rough wagon road that crossed over Walden's Ridge. The army's mules, however, soon became exhausted from pulling heavily laden wagons along this steep and treacherous track between Chattanooga and the Federal supply depot at Bridgeport, Alabama, about sixty miles away. Complicating matters, heavy rains at the end of September washed away stretches of the tortuous route. Worse still, Confederate cavalry under Joseph Wheeler began to raid the supply convoys. In October, for example, the Rebels attacked a supply train of eight hundred wagons, burning hundreds and killing the mules. The poor condition of the road and continued Rebel attempts to cut Rosecrans's meager supplies forced the soldiers in the Army of the Cumberland to continually cut rations to near starvation levels and to either watch their horses and mules die of malnutrition or eat them.

Lincoln, Halleck, and Secretary of War Edwin M. Stanton were working desperately to save the Army of the Cumberland by sending more troops to break the siege. Major General Joseph Hooker and two corps (about twenty thousand men) from the Army of the Potomac were on their way to Bridgeport, Alabama, and a corps of four divisions under Major General William T. Sherman was en route from the successful siege of Vicksburg, Mississippi.

Dissension in the Army of Tennessee

If Bragg lacked enough combativeness to drive the Federals from their stronghold, he exhibited more than enough to assail his own generals. Shortly after Chickamauga, he suspended both Polk and Hindman from command, ostensibly for their dismal performances in the recent campaign. Several of the army's most prominent generals retaliated by petitioning President Davis for Bragg's removal. Again, as after Murfreesboro, the Army of Tennessee's leadership ignored the Federals and engaged in an internal power struggle. Jefferson Davis traveled to Bragg's headquarters in mid-October intending to end this crippling dissension. Instead, he only made it worse. After hearing the candid recriminations of both sides, Davis chose to sustain Bragg. Bragg used the president's declaration of support as an opportunity to rid the army of more of his enemies. The vindictive general relieved both Major Generals D. H. Hill and Simon Buckner and received Davis's permission to restructure the army. Officially, Bragg's decision to break up established divisions and reshuffle their brigades was intended to mitigate the effects of battlefield losses on a particular state or region. Unofficially, it was intended to destroy the anti-Bragg cliques in his divisions, especially those Tennesseans and Kentuckians in the divisions of Breckinridge and Cheatham.

The squabbling among the army's high command naturally affected the men in the ranks. Dismembering units eroded both morale and faith in Bragg. Many soldiers abandoned the army and the Southern cause rather than serve under their despised commander. And it was not only the reshuffling of brigades that drew their wrath; the supply situation, critical after Chickamauga, had deteriorated further. When President Davis reviewed the army in October, he was met with cries for food from the thin, ragged ranks. Although accustomed to privation, the men had never endured such a shortage of rations, clothing, and shelter.

Opening the Cracker Line

On September 29, the Union military landscape in the Western Theater changed when Lincoln appointed Grant commander of the newly created Military Division of the Mississippi, bringing the territory from the Appalachian Mountains to the Mississippi River under a single commander for the first time. The War Department ordered Grant to Chattanooga and gave him the option of retaining Rosecrans as commander of the Army of the Cumberland or replacing him with Thomas. Grant traveled the treacherous roads and arrived in Chattanooga on October 23, ready to determine which course of action he would take. While he disliked both men and both disliked him, in the end he chose to relieve Rosecrans and elevate Thomas.

The question now was how to break the Rebel demi-siege in order to feed the starving men and surviving animals.

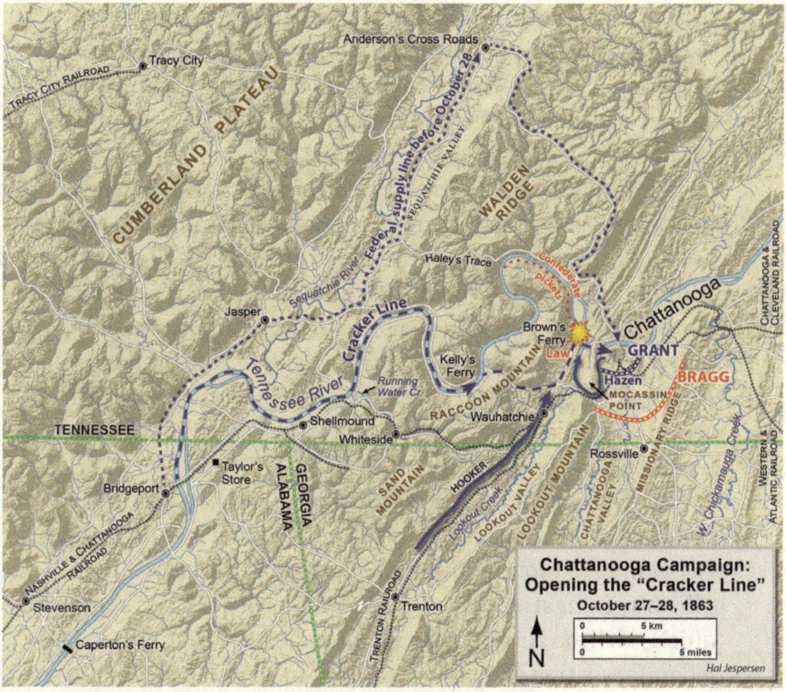

Map by Hal Jespersen, www.cwmaps.com.

A shocked Grant learned that Rosecrans and his chief engineer, Brigadier General William F. "Baldy" Smith, had already devised a plan to open a circuitous but stable supply line by seizing Brown's Ferry west of the town. Unable to fathom why Rosecrans never got around to organizing the operation, Grant adopted the plan and ordered Thomas to execute it immediately.

Brown's Ferry was on the east side of the Tennessee River and was separated from Chattanooga by Moccasin Bend. If the Yankees seized the ferry and crossed to the west side of the river, they could gain access to a road there that cut through the foothills and turned south through Lookout Valley to Wauhatchie Station. From there, the road continued farther west to Kelly's Ferry on the Tennessee, which could be reached by Federal supply boats coming from the supply hub at Bridgeport, Alabama.

The plan called for Hooker to advance from Bridgeport to Lookout Valley with elements of his corps from the Army of the Potomac. Meanwhile, most of Brigadier General William B. Hazen's brigade would drift downriver on flatboats and pontoons on the moonless night/early morning of October 27–28 to seize the west bank of the Tennessee. A second brigade under Brigadier General John B. Turchin would simultaneously march across Moccasin Bend and be ferried across in support.

Hooker's movement toward Lookout Valley prompted Bragg to order Longstreet, who oversaw that sector of the Rebel line, to move additional troops into the valley. Inexplicably, Longstreet disregarded the order. Hazen's men quietly drifted through the fog unmolested, past the Confederate position on Lookout Mountain, and then seized the high ground above the ferry just before dawn. Longstreet somehow did not realize the gravity of the situation and did nothing until Bragg demanded the position be retaken immediately. Still Longstreet ignored his superior officer.

As Hooker's divisions approached Wauhatchie near the ferry, Bragg changed tactics and ordered Longstreet to attack there instead. Again, apparently not realizing the gravity of the situation, Longstreet ordered a badly coordinated night attack that failed, forcing the Rebels to retreat to Lookout Mountain and surrender the valley to the Federals. The capture of Brown's Ferry and the opening of a supply line to the Federals in Chattanooga spelled disaster for the Confederates. Without the specter of slow starvation, they now had no hope of forcing the Yankees out of the city, and

Bragg's efforts thus again had come to naught. This new Federal line of supply, dubbed the "Cracker Line," would undoubtedly now bring Union reinforcements in even greater numbers. Bragg's one hope of accomplishing anything at Chattanooga vanished, and the situation was about to get even worse for him and the Army of Tennessee.

Longstreet Departs for Knoxville

While Bragg was focused on the disaster at Brown's Ferry and Wauhatchie, events to the north soon grabbed his attention. He had been concerned for some time that Burnside's army at Knoxville might move southward toward Chattanooga. On October 17, he ordered Major General Carter L. Stevenson to move his division and two cavalry brigades toward Knoxville. Less than a week later, he added another division under General John K. Jackson, giving the force about eleven thousand men. Bragg considered sending more troops and placing General Breckinridge in charge of an advance all the way to Knoxville. However, on the orders of President Davis, Bragg replaced Stevenson's and Jackson's divisions with the willful Longstreet and his men from the Army of Northern Virginia. The arrangement made sense in that Longstreet and his men would eventually have to return to Lee in Virginia, and the railroad connections from Chattanooga to Knoxville and on to Bristol offered a plausible way to make that return provided that Longstreet's force could clear the Federals out of the Great Valley of East Tennessee. The move, however, seriously weakened Bragg's army.

Longstreet planned to travel by railroad to Sweetwater, approximately halfway to Knoxville, but it was a journey fraught with problems. It took eight days for all the men and equipment to travel just sixty miles to Sweetwater because of the underpowered locomotives, and when they did finally arrive on November 12, there was no food or winter clothing waiting on them. The campaign to force Burnside out of East Tennessee was off to an unimpressive start.

As unimpressive as it was, Longstreet's movement toward Knoxville worried both Grant and Burnside. Burnside decided to take five thousand men and advance toward Longstreet. He planned to initiate contact and conduct a fighting retreat back to Knoxville, slowing the Rebels to buy time for establishing defenses in the city. Longstreet saw the move as an opportunity to crush Burnside's smaller force if he could move fast enough to surround it. On November 14, the Rebels bridged the Tennessee River west of Loudon and, following a parallel route, raced the retreating Federals toward Campbell's Station, a small village on the road to Knoxville. Burnside force-marched his men, and on a rainy November 16, the weary Federals reached the vital intersection first. But the Rebels were close behind. Longstreet attempted a double envelopment of the Federal line that failed because of poor coordination. Staving off disaster, Burnside and his exhausted men escaped to the defenses of Knoxville. On November 17, Longstreet attempted to put the town under siege, yet with his supplies low, no prospect for reinforcements, and inadequate artillery to bombard the Federal works, the best he could do was wait for developments while looking for a weak point in the Federal defenses in case he was forced to attack.

Battles for Chattanooga

Meanwhile, Grant was preparing to break what remained of the Confederate demi-siege at Chattanooga. While waiting for Sherman's corps to arrive, Grant charged Thomas and Smith with the task of developing a preliminary plan to not

C. E. F. Hillen sketch, Union pickets approached by Rebels in cedar bushes near Chattanooga. Library of Congress.

only break out of Chattanooga but also to destroy the Rebel army. After reconnoitering the Confederate positions, the Union generals met on November 14 to discuss their strategy. They proposed what would be a surprise strike on the Rebel right flank. Sherman's troops would pass through the hills north of Chattanooga, taking a route that was not visible from Rebel positions on Lookout Mountain or Missionary Ridge. Smith, meanwhile, would assemble pontoon bridges to allow Sherman's corps to cross the Tennessee River near the mouth of the South Chickamauga Creek. Sherman would then advance onto the northern edge of Missionary Ridge (Bragg's right flank), roll up the Rebel

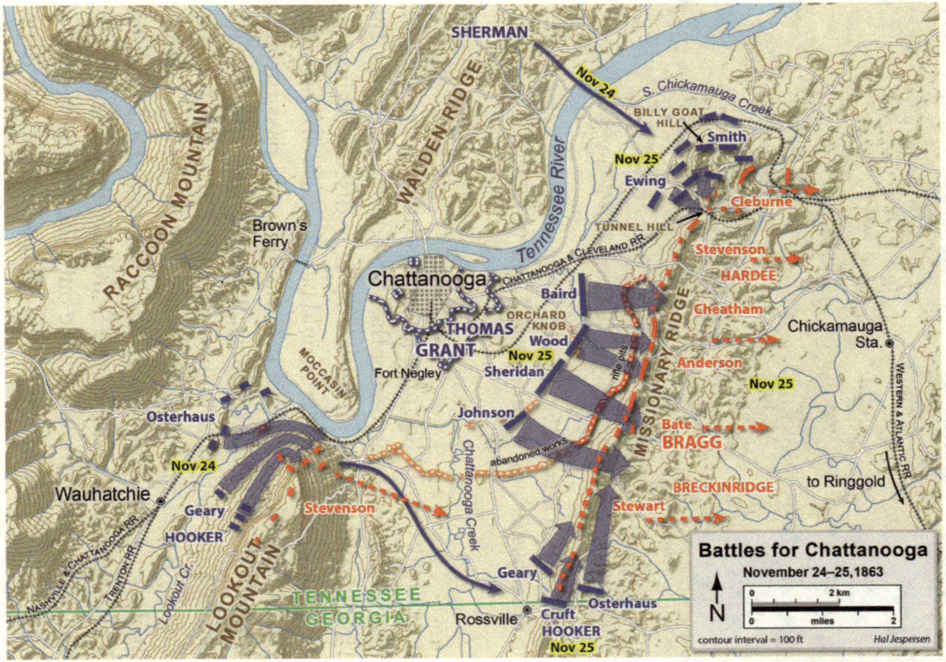

Map by Hal Jespersen, www.cwmaps.com.

position, and push them across the ridge. Thomas would support this main assault by positioning his men near the base of Missionary Ridge, threatening the Confederate center and thus preventing the Rebels from focusing solely on Sherman. As Sherman swept Missionary Ridge of its Rebel defenders and Thomas threatened attack, Hooker would storm Lookout Mountain on Bragg's left flank, drive away its defenders, and then continue on to Rossville, where he could cut off any Confederate retreat to the south. It was a well-designed plan. Sherman arrived ahead of his men on the evening of November 15 and was briefed on his key part in the operation. Although Grant had hoped to begin offensive operations on November 21, by November 20 only one of Sherman's brigades had crossed over Brown's Ferry; thus the attack had to be postponed.

As November faded, two major actions were developing in East Tennessee. Longstreet, with about seventeen thousand men, was hoping to be reinforced either by Bragg or by a small Confederate force in Virginia before he faced Burnside's twelve thousand soldiers for control of Knoxville. At Chattanooga, Hooker's and Sherman's corps, together with Thomas's Army of the Cumberland, had given Grant approximately sixty thousand men to face Bragg's forty-two thousand veterans, with a promised three thousand reinforcements coming from Mississippi. The climactic battles for East Tennessee were about to begin.

Having dispatched most of his cavalry with Longstreet, Bragg had little means of gathering intelligence. He thought Sherman's corps might be heading toward Knoxville, and he believed that the main Union assault would probably occur on his left flank at Lookout Mountain. Both assumptions were wrong. Still, Bragg adjusted his lines and bolstered his left flank. Hardee's corps would now be responsible for holding Lookout Mountain and the portion of

Chattanooga Valley on the west side of Chattanooga Creek. Breckinridge's corps would deploy from the east bank of the creek and along the base of Missionary Ridge from north of the Rossville Road to near Tunnel Hill, where an elite division under Cleburne guarded the Confederate right. After a bit of maneuvering, the Rebels settled into soggy positions and waited for either the rains to stop or the Federals to move. They would not have to wait long for either.

Orchard Knob, November 23

On November 23, the Union army observed columns of Rebel troops marching away from Missionary Ridge. Grant feared that Bragg was reinforcing Longstreet, and he wanted Thomas to disrupt the movement with a demonstration of force. Thomas ordered four divisions to move just outside Chattanooga's defensive works toward a small knoll around two thousand yards away known as Orchard Knob. At 1:30 p.m., as signal cannon boomed, fourteen thousand Union soldiers swept toward the hill and overran the small Rebel force there. The sudden movement stunned Bragg. He recalled Longstreet's reinforcements and pulled troops from his left wing on Lookout Mountain to strengthen his far right at Missionary Ridge. He assigned Hardee to command his now critical right flank, turning over the left flank to General Stevenson. In the center, he ordered Breckinridge to begin fortifying the crest of Missionary Ridge, a task that should have been completed weeks prior.

Lookout Mountain, November 24

Sherman crossed the Tennessee River on November 24. At first the advance appeared to go well; however, as Sherman's men ascended the north end of Missionary

Ridge, they soon realized the topography was not what they expected. They were in rough terrain and on detached hills far from the Rebel lines, and, even worse, Missionary Ridge was not as smooth as it had appeared from a distance and was in fact a series of undulating heights and depressions. Essentially the ridge was a group of hills with the highest on the north end, making it easy to defend and difficult to traverse. Sherman's men would struggle all day against both the terrain and the determined Rebel resistance.

While Sherman's men were plodding across the broken ground, Hooker's force had managed to storm Lookout Mountain. Although the vastness of the mountain looked intimidating to an attacker, the enemy's defenses were anything but. The Confederates simply did not have anywhere near the number of troops needed to defend such a large area. Hooker's men moved along the slope of Lookout Mountain and drove the Rebels from their defenses along a flattened position, or "saddle." By about 3:00 p.m., thick fog enveloped the mountain, obscuring the fighting from the valley below. This eerie scene led newspapermen who covered the battle to call the action the "Battle Above the Clouds." By evening, as Sherman's men were taking up their position at the northern end of Missionary Ridge, Hooker's forces were driving the last of the Rebels from the slopes of Lookout Mountain. Realizing the mountain was lost, Bragg abandoned it. At midnight, the fog cleared and, under a lunar eclipse, the retreating Rebels from the left flank crossed Chattanooga Creek, burning the bridges behind them.

Later that night, Bragg ordered the army to pull back to a position atop Missionary Ridge, where he questioned his corps commanders as to whether the army should retreat or stand and fight. Hardee counseled a retreat, but Breckinridge objected and convinced Bragg to hold the ridge. The Rebels would stay and fight. Hardee's corps would hold the right around Tunnel Hill while Breckinridge would hold the center and left to the Rossville Road. During the night, Confederate divisions began moving from the valley toward the summit of Missionary Ridge. Instead of concentrating their forces at the crest, however, Bragg and his corps commanders split their strength between rifle pits along the ridge's base and newly dug entrenchments farther up the steep slope. This illogical deployment created several potentially disastrous problems. First, if the Federals broke the first line of resistance along the base, the retreating Rebels would be mixed in with the advancing Yankees, blocking the fire of their comrades farther up the ridge. Second, because they would be spreading their small army over two, or in some cases three, successive rows of entrenchments, the Confederate commanders would have few or no troops left for a tactical reserve to plug any breaks in their line. Moreover, although Breckinridge had started to fortify the ridge as early as November 23, more breastworks would have to be built that night, and supporting artillery would have to be placed in the dark without proper sighting. This meant that the Confederates wound up placing most of the hastily dug entrenchments without regard to proper fields of fire or the elevation of the ridge. This created blind spots that would allow the enemy to reach the top nearly unmolested while the defenders would have to expose themselves in order to get a clear shot. The Confederate defenses, such as they were, could not stop a determined attack.

Missionary Ridge, November 25

The next day dawned clear and cool, and with it came a Federal assault aimed at the Confederate right. Unfortunately for Sherman, the problem of navigating through the rough terrain was only one obstacle he faced. Patrick Cleburne's

Alfred Waud sketch of the Battle of Missionary Ridge. Library of Congress.

crack division had now blocked every Federal attempt to move forward. The struggle lasted until mid-afternoon and ended with a complete Yankee failure. Sherman was stymied. Meanwhile, at the other end of the Federal line that morning, Hooker's men had found the summit of Lookout Mountain abandoned by the Rebels and raised the US flag to the cheers of all troops that could see it. Hooker sent his men toward the left or southern flank of Bragg's line on Missionary Ridge. However, at Chickamauga Creek (at the midpoint between Lookout Point and Missionary Ridge), the Federals discovered that the Rebels had burned the bridge. This forced them to delay their advance while they built a new one.

Impatient at his headquarters on Orchard Knob, Grant sought a way to support Sherman's floundering attack. He ordered Thomas to send the Army of the Cumberland against the rifle pits at the base of the ridge, hoping that the threat to the center would force Bragg to pull men away from Sherman's sector.

Meanwhile, in the center of Missionary Ridge, the Rebels waited. As the sounds of battle drifted from the Confederate right, Breckinridge's front remained quiet. However, around noon, increased Federal activity in the valley caught the Rebels's attention. Fearing an attack, Breckinridge repositioned his men. By 3:30 p.m., the better part of four Federal divisions had assembled in the valley below. The dress-parade formations awed the Rebels. A six-gun cannonade echoed across the valley, and a blue wave advanced. For a few moments, the Yankees marched unmolested. Then the thunderous peal of Confederate artillery pierced the silence. Despite the frightening noise, the shelling proved largely ineffective. The Rebel artillerymen overshot their targets.

As the Federals approached the base of the ridge, confusion and panic gripped the Rebel defenders in the rifle pits. Some, unsure of their mission as skirmishers, attempted to hold their position, while others simply fired a volley or two and scampered up the slope, leaving behind their steadfast comrades to be flanked and routed. Before long, all the rifle pits had fallen to the Yankee assault, and hundreds of scared Rebels scrambled toward the main line. While the Federals consolidated their hold on the base of the ridge, artillery and small arms fire from higher up ripped into their ranks, exacting a deadly toll. Instinctively and completely without orders, the Union troops emerged from the trenches and advanced. One Rebel veteran along the ridge recalled that "the enemy came on, crawling up the steep ascent like bugs, and were so thick they were almost in each other's way."

Fearing a bloody repulse, Grant became furious. As he witnessed the advance, he turned to Thomas and demanded to know who had ordered the assault up the ridge. Even though Thomas was as surprised as his commander, he knew without a doubt that he would be blamed if the attack failed. Against all odds, however, it succeeded. The Union forces surged up the ridge, exploiting the poor placement of the Rebel defense. By 4:30 p.m., the center of Bragg's line had been broken completely, and the Rebels were fleeing in panic. Some of Thomas's veterans chanted "Chickamauga! Chickamauga!" at the fleeing Rebels as Missionary Ridge was taken and the defeat at Chickamauga Creek avenged. Among the Rebel leaders, only Cleburne attempted an orderly withdrawal as chaos reigned around him and his men.

Retreat and Pursuit: Ringgold Gap, November 26–27

The coming of night saved Bragg's shattered army and allowed it to withdraw toward Chickamauga Station on the Western and Atlantic Railroad. The next day, Bragg sent the army on its way toward Dalton, Georgia. The Federals attempted a pursuit, but it ended on November 27 when Hooker ran into the Confederate rear guard under the command of Cleburne at Ringgold Gap. Outnumbered three to one, the Rebels held their ground, which allowed the rest of the army with its wagon and artillery train to pass through the gap.

Grant called off any further pursuit and prepared to send immediate aid to Burnside in Knoxville. Although numbers vary, casualties for the Union in the Chattanooga campaign amounted to around six thousand of the approximately fifty-six thousand engaged. The Rebels suffered at least seven thousand casualties out of about forty-four thousand engaged. Most of the Rebel losses were prisoners who were swept up in the Union tide or simply gave up rather than continue what many were now viewing as a hopeless struggle. Meanwhile, an angry, sullen, and vindictive Bragg accused Breckinridge of drunkenness during the struggle for Chattanooga and relieved him of command. Furthermore, he blamed his generals and the cowardice of his men for the Confederate fiasco. He then tendered his resignation on December 1, which Jefferson Davis wisely accepted. Davis placed Hardee and later Joseph E. Johnston in command of the Army of Tennessee. Although Bragg was disgraced, Davis would elevate his friend to the position of his personal military adviser, a position once held by Robert E. Lee. Bragg's influence on the war was far from over.

End of the Knoxville Campaign: Fort Sanders, November 29

Back around Knoxville, Longstreet continued to hold his position and await developments. He became increasingly worried that his lines of communication and supply with Bragg were in danger. An attempt to secure those lines failed at Kingston when two divisions of cavalry under Joseph Wheeler could not dislodge Federal infantry and cavalry.

Anxious to end the stalemate, Longstreet decided to attack the defenses in Knoxville at Fort Sanders, which he believed to be a vulnerable point. The fort, named in honor of recently slain cavalry officer Brigadier General William Sanders, stood on a hill just northwest of Knoxville. Longstreet planned to quietly assemble an assault force at night

Battle of Fort Sanders. From *Harper's Weekley,* January 9, 1864.

below the fortifications and overwhelm the defenders and seize the fort just before dawn. Following a brief artillery barrage, the three hidden Rebel brigades charged. However, instead of surprising the Yankees, they were the ones surprised. The Rebels immediately ran into telegraph wire stretched low between tree trunks that either tripped the onrushing infantry or slowed them to a dangerous trot as they carefully maneuvered the entanglements. However, the true obstacle was an outer ditch unseen by the Confederates planning the attack. The ditch, approximately twelve feet wide and between four to ten feet deep with steep sides, butted against the fort's nearly vertical walls. As the attackers, who lacked scaling ladders, piled into the ditch, they could not advance or retreat and became pinned as artillery and rifle fire ripped through their ranks. It was

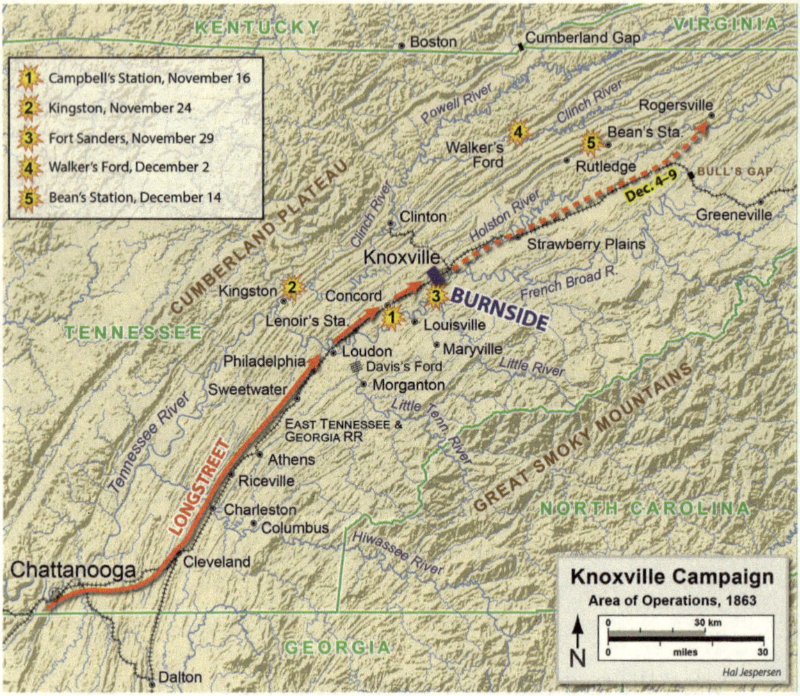

Map by Hal Jespersen, www.cwmaps.com.

a death trap. The attack lasted only twenty minutes and was little more than a slaughter, with the Federals suffering only a handful of casualties compared to more than eight hundred for the attackers. Longstreet had failed to break the Knoxville defenses, and he could not continue to hold his position outside the city.

A small battle occurred on December 2 at Walker's Ford north of Knoxville as Federals moving from Cumberland Gap began to probe into East Tennessee. Longstreet's situation was precarious. His men needed supplies and warm clothing as winter approached, and he was no closer to taking Knoxville than he was before the assault at Fort Sanders. As he contemplated his next move, he received word that Bragg had been routed and was in retreat into Georgia. Although Bragg ordered Longstreet to rejoin the Army of Tennessee, Longstreet had already decided that he would return with his command to Virginia. He did commit to maintaining his position at Knoxville as long as possible to prevent Burnside from joining Grant immediately. However, when Grant sent Sherman with twenty-five thousand men to drive the Confederates from Knoxville, Longstreet abandoned his siege on December 4 and withdrew toward Rogersville, Tennessee, sixty-five miles to the northeast. Although another small battle at Bean's Station occurred on December 14 as Longstreet turned on the Federals pursing him, that would be the last significant action in East Tennessee. The Yankees continued to harass Longstreet but would not confront him as both sides went into winter quarters, and he waited until spring to rejoin Lee.

Tennessee in Union Hands

The battles across East Tennessee in November 1863 finally gave Union forces undisputed control of the region, liberated the long-suffering loyalists, and placed virtually the entire state in Union hands. The struggle for the Volunteer State had been long and arduous and had stretched across several years. Back in the winter and spring of 1862, it had looked as if Tennessee and perhaps the entire Western Theater of the Confederacy would collapse quickly and easily as the Federals gained control of the Cumberland, Tennessee, and Mississippi Rivers, along with the key cities of Nashville and Memphis. The Rebels made a concerted effort to reclaim the state at Shiloh and again with Bragg's invasion of Kentucky, but both offensives ultimately failed and left only a sliver of Middle Tennessee and the loyalist bastion of East Tennessee under Confederate control. A string of disasters in 1863 at Vicksburg, Gettysburg, and Tullahoma rocked the Southern republic to its core, yet perhaps the greatest disaster of that year came with the near destruction of the Army of Tennessee at Chattanooga and the loss of East Tennessee. The Federals now held virtually the entire Volunteer State and were poised to drive deeper into the Confederate Heartland. Tennessee's cities, especially Nashville and Chattanooga, would serve as the main supply and logistics hubs for the drive into Georgia toward Atlanta. Yet while it appeared that major military operations were over in Tennessee, this would not be the case. Middle Tennessee's strategic importance to Federal operations in Georgia would make it the objective for one last Rebel offensive. Tennessee was simply too important for the Confederates to abandon.

SIX

The Final Campaign

★ ★ ★

AFTER THE DEVASTATING Confederate defeats in the battles around Chattanooga in November 1863, the war in the Western Theater shifted to Georgia. In March 1864, President Lincoln promoted Ulysses S. Grant to lieutenant general and made him general in chief of Union forces, replacing Henry Halleck who would now serve in an administrative role as the army's chief of staff. Grant immediately charged Major General William T. Sherman with destroying the Army of Tennessee and capturing the important rail hub of Atlanta. In Tennessee, Nashville and Chattanooga became the primary logistics hubs for the massive army group assembled under Sherman. Sherman commanded approximately one hundred thousand men, divided into the Army of the Cumberland under Major General George H. Thomas, the Army of the Tennessee under Major General James B. McPherson, the small corps-sized Army of the Ohio commanded by Major General John Schofield, and some cavalry. Facing Sherman at Dalton was the Army of Tennessee under General Joseph E. Johnston. This smaller army of about sixty thousand consisted of three corps commanded by Lieutenant Generals Leonidas Polk, William J. Hardee, and John Bell Hood.

The Fight for Atlanta

The first stage of the campaign began in Dalton. Johnston hoped that while his troops waited behind heavy fortification there, Sherman would commit to massive frontal assaults. If so, Johnston's men would be ready and able to inflict grievous casualties on the Yankees and break their resolve. Sherman, however, adopted a consistent and prudent strategy of avoiding large assaults against entrenchments and instead concentrated his larger force on flanking the Rebels from their positions. He continued this pattern at Dalton from May 8 until May 12; at Resaca from May 13 to May 15; at the Adairsville Line on May 17 and the Cassville Line on May 19; at New Hope Church, Pickett's Mill, and Dallas from May 25 through June 3; at the Mountain Line from June 5 to June 14; at the Gilgal Church Line from June 15 to June 16; and at the Mud Line from June 17 to June 18. As a result, the Federals suffered few casualties and drove the Rebels ever toward their supply base at Atlanta. Sherman did switch tactics once when he tried a large but unsuccessful assault on Johnston's lines at Kennesaw Mountain in June before resuming the campaign of maneuver in early July. He forced Johnston to abandon the Smyrna Line (July 3–4) and the Chattahoochee River Line (July 5–9). The Federals were now at the gates of Atlanta, and the prospect of the Rebels holding the city looked bleak. From May until July 1864, Sherman's strategy had clearly worked, and Johnston's strategy, such that it was, had not.

Chattanooga, Tennessee, ca. 1864. Library of Congress.

Johnston appeared unable to stop Sherman, and Jefferson Davis feared that he might abandon Atlanta. The Confederate president, therefore, removed him from command and replaced him with Hood. Davis had few options for a new army commander, and Hood appeared to be a viable choice. The Texan had earned a distinguished combat record with the Army of Northern Virginia and had modeled his fighting style on that of his mentor and idol, Robert E. Lee. Indeed, Hood always tried to emulate the success of Lee and his army. In a series of battles around Atlanta (Peachtree Creek, July 20; Atlanta or Bald Hill, July 22; and Ezra Church, July 28), he used elaborate and brilliantly conceived plans to isolate and cripple part of Sherman's army group. However, Hood's plans were beyond his army's ability, and his general officers followed the Army of Tennessee's long-established pattern of willfulness, disobedience, and incompetence. As a result, Hood's attacks failed.

Hood then attempted to cut Sherman's supply line to Chattanooga and force the Federals to retreat or starve. In August, he ordered Major General Joseph Wheeler to take four thousand troopers and strike the Western and Atlantic Railroad below Chattanooga, then advance beyond the town into Middle Tennessee, damaging the railroads south of Nashville. Wheeler was then to return with the bulk of his men while leaving a sizable force in Tennessee to continue disrupting the railroads.

Wheeler set out on August 10 and began tearing up track at Marietta, Resaca, and Dalton. However, strong Union garrisons prevented him from striking all along the Western and Atlantic. Inexplicably and contrary to his orders, Wheeler took his men into East Tennessee and then turned toward Middle Tennessee, but they only managed to inflict slight damage to the railroads before moving into Alabama. His raid was a total failure in that all damage was easily and quickly repaired and Sherman's army group suffered no serious supply problems.

Forrest's West Tennessee Raid

Wheeler's raid was not the only Confederate attempt to disrupt Union logistics in Tennessee. Even as Sherman prepared for his advance into Georgia, he was concerned about Confederate guerrillas and cavalry raiders operating against his rail supply lines stretching through Kentucky and Tennessee. He was particularly worried about operations by Nathan Bedford Forrest, who had become a thorn in the side of Federals in Tennessee. As Sherman attempted to amass supplies for the coming offensive, Forrest, now

Fort Pillow Massacre. Library of Congress.

in independent command, initiated a raid through Kentucky and his native West Tennessee to recruit and disrupt Union activities. Many of the region's Union garrisons had been reduced in quantity and quality to provide troops for Sherman. Forrest, therefore, could essentially roam freely.

Forrest struck at the Federal depots at Union City, Tennessee, and Paducah, Kentucky, in March 1864, wreaking havoc by destroying or capturing supplies and horses and forcing the surrender of Federal troops. The Rebel horseman humiliated a Tennessee Unionist cavalry regiment near Bolivar, Tennessee, before heading to Fort Pillow on the Mississippi River about forty miles north of Memphis. There, on April 12, 1864, Forrest's veteran cavalry demanded that the post surrender. When it did not, the Rebels overran the fort, offered no quarter, and subjected the garrison of White Unionist Tennesseans and African American artillerymen serving in the United States Colored Troops (USCT) to a bloodbath. Out of the garrison of 550, roughly 250 were killed, with another thirty-one eventually succumbing to their wounds. More than two-thirds of the fatalities were among the USCT soldiers; only sixty-two survived the battle. The Rebels, meanwhile, suffered fourteen killed and eighty-six wounded. Forrest intended to send a clear message to Tennessee Unionists about the dangers of collaborating with the Yankees and mobilizing Black troops.

News of the "Fort Pillow Massacre" spread like wildfire throughout the North and became a powerful propaganda tool. The US Congress Joint Committee on the Conduct of the War investigated and condemned Forrest for his butchery. "Remember Fort Pillow" became a popular rallying cry in the North, and many USCT units wore badges emblazoned with the slogan.

Forrest soon abandoned Fort Pillow and headed northward to Jackson, Tennessee. The raid convinced Sherman to choose a new commander for West Tennessee, Major General Cadwallader C. Washburn, whom he charged with protecting the region from Forrest. Forrest eventually moved into Mississippi but planned to return soon to disrupt Sherman's supply lines. However, the Federals launched cavalry raids of their own into Mississippi to occupy the Rebel general's attention. Although Forrest was stunningly successful against the Union forces, they did their job of keeping him from interfering with Sherman's campaign in Georgia. By August 1864, however, Forrest was able to launch a raid of about fifteen hundred horsemen on Memphis, where he exploited the city's weak defenses and unprepared garrison. While there, Forrest's men looted Federal supplies and captured hundreds of soldiers before leaving the humiliated Union commander behind. Although Forrest's cavalry and other Confederate raiders failed to stop Sherman's advance into Georgia, they did keep the Union general worried and compelled him to detach badly needed soldiers for garrison duty. There could be no peace in Tennessee with raiders such as Forrest about.

The Western and Atlantic Line

Meanwhile, Sherman had cut loose from his supply line, the Western and Atlantic, in August 1864 and severed the last Rebel rail links to Atlanta, forcing Hood to abandon the city on September 2. Hood took his demoralized army southward while the victorious Yankees occupied Atlanta. As Sherman contemplated his next move, Jefferson Davis arrived at Palmetto, Georgia, in the rain on September 25 for his last visit with the Army of Tennessee. The fall of Atlanta had severely shaken Southern morale, and in an attempt to strengthen the public's resolve, the president had decided to tour the Confederate Heartland. He also hoped to revive the esprit of Hood's battered army, on which so much now depended. Davis spent three days visiting the soldiers, conferring with his generals, and formulating a strategy to reverse the tide of war in the West.

The army Davis found in the muddy camps at Palmetto was in appalling shape. The men were without adequate food, clothing, and ammunition, having lost much of their commissary, quartermaster stores, and ordnance in Atlanta. Thousands of soldiers were without shoes, and winter was fast approaching. Moreover, the carnage of the unsuccessful battles around Atlanta had destroyed the men's faith in Hood's leadership. Likewise, his general officers no longer trusted in their commander, and dissension was again growing within the army. All three of the army's corps commanders, Hardee, Lieutenant General Stephen D. Lee, and Lieutenant General Alexander P. Stewart (Polk had been killed during the campaign), recommended that the president replace Hood, preferably with Johnston. Hardee and Hood continued to blame one another for the capture of Atlanta, and Hardee asked again to be relieved if Hood remained in command. Humbled and humiliated by his generals, Hood tendered his resignation, but Davis refused it. Instead, the president sustained him and reassigned Hardee to the Atlantic coast, which elevated Major General Benjamin F. Cheatham to corps command. Nevertheless, the public outcry over the fall of Atlanta compelled Davis to reorganize the command structure in the West. Unwilling to restore Johnston, Davis appointed his old nemesis, Beauregard, to command the newly created Division of the West (essentially the old Department of the West). Ostensibly, Beauregard now controlled all Confederate forces in the Western Theater, including the Army of Tennessee. In reality, however, Davis intended for the position to be mostly advisory and supervisory. Hood would still be leading the Army of Tennessee.

The question of where Hood would now lead the army was also decided at Palmetto. Hood proposed to Davis that he move against Sherman's supply line—the Western and Atlantic Railroad. Once the Rebels were astride the railroad, Sherman would be forced to attack Hood or head south to open a new supply line on the Gulf or Atlantic coast. If the Federals attempted to clear the railroad, Hood would continue to lure the Yankees northward or fight on ground of his choosing. If Sherman advanced southward, Hood would shadow him, striking when and where he could inflict the most damage.

Davis concurred. However, to prevent Sherman from moving deeper into Georgia, the president advised Hood to move quickly. On September 29, two days after Davis's departure, the Army of Tennessee began crossing the Chattahoochee, heading northeast. Hood's army seized the railroad north of Atlanta on October 2 and advanced northward, demolishing track and capturing Yankee garrisons along the way. By the end of the first week of October, just as Hood had planned, Sherman sent a portion of his army northward to prevent the Rebels from cutting his supply line. Ironically, the two forces now retraced their footsteps across the same terrain they had fought over the previous summer. The Federals closely pursued the Rebels as Hood drew them ever northward. However, although Hood had succeeded in demolishing a few blockhouses guarding the Western and Atlantic and capturing small garrisons, he lacked the fighting strength to do much more. Indeed, when a full division of Hood's army attacked a brigade of the Army of the Tennessee at Allatoona Pass under Brigadier General John M. Corse, the Rebels were bloodily repulsed.

Following the defeat at Allatoona, Hood grew frustrated with his army's poor showing in northwest Georgia. The Federals had quickly repaired any damage to the railroad his men had inflicted, and Sherman showed no sign of chasing him with the bulk of the Union forces in Atlanta. Hood moved his army westward toward Rome, Georgia, and then headed northward toward Resaca. From Resaca, he moved westward toward Gadsden, Alabama, in mid-October. Along the way, Hood began to rethink his strategy. Instead of establishing a strong defensive position and baiting the Federals to attack, he envisioned enticing them even farther northward. Rather than simply rip up track, Hood now planned to cross the Tennessee River and strike Sherman's depots at Stevenson and Bridgeport, Alabama.

He reasoned that Sherman would have to follow. By the end of October, however, Sherman's patience had reached its limit, and he finally ended the chase.

Like Hood, Sherman had grown equally frustrated with the military standoff and had no intention of continuing to chase over the same ground in northwest Georgia. He therefore requested that his superiors in Washington allow his army to break away from the Western and Atlantic supply line and plunge into the heartland of Georgia toward Savannah and the coast. This "March to the Sea" would humble and humiliate the South and demonstrate the Confederacy's inability to protect its citizens. It would also destroy valuable infrastructure that could cripple the Rebels. The Federals would emerge at Savannah, take the city, and be resupplied by the Union navy. And as they made their way to Savannah, Sherman's men would live off the bounty of the east Georgia countryside. Lincoln, Stanton, and Grant agreed, and Sherman began his campaign to break the back of the stubborn Rebel nation.

Hood's New Plan: To Nashville and Beyond

The Confederates did not learn of Sherman's redeployment until November 17. By then, Hood had already moved his army to Florence, Alabama, taking it well out of position to follow Sherman. Hood, however, was not overly concerned. He envisioned advancing in the opposite direction away from Sherman and deeper into Alabama where he would cross the Tennessee and advance into the Volunteer State, eventually drawing Sherman after him and breaking the Federal rail links to Chattanooga. The Rebel general even envisioned reorienting the entire strategic situation in the Western Theater by moving to Nashville and perhaps beyond into Kentucky, sowing chaos and breaking Federal resolve. With few options, Davis tacitly approved the new plan.

Hood led his troops across northern Alabama all the way to Tuscumbia in search of a suitable crossing point. The army waited three weeks there for reinforcements and supplies. The mild weather of October soon yielded to the rainy days and frigid nights of November, and Hood's logistical challenges were further exacerbated by the cold, damp conditions. The ramshackle railroads and broken-down wagon trains along the route through Alabama had created serious supply problems. Many shivering Rebels, still without shoes, resorted to tying freshly cut cowhide around their feet while trying their best to ignore the smell.

Hood's veterans crossed a pontoon bridge on November 15 as bands played and Rebel yells echoed across the icy river. The army advanced to Florence, where it halted. Hood had left most of his cavalry under Joseph Wheeler in Georgia to operate against Sherman, and Beauregard had arranged for new cavalry support for the campaign into Tennessee. Within a week, Hood established contact with Nathan Bedford Forrest, whose cavalry would spearhead the army's advance. On Monday morning, November 21, still woefully short of supplies, the army set out from Florence toward Nashville. Snow began to fall as the thinly clad Rebels trudged forward. Private William Worsham from the Nineteenth Tennessee recalled, "The wind blew almost a hurricane in our faces, and with the snow, was almost blinding. All day long we plodded through the storm, so slow we could hardly keep warm." Freezing groups of Rebels would huddle for warmth at the bonfires along every few hundred yards of the road before moving to the next fire.

Hood's army as it left Florence stood at about thirty thousand infantry with some eight thousand cavalry.

Opposing him on the way to Nashville would be an ad hoc force hastily assembled by George H. Thomas. Sherman had given Thomas two corps, and Thomas would gather any additional men he needed from Union garrisons spread out across Tennessee. Another force, a detachment from the Army of the Tennessee under Major General Andrew Jackson (A. J.) Smith, was en route from Mississippi. Thomas could certainly amass the manpower he needed, but assembling the scattered forces at Nashville would require time. He, therefore, ordered Schofield to take the two corps and block Hood's advance on Nashville. Schofield chose to position his men at Pulaski, Tennessee, about seventy-five miles south of Nashville and fifty miles northeast of Florence.

Apparently, Hood was ignorant of the strategic situation and believed that Schofield was the only Federal force of any significant size he faced in Tennessee and that he was racing the Yankees to Nashville. To speed the advance, Hood sent each of his corps via a different route while he opted to accompany Cheatham's men, who covered around twelve miles that day before camping at Rawhide near the Tennessee–Alabama border. The bone-numbing cold and slushy roads had exhausted the men. The winter storm intensified the next day, but Cheatham pushed his corps from sunrise to dark, marching eighteen miles and camping only fourteen miles from Waynesboro. While struggling through the biting wind and snow, the Rebels had passed an ominous road sign that read "Tennessee, A Grave or a Free Home." Such was the spirit of the shivering veterans in the Army of Tennessee.

By November 22, Stewart's corps had advanced some forty miles from Florence to Lawrenceburg, Tennessee, which was located about twenty miles northwest of Schofield's position at Pulaski. Part of Hood's army had managed to get behind Schofield, who frantically pushed his men north in an attempt to overcome the Rebel lead. On November 24, Hood's army was reunited along the Waynesboro-to-Mount Pleasant Pike. Although Forrest warned Hood that Schofield was moving northward from Pulaski, the Texan still believed he would beat Schofield to Columbia, Tennessee, where the road to Nashville crossed the Duck River. This would place the Rebels between Schofield and Nashville. Over the next two days, Schofield marched his men hard as they headed toward Columbia while Hood's men raced toward the same spot on parallel roads. Both commanders understood the importance of winning this race. Columbia was a key town on the road to Nashville for both sides because of its bridges crossing the Duck River.

On the evening of November 26, the Rebels reached Columbia and were shocked to find entrenched Federals waiting for them. Schofield had won the race, but Hood, undeterred, still held out hope that he could maneuver his army between Schofield and Nashville. For the next several days, he assembled his army facing Schofield's entrenched men. He had no intention of attacking entrenchments, however, and instead began looking for a way to flank the Federals. Schofield anticipated Hood's plan, and on the late night/early morning of November 27–28, he moved all his men to the north bank of the Duck River and destroyed the bridges across it. Unaware of the Federal move, on November 28, Forrest's horsemen found Davis's Ford upstream, and Hood prepared a plan to flank the Federal position. Leaving Lee's corps, along with the army's artillery train, on the south bank of the Duck River to trick Schofield into thinking the Rebels were still there, Hood would take his other two corps along with Forrest's troopers across the Duck and northward to Spring Hill, Tennessee, about twelve miles north of Columbia. From there, the Confederates could either hit Schofield's rear or continue the advance on Nashville.

The Spring Hill Affair

The day became increasingly balmy as the warm temperatures returned, and the flanking column cleared the Duck River. Meanwhile, Forrest's troopers rode ahead, clashing with Yankee infantry at Spring Hill. As it became clear that at least part of Schofield's force was retreating toward Spring Hill, Hood ordered the cavalry to hold its position while he brought the flanking column into position.

The head of the Confederate flanking column arrived at Rutherford Creek around 3:00 p.m., still two and a half miles from Spring Hill. There, Hood heard the crackle of small arms fire in the distance and rode ahead to investigate. Observing Federal forces moving northward along the Columbia Pike, Hood now realized that the road would have to be seized to prevent Schofield from escaping the trap. He returned to Rutherford Creek and outlined a plan for Cheatham. Hood would personally lead Patrick Cleburne's division across the creek and move it toward the pike. Meanwhile, Major General William B. Bate's division, still strung out in column, would close up. Cheatham would lead them to Cleburne's support. Hood would then return to the creek and direct Major General John C. Brown's division forward to join Cleburne and Bate. Stewart's corps would remain at the creek in reserve.

However, as Cleburne moved toward the Columbia Pike, contact with a strong Yankee force on his right forced him to swing his entire division northward toward Spring Hill, well short of the pike. Making matters worse, at this point Cheatham and Hood began issuing contradictory orders. Cheatham failed to conduct Bate to the battlefield, but when Bate wandered forward, he encountered Hood, who ordered him to advance on Cleburne's left and seize the pike. Later, as Bate's men pushed to within a few hundred yards of their objective, Cheatham then ordered Bate to pull back his division from the pike and move northeast to close up on Cleburne's left. When Brown's division arrived, Cheatham ordered it northward to support Cleburne's right flank.

As a result of Cheatham's orders, the Rebel divisions were not where Hood thought they were. Moreover, after sending most of Cheatham's corps to seize the pike, Hood left the field without seeing that his orders were carried out. By 5:00 p.m., Cheatham had not only failed to capture the pike but was also planning a full-scale assault on Spring Hill. Brown's men were to initiate the attack, with the sound of their musketry being the cue for Cleburne and Bate to advance. The Rebel brigade and division commanders, however, became convinced that Federals were about to strike and advised Cheatham against the attack. The end result was that the Rebel divisions were not securing the pike as Hood wanted, and thus not blocking Schofield's line of retreat. It was now after 6:00 p.m., and darkness was falling. As a new corps commander, Cheatham was unwilling to risk an assault without Hood's approval. He therefore postponed the attack and rode to Hood's headquarters. Inexplicably, an apparently confused Hood permitted Cheatham to bivouac his men, which left the pike and the Federal route of retreat open. Hood was exhausted from being strapped to his saddle all day because of his missing leg (amputated following the battle of Chickamauga), and he turned in early. At one point he was awakened and informed that the road was still open, so he issued orders for it to be closed. However, he went back to sleep without seeing that his orders were carried out. As had happened so many times with the Army of Tennessee's high command, willfulness and incompetence prevented the execution of the most sensible of actions. Somehow two Rebel corps and strong cavalry elements had failed to brush aside the outnumbered Federals in the town, capture the pike, and prevent Schofield from moving his entire army past them in the night.

When dawn arrived on November 30, broken-down wagons and abandoned equipment along the Columbia Pike bore witness to Schofield's escape. Hood awoke to learn of the disaster. Furious, he lashed out at his subordinates (especially Cleburne, Brown, and Cheatham), accusing them of negligence and blaming them for Schofield's escape. Recriminations flew as his generals sought to blame anyone but themselves for the debacle.

Battle of Franklin

Hood ordered Forrest's troopers to pursue Schofield's column, while Cheatham and Stewart advanced toward Franklin, some twelve miles away. The clear, balmy weather and the sight of abandoned Yankee equipment raised Confederate spirits as they marched along the Columbia Pike. The morale of the troops was also lifted by local citizens lining the road and shouting encouragement. By noon, Forrest's troopers and the leading units of Stewart's corps had overtaken Schofield at Franklin, where they found the Federals frantically trying to bridge the Harpeth River. All of Stewart's and Cheatham's soldiers arrived on the field during the next couple of hours. From atop Winstead Hill, Hood and his generals could observe the two-mile open plain to the Yankee positions around the town. A sharp bend in the Harpeth protected Franklin's western, northern, and eastern approaches, and an extensive line of earthworks guarded its southern approach. Union artillery was placed so that it could sweep the plain in front of Franklin with deadly accuracy.

Despite Schofield's formidable position, Hood stunned his generals by directing them to prepare for an assault on the town. Forrest, Cheatham, and Cleburne protested and advocated instead another flanking march. Hood remained adamant, however. There would be no more intricate flanking maneuvers. The Army of Tennessee would now charge head-on into the enemy, and Cheatham's men would lead the way.

There appeared to be only one apparent weak spot in the Federal defense: the center, where the Nashville–Columbia Pike passed through the entrenchments. Hood ordered the main effort to be directed here. The "honor" of assaulting this point fell to two of Cheatham's divisions. Brown's men would advance northward on the left side of the pike, and Cleburne's would advance on the right. Brown's division was Cheatham's old command and arguably the toughest in the Army of Tennessee—rivaled only by Cleburne's stalwart veterans. These two crack divisions, the army's shock troops, would contend side by side. Meanwhile, on the Confederate left, cavalry along with Bate's division of Cheatham's corps would assail the Yankee works while Stewart's corps would assault the Federals on the Rebel right.

The Confederate regiments crossed Breezy and Winstead Hills around 2:45 p.m. At the base of the hills, the men rested and chatted while awaiting the order to advance. At approximately 4:00 p.m., as the late afternoon shadows crept across Franklin, that order came. About eighteen thousand ragged but determined Rebels advanced forward, the sun glinting off their bayonets and a warm breeze catching their tattered battle flags. Bands struck up "The Bonnie Blue Flag" and "Dixie" as the last great spectacle of the Civil War unfolded.

The men halted about half a mile in front of the main Federal line, formed into two battle lines, and surged forward. Several hundred yards in front of the main Federal works, Brown and Cleburne encountered a Yankee division entrenched on high ground across the Columbia Pike. The Federals loosed a fusillade into the onrushing Rebels, but they were not to be stopped. Brown's and Cleburne's men overran the position and sent the Federals fleeing along the pike and through the gap in the main fieldworks. The Rebels, now a yelling mass of intermixed units, followed close behind. The Federals occupying the main line held their fire as long as possible for fear of hitting their retreating comrades, but as the Confederates drew closer, they unleashed a withering mixture of artillery and musketry.

As they surged across a large ditch fronting the entrenchments, Brown's and Cleburne's men breached the Federal works on both sides of the pike. Brown's men advanced beyond the Carter farmhouse, pushing the dazed Yankees back, while Cleburne's soldiers engaged in a savage hand-to-hand struggle at a nearby cotton gin. This was the high tide for the attackers, however. They could not and would not expand their breakthrough. Elements of several Federal divisions counterattacked and gradually forced Brown's and Cleburne's men back with heavy casualties—including both division commanders.

Brown's men retreated to the outer edge of the fieldworks, where they halted and exchanged fire with Federal troops positioned behind a hastily constructed barricade some two hundred yards away in the Carter House garden. With the intermingling of regiments and the loss of many officers, Rebel command and control broke down completely. Instinct and combat experience took over as small groups began to operate independently.

Brown's men continued to launch uncoordinated assaults against the Federals in the garden into the night, but to no avail. The Rebels lacked the numbers for a breakthrough.

While they could not advance, neither could they retreat without subjecting themselves to Federal fire. Worse yet, as long as they remained in their present position along the fieldworks, they were exposed to enfilading fire from their right due to an angle in the Federal line east of the pike. By nightfall, Brown's division was decimated. While the bravest continued to scale the works and fire at the Yankees, most huddled in the large ditch at the base among the piles of dead and groaning wounded. Across the road, Cleburne's division and part of Brown's suffered such slaughter from enfilading fire that the proud veterans called for mercy and many surrendered.

In the meantime, the Rebel assaults against the Federal flanks had also failed. These attacks were poorly coordinated and did not actually occur until Brown's and Cleburne's men had been forced to retreat to the outer earthworks. This disjointed effort did nothing to relieve the pressure on the Confederate center. A night assault by one of Lee's divisions near Brown's position likewise accomplished nothing. Bereft of support, Brown's and Cleburne's divisions—the finest in the army—were simply torn to shreds.

Meanwhile, Hood remained at his headquarters on Winstead Hill, oblivious to his army's condition. Around midnight, he met with his corps commanders and outlined his plan to renew the attack in the morning. Mercifully for Hood's broken army, however, there would not be another assault. Around 2:00 a.m., the light of a burning bridge announced the Federal withdrawal. Two hours later, Rebel forces entered the town. A cold wind blew across the battlefield, carrying the cries of the wounded. Cheatham walked over the field where Brown's men (his old division) had stormed the works. There, by the glare of torchlight, Rebel veterans watched as "great big tears ran down his cheeks and he sobbed like a child." All around Cheatham lay those he called "his boys."

The true dimensions of the tragedy became apparent as dawn broke. While the Federal forces had sustained just over 2,000 casualties, the Confederates had suffered more than 6,200—1,750 of them killed. Moreover, the army's officer cadre, especially in Cheatham's and Stewart's corps, was decimated. The greatest single loss was the death of Patrick Cleburne, arguably the most capable officer ever to serve in the Army of Tennessee. In all, six generals were killed, five wounded, and one captured. Fifty-four regimental commanders were also killed, wounded, or captured. Even by Civil War standards, the carnage was extraordinary. Private Sam Watkins, who served in Brigadier General John C. Carter's brigade of Brown's division, was forever affected by what he experienced at Franklin. Decades later he reflected: "I was there. I saw it. My flesh trembles, and creeps, and crawls when I think of it today. My heart almost ceases to beat at the horrid recollection. Would to God that I had never witnessed such a scene!" Private Worsham declared, "Oh! this one scene of butchery will go down the ages in history as a black page in the memory of our lost cause."

Pursuit to Nashville

Despite essentially wrecking his army at Franklin, Hood clung to the delusion of capturing Nashville and ordered an immediate pursuit of Schofield. The battered Confederates arrived above the city on December 2. Schofield had delayed Hood long enough to allow Thomas to assemble a force that, when added to Schofield's men, numbered nearly sixty thousand strong (twice the size of Hood's army). Moreover, because Nashville was such an important logistics hub, the Federals had constructed elaborate defenses over the years, making it arguably the most heavily defended city in the entire country. Hood's men could not possibly storm Nashville, and the Rebels lacked the manpower to even encircle the city for an attempted siege. After viewing the Federal dispositions, even Hood realized that attacking was out of the question, but still unwilling to admit defeat, he decided to take a defensive position outside the city and invite a costly Federal assault.

The Rebels, therefore, entrenched along a five-mile line south of the city. This line covered only three of the seven major routes running south from Nashville, which left the army vulnerable to a Federal turning movement. Making matters worse, Hood ordered Forrest's cavalry and Bate's division to raid Murfreesboro, thereby weakening his army in the face of a much larger foe. This left only about fifteen thousand men to cover the entire Rebel line at Nashville.

Bate was ordered to destroy the railroad and blockhouses between Murfreesboro and Nashville and then join Forrest for further operations. On December 4, Bate's men attacked Blockhouse No. 7, but his troops were driven off. On the morning of December 5, Forrest seized a fort and Blockhouse No. 4, both at La Vergne, capturing the garrisons. Outside La Vergne, Forrest joined Bate's division, and the command advanced on to Murfreesboro along two roads, driving the Union forces into their fortifications (known as Fortress Rosecrans). The Rebels then encamped and waited for reinforcements from Hood, which arrived the next day. However, even with the reinforcements, the Rebels felt the fortifications were too strong for a direct assault. On the morning of December 7, Union Major General Lovell Rousseau, commanding all the forces at Murfreesboro, sent two brigades against Bate's troops. The men broke and ran. Forrest's command conducted an orderly retreat from the field and encamped for the night outside Murfreesboro.

Forrest had accomplished all he could by destroying railroad track and blockhouses, yet the foray had done nothing to hurt the Yankees or improve Hood's situation.

A winter storm descended on the region during the second week of December. Rain, sleet, and eventually snow pelted the shivering Confederates, and frigid winds buffeted their camps. One Rebel veteran vividly recalled the scene: "We were out in the open fields on an elevation, without protection from the wintry blasts, and were thinly clad—many of us without shoes—with nothing whatever to keep our sore and bleeding feet from the cold and frozen ground. We were without tents, and with but one old worn blanket to each man, with which to cover at night, and our only bed the frozen ground, and that covered with ice and snow."

Battle of Nashville

In the bitter cold, both armies eyed each other warily. In Washington, Grant was eager for Thomas to destroy Hood's army to prevent it from moving northward and creating a panic. Thomas, however, waited. He had supply problems and needed horses to remount his cavalry. Grant continued to push Thomas over the next week and a half and even considered removing him from command because of his unwillingness to attack. Just as Grant prepared to replace the Union general, the weather cleared, and Thomas was finally ready to assault the Rebels.

Planned for the morning of December 15, a series of obstacles delayed the assault until midday. Thomas ordered a diversionary attack against Hood's right by elements of Major General James B. Steedman's Provisional Detachment. The inexperienced troops, including a brigade of USCT soldiers, fought bravely but were no match for the

Rebel veterans they faced. The main Federal blow, however, came on the Confederate left where Thomas initiated a huge wheeling movement. Smith's corps, with Major General James H. Wilson's cavalry corps on their right flank and Schofield's corps in reserve, launched an attack on the Confederate left. There, Hood had bent back his line in a sharp ninety-degree angle. This section of the line was composed of a series of hilltop forts or redoubts, which were strong points anchoring the west end of the Rebel line. Smith's men stormed the redoubts, assisted by Wilson's dismounted cavalry still on their right. By 4:30 p.m., as dusk approached, the redoubts had fallen, and Hood's left flank began to dissolve against the relentless Federal hammering. Stewart's battered corps broke, prompting elements of Lee's corps to shift to meet the threat and act as a rearguard to prevent a complete rout. With the collapse of the Confederate left, Cheatham's and the rest of Lee's corps followed Stewart's men into the darkness. The Federals suspended the advance as night fell, giving Hood the opportunity to pull back to a new defensive position two miles to the south near the Granny White Pike. By 8:00 p.m., the exhausted men of the Army of Tennessee were at work digging entrenchments in the frozen ground along a three-mile line, which was more compact and stronger than the previous one. It stretched along a line of hills from Peach Orchard Hill on the right to Compton's Hill on the left. Compton's Hill would become a key point in the next day's battle and would be renamed Shy's Hill after Colonel William M. Shy, a Confederate officer who died defending it. Along his new line, Hood placed Lee's corps on the right, Stewart's in the center, and Cheatham's on the left.

The next morning, Thomas called for essentially the same plan as the previous day. A feint on the Rebel right flank was to be followed by the main attack on the left.

The Battle of Nashville. Library of Congress.

The feint worked in forcing the Rebels to shift troops away from the main target on the left flank. The main assault, however, was delayed by Schofield's unwillingness to move against the Rebels. When the Yankees did initiate the attack on the left, it was piecemeal and uncoordinated. Despite constant Union probing and shelling throughout the day, by mid-afternoon, amid a cold drizzle, the Rebels still held their ground. Around 4:00 p.m., a division from Smith's corps acting on its own initiative stormed Compton's (Shy's) Hill while Wilson's cavalry hit Cheatham's flank and rear, creating panic in the Rebel ranks. Beginning with the corps on the left and spreading along the Rebel line to Stewart's corps in the center, the Confederates began to give way

Confederate Camps, Battle of Nashville. Library of Congress.

and flee in fear. Lee's corps held on and again acted as a rearguard protecting Stewart's and Cheatham's men, who were now little more than a mob fleeing southward. Under Federal pressure, Lee's veterans gradually retreated as they, too, abandoned the field. Nightfall again saved Hood's army from annihilation.

Retreat and Pursuit of Hood

The army retreated several miles before bivouacking along the road to Franklin. The disaster at Nashville had cost the Confederates around ten thousand casualties compared to a third of that for the Federals. The battle had also destroyed the army as a viable combat force. There would not be another defensive stand at Nashville. The Army of Tennessee was finished, and with its demise, the war in the Western Theater was essentially over. By the time the army reached Columbia, Hood had decided to abandon the state and move south of the Tennessee River. Forrest's cavalry would serve as the army's rearguard, but they needed infantry support as well. Hood chose Major General Edward C. Walthall to command the infantry detachment, which consisted of the remnants of eight understrength brigades totaling fewer than two thousand men. Forrest's troopers and Walthall's tiny force would be all that stood between Hood's army and destruction.

Nature offered no respite to the Rebel rearguard or the pursing Yankees. A mixture of cold rain, sleet, and snow fell almost daily, and temperatures again plunged. Hundreds of the retreating men were still without shoes or winter clothing, and icy roads often sliced the naked feet of the retreating Rebels, leaving a bloody trail for the Federals to follow. However, the miserable weather served as their ally in one respect: mud and swollen streams slowed the Yankee pursuit.

Forrest's and Walthall's men skirmished continually for several days, holding the pursuing Federal cavalry at bay. As the Federals moved southward, they passed the debris of the retreating Rebels. Frozen horses and mules lay by the roadside, and broken-down wagons and cast-off accoutrements littered the ground. On Christmas Eve, the Rebel rearguard occupied Pulaski and destroyed much abandoned equipment. They had by now overtaken Hood's main force, trudging along with forty miles still to go before reaching the Tennessee River. To relieve pressure on the main column, Forrest and Walthall prepared an ambush for the Federal pursuers.

The site chosen for the trap was Anthony's Hill, about seven miles south of Pulaski. There broken ground and dense woods would screen Walthall's men until the last possible moment. When the Federal horsemen ran into Rebel pickets, they dismounted and charged. Hidden Rebel batteries then opened fire, and Walthall's men countercharged, driving the Federal cavalry back in disorder. At sunset, the Rebels retired and marched toward Sugar Creek, Alabama. The rearguard crossed the Tennessee River on December 28 via a pontoon bridge at Bainbridge, safe at last from Federal pursuit.

Once across the river, the army continued south, finally establishing a new base at Tupelo, Mississippi, on January 13. Only seven thousand effective infantry remained in the Army of Tennessee. Most of the artillery, along with horses, mules, and wagons, was gone, leaving the army unable to provide necessary transportation. Food, clothing, and shelter were scarce. To ease the logistical burden, Hood furloughed many of the men from Alabama, Mississippi, and Middle Tennessee. Some, believing the war lost, would never return. Broken emotionally and physically, Hood wrote to Richmond, asking to be relieved—a request the War Department quickly granted. Lieutenant General Richard Taylor temporarily replaced Hood while Richmond decided the fate of the army. The wait was short. With Sherman at Savannah, Georgia, poised for a march through the Carolinas, most of what had once been the Army of Tennessee was ordered to proceed eastward to North Carolina, where they would join an amalgamation of units under the command of Joseph E. Johnston. Most of the Rebel Tennesseans still willing to take up arms for a dying country headed far from home to fight it out to the bitter but inevitable end.

The Confederate situation was hopeless, however.

Johnston could not stop Sherman's advance through the Carolinas, so he moved northward, anxious to link up with Robert E. Lee. On April 9, 1865, however, he learned that Lee had surrendered his army at Appomattox, Virginia. With hope of Southern independence crushed, Johnston ordered his troops to Greensboro and met there with Jefferson Davis. Johnston requested permission to negotiate with Sherman for the surrender of his army. A shaken Davis agreed. For a week and a half, Johnston and Sherman met intermittently, and on April 26, the Army of Tennessee, the last major Confederate force east of the Mississippi, capitulated. Johnston attempted to keep the army together until a formal disbanding, but many men slipped off and headed for home. By May 3, the Confederates had stacked their arms and received paroles. The army then marched to Salisbury, fifty miles to the southwest, to disband officially. At Salisbury, Cheatham drew up his division of Tennesseans for one last inspection. He moved down the line, shaking hands with each of his remaining veterans, as tears coursed down his broad face. These Rebel Tennesseans, like their fellow Confederates, now had to come to terms with defeat and rebuild their lives. What those lives would be like and where they would be lived remained to be seen. Unfortunately, no peace was coming to Tennessee. The conflict had reached far beyond the battlefields and into the home front, and it had opened deep wounds that could not and would not be healed easily.

SEVEN

Tennessee's Home Front

★ ★ ★

FOR FOUR LONG and arduous years, Confederate and Union forces struggled to control the Volunteer State and its resources. While thousands of Tennesseans fought on battlefields across the state and throughout the South, their friends and family at home endured a different but no less brutal war of their own. Faced with hunger, deprivation, occupying armies, and guerrilla and outlaw bands, they struggled to maintain their homes and their very lives in the maelstrom of war.

The Military Governorship of Andrew Johnson

The collapse of the Confederate defensive line in the Western Theater in early 1862 offered the Lincoln administration two great opportunities. First, there was a possibility of ending the war quickly provided the Rebel armies could be

A refugee family arriving at a Union Army post in Tennessee. Library of Congress.

crushed and the Confederate Heartland overrun. Second, as most of Middle and West Tennessee fell before Union armies, Lincoln saw a chance to attempt a speedy reintegration of the rebellious state back into the Republic. As Federal forces occupied Nashville, Lincoln chose Andrew Johnson to shepherd Tennessee back into the fold by appointing him military governor of the state.

Lincoln had known Johnson casually from Congress since the 1840s and considered him to be the logical choice for the job. The president was impressed with Johnson's dedication to the Union. Indeed, immediately after Johnson took office, Lincoln charged him with dispensing Federal

Union refugees coming into Federal lines. *Harper's Weekly*, November 5, 1864.

patronage in Tennessee despite their political party differences. This surprised and angered many Republicans who did not like the Democrat, but Lincoln would not be swayed. Johnson was loyal, and he was a Southerner.

For his part, Johnson worked tirelessly to keep Tennessee in the Union throughout the secession crisis. When Congress adjourned in the spring of 1861, Johnson returned to Tennessee to campaign against separation from the Union in the state's upcoming June referendum. He allied himself with former political rivals from the old Whig (Opposition) Party in Tennessee, such as William G. "Parson" Brownlow and Thomas A. R. Nelson, because he believed the Union's survival transcended political differences. By concentrating their efforts on East Tennessee, Johnson and the other

Unionists hoped to win enough votes to sway the election. At great risk to his life, Johnson spoke out against secession in openly hostile areas. On June 8, however, the state voted overwhelmingly for independence. Disappointed and still fearing for his life, Johnson fled Tennessee. He continued to give speeches in favor of the Union in Kentucky and Ohio before returning to Washington and retaking his seat in Congress. Johnson's loyalty to the old Union made him a hero to the North and a strong ally of Lincoln, and Lincoln's support would be critical as Johnson entered the next phase of his career.

Johnson's vision of the war paralleled the president's, and they shared a set of assumptions about secession and its leadership. Both believed that the Confederate states were not really out of the Union, and both believed that the state governments had been usurped by ambitious politicians and large slaveholders. These unscrupulous men had misled the general population of the South into believing Lincoln, the Republican Party, and the old Union represented a threat to their traditional political, economic, and social systems. Lincoln and Johnson presumed, therefore, that as Federal armies regained control of Confederate territory, a strategy of suppressing the small but vocal secessionist element while offering a conciliatory policy toward the rest of the population would regain their allegiance and end the rebellion quickly. In this, both were badly mistaken. They had seriously underestimated the strength of Confederate patriotism in Tennessee and, indeed, throughout the South.

In addition to miscalculating the depth of Rebel sympathy, the two men also miscalculated Johnson's popularity in Tennessee. Johnson had always been more highly regarded in East Tennessee, which still remained under Confederate control. The largely pro-secessionist citizenry of Middle and West Tennessee considered Johnson a traitor for supporting Lincoln and the hated Yankee invaders. Moreover, Johnson's personality made him more enemies among even those who agreed with his Unionism. He was prone to being argumentative, stubborn, dogmatic, and self-righteous when he thought he was on the right side of a dispute, and worse, he was vindictive to those who crossed him. These were hardly the best qualities for a man sent to woo a rebellious people.

Still, when Johnson arrived in Nashville in March 1862, he was optimistic that he could handle the task of restoring Tennessee to the Union. In essence, he planned a carrot-and-stick approach. On March 18, he issued "An Appeal to the People of Tennessee" in which he outlined the course of his military governorship and attempted to persuade the population to support his efforts. He declared that his goal was the quick restoration of Tennessee to the Union and offered amnesty to those who would renounce the rebellion and accept the old Union. Yet, punishment awaited those who remained disloyal.

Johnson's offer fell largely on deaf ears, and true to his word, he began to lash out at secessionists. Within weeks of his arrival in Nashville, he had arrested the mayor, Richard B. Cheatham; a former governor, Neill S. Brown; and several secessionist ministers. He removed all local politicians who would not take an oath of allegiance to the Union, shut down several secessionist newspapers, and even closed the Baptist and Methodist publishing houses. Throughout his tenure, Johnson would resort to forced oaths, censorship, prison, and even banishment to break or punish defiant Rebels. He was determined to root out secessionist sentiment regardless of how harsh he had to be. In retaliation, Confederate authorities in East Tennessee seized his home and property, including his slaves, and expelled his family from the region.

Johnson could even be harsh with his allies. With his governorship came the rank of brigadier general, and he relished this authority. His cantankerous nature often conflicted with the Union military commanders in Tennessee. Initially he argued with Major General Don Carlos Buell over efforts to protect Nashville, and he therefore supported the effort to oust the general. He also clashed with Buell's replacement, Major General William Rosecrans, over jurisdictional matters. In 1863, Johnson even traveled to Washington to gain clarification from the War Department on the extent of his authority compared to that of Rosecrans. Surprisingly, Lincoln and his administration supported Johnson. In fairness, Johnson was right to be concerned over the safety of Nashville; Confederate guerrillas, Rebel cavalry raiders, and the Confederate Army of Tennessee remained threats to the city and region throughout 1862–63. This concern, along with the growing realization that he could not win over the secessionists, prompted a change in Johnson's attitude. He became increasingly convinced that Tennessee's Rebel population had to be punished; conciliation had clearly failed.

While Lincoln continually pushed for state and local elections, military circumstances and Johnson's own reluctance slowed the process. Congressional elections in 1862 were canceled, and no elections were held in 1863. However, Union victories in 1863 brought virtually all of Tennessee under Federal control and ended any real Confederate threat to the state. With the Rebel menace gone, Johnson now made a real effort to reestablish a civilian government. This did not come easily, however, and over the fourteen-month period from January 1864 to February 1865, he used coercion to control the process and to ensure that his vision was realized and his candidates had an advantage.

Although Johnson had reached out to the state's Unionists since arriving in Tennessee, many had become disenchanted with the military governor for a number of reasons. Old political animosities existed between Johnson, who was a Democrat, and the Unionists who were former Whigs. Also, Johnson's overbearing personality and his constant reluctance to share power continued to breed resentment among the loyalists. These differences paled in comparison, however, to the one issue that drove the deepest wedge between Unionist ranks: emancipation.

Like most War Democrats, Johnson had wanted to preserve the Union, but he had not supported radical social change, especially regarding slavery. In fact, he had been firmly against emancipation before the war and in the early stages of the conflict. When Lincoln issued the preliminary Emancipation Proclamation in 1862, Johnson convinced the president to exempt Tennessee. He saw the measure as potentially damaging since many Tennessee Unionists, including himself, did not support Black freedom. Gradually, however, Lincoln's cajoling and his own class envy reversed his opinion, and he came to view emancipation as a necessary means to an end. It could weaken Southern resolve and separate the yeoman farmers of the South from the aristocratic slaveholders that Johnson held responsible for secession and the war. So the man who initially persuaded Lincoln to exempt Tennessee from the Emancipation Proclamation in early 1863 had by the end of the year become convinced that the institution must end.

Most of Tennessee's Unionists felt betrayed. Indeed, their sacrifices had been in vain if the Lincoln government followed the very same abolitionist agenda that the secessionists had warned Tennesseans about. For these men, union and slavery were synonymous. The Unionists of Tennessee quickly split into either "conservative" Unionists who wished for the Union to be restored as it had been, or absolute and unconditional Unionists like Johnson, who wished to punish the Rebels and initiate emancipation.

While Johnson grudgingly supported emancipation, he certainly did not believe in Black equality and resisted recruiting Black soldiers for the Union army in Tennessee. Eventually, however, under pressure from the Lincoln administration, he again relented and helped put some twenty thousand former slaves into uniform. These changes in his attitude toward emancipation brought him into conflict with many Tennessee loyalists who had always supported both the Union *and* slavery. Ultimately, for Johnson, the preservation of the Union was far more important than any other consideration. Johnson expected all Tennessee Unionists to follow his lead on the issue, but his dogmatic nature turned his difference of position into entrenched lines of conflict that split the Tennessee Unionists into two camps.

Johnson's evolution of thought is clearly demonstrated in some fifteen public speeches from 1864, the majority of which contained comments about slavery and emancipation. He even advocated for a state constitutional amendment ending slavery. While attending a Unionist convention in Knoxville in April 1864, Johnson witnessed the pronounced differences among Unionists over the idea of emancipation. Despite significant opposition, he led the efforts to get resolutions passed calling for the end of slavery. On October 24, 1864, he broadcast perhaps his most famous speech on the subject. A huge torchlight procession of Black people calling for freedom ended at the steps of the state capitol. The crowd insisted that Johnson speak. Caught up in the emotion of the moment, he declared, "I, Andrew Johnson, do hereby proclaim freedom, full, broad and unconditional, to every man in Tennessee." Johnson spoke dramatically of his hope for a Moses to lead them to the "Promised Land" of freedom. The crowd chanted for Johnson to be their Moses, and he reluctantly agreed to assume that epic role. In mid-November, another parade of some four thousand Blacks marched to Johnson's home, and he rewarded their faith in him with a paternalistic speech on the importance of hard work, education, strong morals, and the virtues of marriage. He went so far as to proclaim, "I claim every honest man, be he white or colored, as my brother." Johnson's new understanding of the Union clearly meant emancipation, and his rhetoric appeared to promise African Americans a new place in the social order of Tennessee.

In 1864, when elections were finally held in the Volunteer State, Johnson stipulated that only those who would take both Lincoln's oath of allegiance as outlined in the 1863 Proclamation of Amnesty *and* Johnson's own oath could vote. According to Johnson, prospective voters must agree to support the Constitution and also desire to suppress the rebellion and extend the Emancipation Proclamation to Tennessee. Everyone had to take what its detractors called Johnson's "Damnesty Oath," which humiliated Unionists who supported the restoration of the Union but not emancipation. The "conservative" Tennessee Unionists had grown weary of Johnson's dictatorial control and protested to Lincoln, but the president supported Johnson. Again in late 1864, as the presidential election neared, Johnson stipulated that potential voters had to swear yet another oath that they did not support negotiations with the Confederacy. In essence, this meant that one could not in good conscience vote for the Democratic candidate George B. McClellan, who advocated a negotiated peace. Lincoln again did not intervene. He had come to trust Johnson and saw much potential in the fiery War Democrat.

Johnson's continued support for Lincoln and his policies had a profound and unexpected effect on his career. Lincoln and the Republicans created the National Union Party by fusing the War Democrats with their own party for the 1864 election in the hopes of securing more votes. They needed a strong running mate for Lincoln and wanted to find an acceptable War Democrat. While many scholars deny that Lincoln influenced Republicans to nominate Andrew Johnson as his vice-presidential running mate, that assertion seems implausible. Lincoln controlled all aspects of his presidency, and he had established a relationship with Johnson. While Johnson may or may not have been Lincoln's first choice, he certainly possessed the credentials for the job. Given Johnson's popularity in the Midwest and his support of Lincoln, he made an ideal candidate. Lincoln apparently agreed that to have a War Democrat join him on the ticket sent a strong message about unity in a time when war weariness was raging in the North.

The Lincoln–Johnson ticket won an impressive victory in 1864, and the future prosecution of the conflict seemed assured. Before leaving for Washington, Johnson worked feverishly to finish establishing a civilian government in Tennessee. A Unionist convention in Nashville in January 1865 set about accomplishing numerous tasks, the most important of which was to elect a pro-Union government for Tennessee. Many delegates tasked with establishing this civilian government were actually Tennesseans in the Federal army. However, the convention was dominated by many of the East Tennessee Unionists who had returned from exile, such as William Brownlow, Horace Maynard, and DeWitt Senter. Brownlow emerged as the president of the convention, and he and his fellow loyalists set to work. The convention repudiated secession, nullified the actions of the Harris administration, and amended the state constitution to abolish slavery. The convention's measures would be submitted to a popular vote on February 22, George Washington's birthday. A general election for state officials would follow on March 4. Given Johnson's control of voting, it was inevitable that the resolutions would pass. Brownlow would win the governor's office and be inaugurated on April 5, 1865. Civil control of Tennessee had returned, yet now it was the Unionists who held power. What they would do with that power remained to be seen.

Johnson issued a self-congratulatory statement outlining the accomplishments of his time as military governor and left for Washington with Brownlow and his supporters in control of the state. Only weeks after being sworn in as vice president, however, Johnson found himself suddenly thrust into the presidency with the assassination of Lincoln on April 14, 1865. The next day, Andrew Johnson was sworn in as the nation's seventeenth president. He faced the enormous task of rebuilding the South and forging a coherent Reconstruction policy. At first, congressional Republicans, even Radicals, were willing to work with the president in shaping policy. What transpired over the next few years, however, would be a disaster that convulsed the nation and tore at the very fabric of the Republic.

Life Under Federal Occupation

While politicians in Nashville and Washington dealt with the larger military and political ramifications of the war, common soldiers and civilians faced more practical but no less important issues. When Union forces entered Tennessee in early 1862, panic ensued among the state's secessionist population. As the whole Rebel line collapsed and much of Middle and West Tennessee fell to the invading Yankees, some Tennesseans fearing murder, rape, and pillage gathered their families and their most valuable possessions (including slaves) and joined the Rebel forces retreating southward. Few, however, relished spending the remainder of the war living as refugees. Most returned home and, like the vast majority of their fellow Tennesseans, resolved themselves to face both their fears and the invaders. Tennesseans were surprised to find that initially the Yankee soldiers they encountered were generally well behaved and sometimes even friendly. Pillaging and vandalism were rare, and there was little destruction and almost no personal violence. The Union forces were even indulgent of displays of Rebel sympathy. Most Union generals were as convinced as Lincoln and Johnson that the South was still part of the Union and that the vast majority of Southerners had been misled into supporting secession. They felt that loyalty could be reestablished through a policy of conciliation. Therefore, Federal officers ordered their men not to mistreat the citizens and to protect their property, including slaves.

Yet, to the shock and chagrin of Lincoln, Johnson, and the Union army, Tennessee's secessionists did not appreciate or acquiesce to this lenient policy. Confederate morale had been shaken, but it did not collapse. In fact, it proved deeply rooted and would endure until the very end of the war, even affecting the course of occupation. Alice Ready of Murfreesboro demonstrated the Rebel tenacity when she wrote in her diary a few days after Union troops arrived in March 1862, "I am a greater rebel than ever before. . . . I cannot feel yet . . . that God has forsaken us. I do not believe it, he will yet smile upon [us]." She, like most of her fellow Tennesseans, resolved to resist Yankee rule. It simply became a question of how and to what degree.

Some acts of resistance were passive, such as displaying Rebel flags. More brazen defiance often came from women, children, or the elderly since they expected little retaliation. Federal soldiers might be jeered at or subjected to renditions of "Dixie" or "The Bonnie Blue Flag." Some Rebel women in Nashville went so far as to hold their noses when they passed Union troops in the streets. Initially, Union soldiers generally tolerated such indignities in the hope that their conciliatory policy would eventually succeed. However, Federal authorities drew the line when it came to more serious forms of resistance such as spying, smuggling, and especially bushwhacking. Bushwhackers (guerrillas) emerged as a serious threat to the Union military. Operating in small, mounted groups in the hinterland, guerrillas would cut telegraph wires, tear up railroad tracks, or ambush Union patrols. Acquainted with the terrain and aided by their neighbors and kinsmen, guerrillas could elude every effort to ensnare them.

While most Rebel guerrillas were part of an insurgency against what they viewed as an occupying force, others were simply brigands using the war to justify brutal crimes. At times, the lines blurred. A perfect example is Richard V. Richardson's Twelfth Tennessee Cavalry Regiment (Partisan Rangers), which operated in West Tennessee. Although "Colonel" Richardson was ostensibly a legitimate military commander leading a Rebel force tasked with disrupting the Federal occupation of the region, his men were often described as mere robbers. Eventually, the unit would be absorbed into Nathan Bedford Forrest's command with new leadership.

Champ Ferguson stands as an example of a brutal bushwhacker who operated as both a partisan and brigand. Even though he committed atrocities throughout Tennessee, Kentucky, and Virginia during the war, he tried to settle down peacefully at its conclusion. However, for his actions, he would be one of a handful of people arrested and

Champ Ferguson, Confederate guerilla, surrounded by prison guards during his trial for war crimes. Library of Congress.

executed for war crimes. Confederate guerrillas in Tennessee would contend not only with Federal soldiers attempting to pacify the region but also Unionist guerrillas. For example, Champ Ferguson's nemesis was David "Tinker Dave" Beatty in the Upper Cumberland region of the Volunteer State. Beatty even testified against Ferguson at the war's end, although his men often used similar tactics of beating, arson, looting, and murder.

The continued resistance to Union authority eventually persuaded Yankee officers and the military governor that appeasement and conciliation would not work. The hostility of the unrepentant Rebels wore on Northern goodwill and patience, and the Yankees gradually became convinced that Southern society had to be reformed and reshaped in the image of the North. This change in attitude generated a harsh policy toward the White population of Tennessee. Earlier restrictions on seizure of private property, especially foodstuffs, were lifted, thus allowing Federal foraging parties to seize anything they needed from local farmers. This liberal foraging inexorably led to pillaging and looting. Moreover, Federal commanders and provost marshals began to muzzle secessionist sentiment by jailing anyone for expressing Rebel sympathies, even women. Ministers, newspaper editors, and publishers were especially singled out for spreading disloyalty. Furthermore, Johnson decreed that all citizens must take an oath of allegiance or face arrest or banishment. Where guerrilla attacks occurred, Union soldiers retaliated by looting or burning nearby homes or even taking hostages. These harsher policies failed to cow the secessionists, who remained determined to resist the Yankees, and savage retaliations did occur. For example, in late 1863 near the village of Mulberry, Tennessee, guerrillas captured five Federal foragers, tied their hands, and executed them. The war had turned hard.

The level of Rebel resistance was linked to the spread of Union authority across the Volunteer State. Throughout 1862 and 1863, Federal forces gradually asserted control over most of West and Middle Tennessee. However, it was not until the end of 1863 that Union troops finally forced the Rebels from East Tennessee. During this long and arduous process, areas of the state often fell under Union, Confederate, or even no authority. Noted historian Stephen Ash observed that as Federal forces advanced into and occupied the South, places like Tennessee were divided into distinct geographical zones that affected the population in a number of ways. Garrison towns formed the first zone, where the Federal forces set up their headquarters, supply depots, barracks, hospitals, and other administrative elements. From such bases as these, Union forces would rest, equip, and prepare to move into Confederate territory.

As they took control of the state, Union troops occupied all of Tennessee's cities, towns, and even some villages. The presence of large numbers of soldiers, runaway slaves, and refugees overwhelmed most of these places, and living conditions deteriorated badly. Memphis, for example, had a prewar population of twenty-three thousand, but by early 1863, this had grown to an estimated thirty-five thousand residents, not counting garrison troops. Overcrowding and scarcity of resources disrupted the local economy, resulting in unemployment, inflation, and shortages of food and housing. Governing the towns was not always easy for the military authorities or the inhabitants. Urban problems exacerbated by the presence of the Federal troops taxed the patience and abilities of the officers-turned-civic administrators. For example, in Nashville, prostitution led to rampant venereal disease. By July 1863, the situation had deteriorated to the point that the provost marshal rounded up several hundred prostitutes and sent them north by train and steamship. When no city would take them, they were forced to return to Nashville by August. Military authorities then established the nation's first system of legalized prostitution requiring women to be licensed and to undergo weekly medical inspections by army surgeons. The system proved successful in controlling venereal disease, and similar practices were adopted in Memphis and other towns in the occupied South. Despite myriad problems associated with the garrison towns, the presence of Union troops did preserve order, and the Federals generally permitted and supported the functioning of schools, churches, and businesses as long as they did not promote secessionism. Furthermore, the army often provided food and clothing to needy inhabitants, especially runaway slaves.

Outside the garrison towns was a second zone of no-man's land. Although Federal forces could project their power into the region at will, they could not be in all places at all times. It was here that the countryside was most barren due to foraging and the prevalence of abandoned farms and homes. It was also here that guerrillas and bandits roamed, pillaging, raping, and destroying. This was a lawless and forsaken landscape. Farmers struggled to feed and care for their families as foraging parties stripped them of their livestock, foodstuffs, and even fence rails (used for firewood). Indeed, as the war continued, many rural Tennesseans faced hunger or even starvation. Adding to the near famine was anarchy. Bandits claiming allegiance to one side or the other preyed on the isolated and helpless homesteads. Travel became so dangerous that families remained close to home for months at a time. Rural churches and schools closed, and community life all but vanished. Unable to bear the violence and hunger, many fled no-man's land for the garrison towns, which only worsened the problem of overcrowding there.

Beyond no-man's land lay a third zone of Confederate territory. While the Confederate military and civilian authorities ostensibly controlled this zone, Federal patrols and foraging parties often penetrated the fringes, meaning that Confederate authorities could offer neither long-term safety nor stability to the inhabitants of these areas.

The borders of these distinct zones ebbed and flowed as the main armies maneuvered and engaged in battles. Eventually, however, Union control of the state grew while Confederate control shrank. Unfortunately, this increased the area of no-man's land, a situation that would remain until the end of the war and even beyond. By 1864, especially after General Hood's forlorn invasion of the state, morale among Confederate Tennesseans withered. Confronted by overwhelming Federal power and by the manifest collapse of slavery, the secessionist citizens of Tennessee, much sooner than those in regions behind Confederate lines, resigned themselves to Northern victory and Black emancipation. The end was coming.

The Collapse of Slavery

Slavery had been an integral part of Tennessee's economy and society throughout its statehood. Only a third of Tennessee families held slaves, and very few slaveholders owned the requisite twenty bondsmen that historians use as a measure for a "planter," the top rung of the slaveholding hierarchy. Still, slaves composed 25 percent of the state's population by 1860 and 34 percent of taxable property. Clearly, slave-owning Tennesseans had a vested interest in protecting and perpetuating the institution. Thus, they were relieved when the Union-occupying forces did not initially interfere with slavery. This would not last, however.

The initial war aim of the North was solely the preservation of the Union. Lincoln's speeches and the Crittenden-Johnson Resolution of July 1861 made it clear that neither the president nor Congress had any interest in interfering with the internal affairs of states (e.g., slave ownership). However, continued Southern resistance gradually changed that stance. The first blow against slavery came with the Confiscation Act of August 1861, in which the US Congress authorized the seizure of any Confederate property by Union forces. Property in this case also meant slaves. Therefore, all slaves that were utilized for the Confederate war effort could be seized as contraband of war, hence the generic term "contrabands" for runaway slaves in Federal camps. These early measures failed to impress the states in rebellion, and the realization that the South would not willingly return to the Union led the House of Representatives to refuse to reaffirm the Crittenden–Johnson Resolution by that December. A second confiscation act passed in July 1862 upped the ante by stating that any Confederate military or civilian official who did not surrender within sixty days of the act's passage would have his slaves freed. Since these acts were only valid in areas of Union control, neither impressed the Confederate population, which simply ignored them. Moreover, the failure of Lincoln's lenient occupation policies, coupled with the increasing cost of the war in blood and treasure, gradually moved the president and the Moderate Republicans closer to the Radicals in the party who had long advocated for an end to slavery. Desiring to end the gruesome conflict as soon as possible, Lincoln offered one last alternative to the rebellious states. His preliminary Emancipation Proclamation of September 1862 threatened to end slavery in areas under Confederate control unless the South capitulated. When his offer was rebuffed, the Emancipation Proclamation of January 1863 went into effect. Always cognizant not to alienate the slaveholding Unionists in the border states, Lincoln exempted those states as well as areas of the South under Federal control such as Tennessee. Emancipation caused a furor in the North and led McClellan and the Peace Democrats to oppose Lincoln's proclamation as part of their 1864 presidential platform. Worse, it only hardened Confederate resolve. Still, Lincoln remained determined to use whatever means necessary to end the rebellion.

While politicians in Washington debated the issue of emancipation, Union soldiers dealt with its ramifications. Federal soldiers reflected the racial sentiments of the society from which they came, and emancipation inspired few of the men initially. The preservation of the Union and its sacred mission to bring representative government to the world was their primary focus for enlistment. However, a firsthand look at the degradation of slavery, coupled with the growing belief that slaveholders were responsible for the war and now had to be punished, convinced increasing numbers of Federals that the institution must end. Moreover, the death of slavery promised to hasten that end by removing a source of labor from the Confederacy. While the preservation of the Union always remained the primary goal, emancipation developed as a means to that end. In sum, the Federal army would become an army of liberation whether some or even most of its officers and men were at best reluctant liberators.

Many runaway slaves eventually found their way to contraband camps near the garrison towns. Grand Junction in West Tennessee was the first of these in November 1862. Eventually some seventeen camps would be created around the state. Conditions in the camps varied; some were dreadful. They often lacked adequate shelter, food, clothing, blankets, firewood, and even medicine. The overcrowding and unsanitary conditions led to widespread sickness and death. Other camps, such as those at Clarksville and Pulaski, fared better, and the inhabitants enjoyed a clean camp, enough food, and even schools run by Northern missionaries.

Federal commanders never intended the camps to be permanent and sought to clear them when possible. Thousands of able-bodied males were used as laborers to build fortifications, railroads, levees, canals, and so on. Those ex-slaves with high-demand skills such as carpenters, brick masons, blacksmiths, and teamsters were especially prized by Union officers. Northern entrepreneurs also sought Black farm labor in order to restart cotton production on the abandoned plantations for the domestic and foreign markets. It must be noted that these men, whether work-

Fort Pickering Contraband Camp, Memphis, Tennessee.
MTSU James E. Walker Library Digital Collections.

ing for individuals or the army, were often compensated for their labor only with rations and shelter, a condition many contrabands recognized as all too similar to slavery.

Another way Federal authorities sought to clear the camps was to encourage young Black men to enlist in the Union army. In the spring of 1863, Brigadier General Lorenzo Thomas was appointed commissioner for the Organization of Colored Troops in Tennessee. By the summer, he had organized three thousand in Memphis. During the fall and winter of 1863, recruiting stations were set up primarily at locations in Middle and West Tennessee such as Fort Donelson, Clarksville, Gallatin, Nashville, Murfreesboro, McMinnville, Columbia, Wartrace, Shelbyville, Lynnville, Pulaski, and Pikeville. The only recruitment effort

Hannah and Adam Watkins escaped enslavement in Middle Tennessee, and Adam joined the 16th USCT Regiment. Courtesy of the Tennessee State Museum.

in East Tennessee was made at Chattanooga. Despite the hostility shown to Black soldiers from many Union officers and politicians, by 1865, more than twenty thousand Black men had joined the United States Colored Troops. Indeed, USCT units formed in Tennessee accounted for about 40 percent of all Union soldiers raised in Tennessee during the war. While no cavalry units were formed, twenty-one regiments of infantry and seven units of artillery were organized, primarily from freedmen coming from the Middle and Western portions of the state. Since the Emancipation Proclamation did not apply to Tennessee but service in the Union army guaranteed freedom, nearly 39 percent of enslaved males in Tennessee obtained their freedom in this manner.

These Black units contributed to the Union war effort in Tennessee in numerous ways. Initially, Union generals were reluctant to allow Black troops into combat. They felt they would be unable to perform well. Black units, therefore, were assigned to labor details, guard duty, and garrison duty. The first taste of combat for these units came as they manned fortifications along the railroads and rivers of the state that were targets for Rebel cavalry raiders—the most infamous incident being the attack on Fort Pillow by Confederate cavalry under the command of General Nathan Bedford Forrest in April 1864. USCT units continued to engage in skirmishes against Confederate raiders until the Battle of Nashville. There Black units were engaged in heavy combat in the defeat of the Army of Tennessee in 1864. While some units were disbanded when the war ended in 1865, others remained in service until 1866, serving as garrison troops in Memphis, Nashville, Knoxville, and Chattanooga. These units proved vital to the Union effort to hold Tennessee, and they proved their bravery and dedication to the Union and Black emancipation. In addition to the dangers of regular military service, USCT soldiers in Tennessee faced mistreatment or even death if captured by Confederate forces. By the war's end, the units suffered a nearly 20 percent casualty rate.

Not all former slaves sought the support of the Federal army. Indeed, many avoided the contraband camps, military service, and contract labor altogether and fled to Black shanty towns that sprang up in Tennessee's larger urban areas. There, they performed odd jobs and attempted to establish lives independent of White supervision and control.

The collapse of slavery in Tennessee stunned White inhabitants. Long accustomed to servile obedience from their slaves, the shock of them fleeing to the Yankees or dropping their guise of feigned respect was too much to grasp. Robert H. Cartmell of Madison County recalled that "to one born and raised in the South & accustomed to keeping the Sons of Ham in their proper place, the impudence of these negroes is hard to endure. They are entirely corrupted." Cartmell and his fellow Tennesseans would have to deal with increasing "impudence" as slaves bargained with their masters, resisted discipline, or continued to run away. The desire for freedom or at least better conditions could not be quelled. The institution dissolved quickly in the presence of Union forces, and by late 1863, one Yankee offered a curt but apt assessment of the situation in Tennessee when he declared, "Slavery is dead."

The Travails of East Tennessee

While Middle and West Tennessee struggled through Federal occupation and the collapse of slavery, the eastern portion of the state endured its own turmoil. East Tennessee's ardent Unionism and the continued presence of Confederate forces made the region an outlier when compared to the rest of the state's home front experience during the Civil War. The area remained under Confederate control until 1863 when Union troops finally managed to drive out major Rebel forces. Still, Confederate raids and guerrilla actions persisted until the end of the war, devastating a region already experiencing banditry, personal feuds, and economic collapse.

Early in the war, the bridge burnings and the disaster at Mill Springs threw East Tennessee Confederates into a panic. Rebel authorities abandoned their conciliatory policies designed to win over the Unionists in favor of mass arrests and confiscations. They now sought to terrorize the loyalists into submission. Unionists had three choices under this new strategy: submit, passively resist, or flee to Kentucky to join the Union army. Many chose the latter. Those crossing the mountains into Kentucky had to elude increased Confederate patrols by using guides called "pilots," who led thousands into the Bluegrass State. In Kentucky, most joined the Federal army in the hope of liberating their homes. Indeed, nearly all of the thirty thousand or so White Tennesseans who joined up came from East Tennessee.

These Federal volunteers were augmented by guerrillas who wished to stay in the area. They had begun raiding the region by the winter of 1861–62, and because of their knowledge of the terrain and the support of the local populace, they proved formidable. They sought revenge for the harshness of Confederate rule by ambushing isolated Rebel soldiers or raiding and burning secessionists' homesteads. As this guerrilla war continued into 1862, Confederate soldiers grew increasingly frustrated with their inability to catch or kill the bushwhackers and more brutal in their attempts to destroy the insurgents. Atrocities mounted on both sides. The region was slipping into anarchy.

Unable to quell Unionist resistance, in March 1862, the Confederate War Department ordered Major General Edmund Kirby Smith to East Tennessee to restore order and defuse the tense situation. Smith and the Confederate authorities in Richmond vacillated between conciliation and coercion, but neither worked. Smith viewed the region as an "enemy's country" and endeavored to convince President Davis likewise. He held no confidence in the loyalty of Confederate troops recently mustered in the region. He believed correctly that the vast majority of East Tennesseans with secessionist sentiments had already joined the army. He, therefore, advised the War Department to transfer locally mustered units to other areas of the Confederacy to prevent their desertion or their aiding Union guerrillas. He also wanted to imprison the region's remaining loyalist leadership in order to curb their influence on the population. He further threatened civil servants who did not comply with the new congressional act requiring loyalty oaths with arrest. In April, Davis finally acquiesced to Smith's pleas for martial law, suspended the writ of habeas corpus in East Tennessee, and granted Smith control of the courts. Smith ordered the families of prominent Unionists such as William Brownlow, Horace Maynard, and Andrew Johnson expelled from the region, and he threatened to expel the families and seize the property of all those fighting in the Union army as well. The harsh initiatives of the Confederate authorities generated a virtual exodus of Unionists heading for Kentucky. Not since the bridge burnings had there been a more polarizing period.

Once Smith had established Confederate authority, he sought to calm the situation and woo the loyalists with acts of benevolence. On April 18, he issued a proclamation offering amnesty to any East Tennessean taking an oath to the Confederacy, including those in the Federal army, provided they returned to the region within thirty days. He also suspended service in the state militia. On August 13 he added a new incentive by offering to buy any arms brought in by East Tennesseans who were leaving Federal service. Smith even suspended Confederate conscription in hopes of mollifying the Unionists and stopping the flood of recruits out of the region and into the Federal army. Yet, despite his best efforts, the hearts and minds of the region's loyalist population did not waver.

During the invasion of Kentucky in the summer of 1862, Smith temporarily left East Tennessee, and the Confederate War Department appointed native East Tennessean John P. McCown and Major General Samuel Jones as his replacements, insisting that they enforce conscription. Jones tried his hand at coaxing the loyalists over to the Rebel cause. He convinced Union leader Thomas A. R. Nelson to issue a public statement condemning the preliminary Emancipation Proclamation, encouraging the acceptance of Confederate rule, and urging Richmond to suspend again the draft in East Tennessee. Nelson's statement, however, fell on deaf ears, as did Jones's call to suspend conscription.

Smith returned briefly to the region in October 1862 but did nothing to change established Confederate policy in the region. He left East Tennessee for good in early 1863 to be replaced by Major General Daniel Donelson, who subsequently would be replaced by Major General Simon B. Buckner in May 1863. Neither Donelson nor Buckner could woo the Unionist population. Confederate policies of conscription, sequestration, and taxation, as well as the increasingly antagonistic attitude of Confederate occupation forces, prevented any hope of a peaceful coexistence. The stubborn resistance of the region's loyalists forced Richmond to accept that East Tennessee was, indeed, an "enemy's country."

During the summer of 1863, Unionist guerrillas, with the open support of the local population, continued to raid the region, and as Buckner moved his forces out of upper East Tennessee by late August 1863 to link up with General Braxton Bragg's army contesting General William E. Rosecrans's advance on Chattanooga, Confederate control began to dissolve. When Major General Ambrose Burnside's twelve-thousand-man army advanced from Kentucky and occupied Knoxville on September 1, 1863, it collapsed outright. As Burnside's men entered the city, East Tennessee Unionists greeted them as liberators, showering them with food and cheers. A little more than a week later, Rosecrans's occupation of lower East Tennessee effectively ended the Confederate occupation of the region.

The years of Confederate rule had taken a heavy toll on the men and women of the region who had remained loyal to the Union. While many men fled East Tennessee to join the Union army or avoid conscription, the women, children, and elderly males stayed to fend for themselves. With the men gone, Unionist women and their children labored in the fields and worked to keep self-supporting farms operating in the face of harassment from secessionist neighbors, confiscations by Confederate soldiers, and raids by Rebel guerrillas. Many of these women even served as couriers, safe house operators, and spies for Unionist guerrillas and Federal soldiers. Early in the war and continuing under Rebel rule, women conducted an "underground railroad" for those escaping into Kentucky. They provided food, shelter, and information to Unionists and escaped Federal soldiers. Their efforts forced Confederate authorities to deploy soldiers desperately needed elsewhere to guard the mountain passes, patrol isolated trails, and search homesteads. Despite their many obstacles and hardships, East Tennessee Unionist women, like their male kin, refused to be subjugated.

While the loyalist–secessionist conflict in East Tennessee was unique to most of the South, the wartime experiences of the region's Black population proved similar to that of others elsewhere in the Confederacy. Due to its geography, East Tennessee had few slaves and masters, yet the

White population, whether loyalist or secessionist, united in their racism and desire to perpetuate the institution of slavery. Slaveholders were found on both sides, and, indeed, many Unionist owners believed that the institution would be better protected in the Union than in what they viewed as a doomed Confederacy. Therefore, Black people in East Tennessee, as elsewhere in the South, had few if any White allies. Like White Unionists, many slaves sought a better life for themselves and their families and crossed over the Cumberland Mountains into Kentucky in a search for freedom at Federal camps as contrabands. This exodus only increased after Lincoln issued the Emancipation Proclamation.

Given the continued resistance of White Unionist men and women, as well as slaves, it is clear that the Confederate government never had full control of East Tennessee. Richmond simply lacked the manpower to garrison the region adequately, and it always faced an active and armed resistance from loyalist guerrillas. Moreover, the inconsistency of Rebel policies, oscillating between conciliation and suppression, only alienated and emboldened a population determined to resist the Confederacy. Given its limitations, it is difficult to imagine that the Confederacy could have done anything politically or militarily to secure the acceptance or loyalty of the region's inhabitants.

By 1863, what little control the Rebels exercised was about to be lost. In the fall of that year, large-scale conventional warfare ushered new horrors into the area. Following his Pyrrhic victory at Chickamauga in September, General Bragg followed the retreating Federals back to their defenses at Chattanooga and attempted to besiege General Rosecrans's army. Lincoln responded swiftly by dispatching General Ulysses S. Grant to take command of the situation. Grant immediately broke the tentative siege and routed Bragg's Army of Tennessee at the Battle of

Missionary Ridge, sending the Rebels into headlong retreat into Georgia. Meanwhile, another small Confederate army under General Longstreet failed to retake Knoxville and subsequently retreated into upper East Tennessee. With the defeat and retreat of both Bragg and Longstreet, all but the extreme northwest corner of East Tennessee was now permanently under Union control, and a new chapter in the region's guerrilla war began.

By the winter of 1863, the only threat to Union authority of the region came from these guerrillas operating out of western North Carolina or North Georgia. They swept through areas of East Tennessee, looting and burning homes and barns and ambushing Federal garrisons. Local militia, loyalist guerrillas, and Federal troops retaliated against both the insurgents and local secessionists, and the bushwhacking escalated. Worse still, an increasing number of deserters from both armies along with brigands with no real allegiance to either side prowled the region in search of the unwary and undefended. Federal attempts at counterinsurgency failed, as had the earlier Confederate efforts. By 1864, East Tennessee and the rest of the state had been relegated to a secondary theater of war as Federal forces prepared for a massive offensive into Georgia. This meant that the violence simply could not be contained given the current resources.

The Federal district commander for East Tennessee, Ambrose Burnside, faced a daunting challenge. Not only did he have to continue to wage war against the remaining Rebel forces both regular and irregular, but he also had to formulate and implement Reconstruction policies for the devastated region. Burnside proved to be an able administrator who was up to the task. His strategy involved immediately crushing any and all opposition to Federal authority. He chose Brigadier General Samuel P. Carter, cousin of the

Reverend William B. Carter, as provost marshal general for the District of East Tennessee and empowered him to exercise martial law throughout the region. Without enough soldiers to enforce this, Carter had to employ members of the local loyalist population as deputy provost marshals for each county. Burnside also established a "secret police" force of loyalists under Robert A. Crawford to be his eyes and ears, and he organized home guard units called the "National Guard of Tennessee" to suppress guerrillas. Burnside attempted a carrot-and-stick approach with the region's secessionist minority, as per Lincoln's December 1863 Proclamation of Amnesty, which among other things offered a pardon to all Rebels except high-ranking officials provided that they took an oath of loyalty and agreed to accept the abolition of slavery. While hopeful of conciliation, Burnside was nevertheless determined to establish Federal control and prepared to imprison or banish secessionists who resisted Union authority. He ordered Confederate prisoners in East Tennessee north to Federal camps by early 1864. Likewise, he deported numerous outspoken civilian secessionists, including some women and ministers, to the Deep South.

Burnside's policies did impress the region's Moderate Unionists such as Thomas A. R. Nelson, who hoped to see an end to the bloodshed and suffering. However, the most influential Unionist in East Tennessee, William Brownlow, did not believe the policies were stringent enough. Arriving on the heels of the Federal army, Brownlow returned from exile to Knoxville with both official and unofficial powers. Officially, he served as special treasury agent for East Tennessee, a post that gave him the authority to issue or withhold licenses to trade, seize goods traded without a license, and confiscate and dispose of property abandoned by traitors. Brownlow energetically and enthusiastically used his office to reward his friends, punish his enemies, and increase his own influence. Unofficially, Brownlow became a demagogue for the Unionists of the region. Through his newspaper, now christened the *Knoxville Whig and Rebel Ventilator*, he spewed forth a torrent of anti-Confederate propaganda and near-obscene calls for retribution against the Rebel population of East Tennessee. Referring to secessionists as "Imps from Hell," he declared that Union men who had suffered at their hands would be "justified in shooting them down on sight." He challenged the manhood of Unionists who did not do so, declaring, "We shall regard hundreds of them [Unionists] as wanting in courage and in resentment if they do not dispatch them [secessionists] whenever they meet their rotten carcasses."

Brownlow's rhetoric fell on receptive ears, and many of his followers joined him in demanding retribution for real and perceived wrongs committed during the Confederate occupation. This placed Burnside in the awkward position of trying to control the violence against former secessionists who accepted Federal rule without alienating the loyalists on whom he greatly depended. Tensions between the region's Unionists and their liberators were exacerbated further by the behavior of Federal troops that often foraged indiscriminately from loyalists and secessionists alike.

As the war dragged on, East Tennessee, always a poor agricultural region, soon faced economic disaster. Guerrillas and brigands continued to destroy homes and barns, steal food and livestock, and murder farmers. Moreover, the region had not recovered from Confederate confiscations before Federal authorities arrived only to continue the practice. Many poor East Tennesseans now moved northward in search of opportunity to cities such as Cairo, Louisville, and Cincinnati, where they received mixed receptions by Northern citizens.

Not all East Tennesseans wanted to leave, nor could they. Those who remained faced starvation and homelessness. Thousands moved to Federal garrison cities such as Knoxville, Chattanooga, and even Nashville, where Union commanders provided temporary shelters and provisions. As Federal military operations in Georgia and Virginia demanded more provisions, however, this aid evaporated. One newspaper correspondent with the *Louisville Journal* recalled the pitiful refugees of Chattanooga arriving daily to beg for food that the military would no longer supply. The situation for Black people was even worse. Black families, crowded into contraband camps in Knoxville and Chattanooga, subsisted solely off military aid in the form of tents, foodstuffs, and other supplies. The lack of sanitary camp conditions led to outbreaks of smallpox that ravaged the refugees. Although Black males in the camps often performed manual labor for the government, in many cases they were not paid and thus could not afford better conditions for themselves or their families. Moreover, while some Black men voluntarily joined the USCT for money and freedom, others were coerced by White Federal officers eager to fill the ranks by any means available.

The economic situation in East Tennessee became so desperate that leading citizens of Knoxville organized the East Tennessee Relief Association. Unable to receive substantive Federal aid, agents traveled to the Midwest and Northeast to secure funds. Naturally, the relief association gave priority to Unionist families, especially those who had suffered for their loyalty. Ironically, while poor Rebel families could obtain aid, Black families, even those with members in the Union army, could not. So widespread was East Tennessee's poverty that the association did not disband until well after the war in 1868.

Poverty was not the only legacy of the war. While most

areas saw an end to organized violence in the spring of 1865 with the surrender of all major Confederate armies, the "official peace" did not extend to East Tennessee. The Unionist–secessionist conflict continued unabated in the coves, mountains, and villages of the region. The great issues of the war concerning secession and slavery had been decided, but the local issue of who would now control the region had not. Moreover, as Unionist guerrillas and those who had joined the Union army returned to the region for good, they were determined to shape the postwar world. Many Unionists wanted revenge for the wrongs they and their families had suffered at the hands of the secessionists. These veterans, like their loyalist neighbors who had remained, were determined to control the politics and economics of postwar East Tennessee, and they initiated a systematic campaign of terror to drive the Rebels from the region. Across East Tennessee, ex-Confederates would endure intimidation, beatings, arson, and even murder as they struggled to rebuild their lives in a region controlled by former neighbors now turned bitter enemies.

A War Within a War

While Tennessee's importance as a theater of war is well established, its historical role in the evolution of Union policies of occupation, wartime reconstruction, and emancipation were equally important. The war years were a period of profound suffering and transformation for the Volunteer State. While Whites in West and Middle Tennessee struggled to retain their secessionist sentiments in the face of Union occupation, their White neighbors in East Tennessee did the opposite, endeavoring to remain loyalty to the old Union against the pressure of a Confederate government. Meanwhile, the state's newly freed slaves fought to maintain their freedom in the face of poverty, racism, and an uncertain future. As the war ravaged the state, the brutality and privation experienced by its inhabitants served as a testament to both their helplessness and their strength. Like other areas of the South, Tennessee's war would eventually draw to a close, and the survivors of the nation's "greatest calamity" would now have to face the realities of a new world.

EIGHT

Reconstruction

★ ★ ★

THE CIVIL WAR ENDED in the spring of 1865. Its conclusion meant that the doctrine of secession had been invalidated by force of arms, and slavery as an institution had been destroyed. Questions concerning other key issues, however, remained unanswered. Who would hold postwar power in the Rebel states? What would be the terms for their readmission to the Union? Who would set these terms and control the process? How would the freedpeople fit into American society? These questions had long been debated in the North. Indeed, as early as 1862, when Federal forces first invaded the Confederacy, Northerners had discussed the future of the postwar South. It soon became obvious that no consensus could be reached, and the attempts to find answers to those questions generated an intense political struggle that would eventually shake the Republic to its foundations. In the end, the return of the seceded states to the Union, or Reconstruction as it came to be called, became an improvised process of compromise that gradually evolved with changing circumstances.

Tennessee's Reconstruction experience was unique to the South. The Volunteer State would reenter the Union quickly and well before the other Confederate states, thereby avoiding much of the strife that occurred under military Reconstruction. This was due to two primary factors: the presence of a large and influential Unionist population in East Tennessee and the fact that Tennessee was the first Rebel state to fall under the control of Federal forces, which meant that the Reconstruction process there under Andrew Johnson's direction began as early as 1862. Still, Tennessee's reintegration into the Union was not easy, and its people—White and Black, free and newly freed, Unionist and secessionist—endured violence, economic deprivation, grief, and countless hardships as they struggled to rebuild their lives amid the ruins of war.

Lincoln's Reconstruction Plan

From the beginning of the Civil War to its end, Abraham Lincoln remained convinced that most Southern White people still harbored a strong devotion to the Union—a belief that colored and shaped his ideas about Reconstruction throughout the war. Lincoln initially hoped that a conciliatory, even lenient policy would entice the region to rejoin the United States. He therefore encouraged his military commanders to respect the civil and property rights of Southerners. He even discouraged them from interfering with slave property. He appointed military governors in occupied areas and hoped to quickly establish civilian governments in the South and return the nation to its prewar status. However, White Southerners were more devoted to

Southern independence than he realized, and they ignored his overtures as the conflict intensified.

Gradually throughout 1862, Lincoln revised his thinking on the Union's restoration and increasingly came to believe that slavery was the chief stumbling block to ending the conflict. He offered the Confederates a chance to return to the Union and retain slavery with the preliminary Emancipation Proclamation in September 1862. The Confederacy ignored his olive branch. The Rebel refusal meant that the official Emancipation Proclamation of January 1863 now freed the slaves in Confederate territory. Still, slavery would exist in states loyal to the Union or former Confederate areas under Union control such as Tennessee. Still hoping to appeal to the overwhelming majority of Southern White people who did not own slaves, Lincoln's Proclamation of Amnesty and Reconstruction, issued in December 1863, outlined his vision further. He offered pardon to almost all Confederates, excluding only high-ranking civilian, military, and diplomatic leaders. Before being pardoned, these former Rebels would first take an oath of allegiance to the United States and pledge to accept all executive orders and congressional resolutions regarding slavery. Amnesty carried with it the restoration of all political rights, including the rights to vote and hold office. Lincoln's proclamation further stipulated that each of the former Confederate states could organize a new state government once a minimum of 10 percent of the number of White male voters from the 1860 presidential election took the loyalty oath. These new bodies would create a constitution establishing a republican form of government, abolishing slavery, and providing education for the freedpeople. Once these requirements were met, the president would recognize the new governments. Lincoln did not advocate prosecuting prominent ex-Confederates or permanently barring Rebels from voting. He did not even rule out compensation for slave property, nor did he insist on giving the freedmen citizenship or voting rights.

While Lincoln developed his vision, Congress was deeply divided over the direction of Reconstruction. Virtually all Democrats and most Conservative Republicans supported Lincoln's so-called "Ten-Percent Plan" and did not want to see any sweeping social or economic changes in the South. For them, the war had been about preserving the Union. However, Moderate Republicans, the largest group, believed that the former slaves should receive some basic civil rights, but they did not support Black suffrage because the majority of their constituents did not. Most Northern states restricted Black civil rights, especially suffrage. Radical Republicans, initially the party's smallest faction, had always called for emancipation and now embraced full civil rights for the freed slaves. Lincoln had to contend with all of these groups while charting a course that most could agree to follow.

Johnson's Reconstruction Plan

Lincoln's future plans for restoration ended with John Wilkes Booth's bullet on April 14, 1865. The next day, Andrew Johnson was sworn in as the nation's seventeenth president. Johnson faced the enormous task of rebuilding the South and forging a coherent Reconstruction policy. At first, congressional Republicans, even Radicals who strongly favored granting civil rights to newly freed slaves, were willing to work with the president in shaping policy. Johnson certainly brought great experience to the office. He had built an enviable political career by serving in local, state, and national offices. His humble origins and ardent Unionism led him to rail against the planter elite of the

President Andrew Johnson. Library of Congress.

South, whom he blamed for the war. In a highly publicized statement, he declared that "treason must be made odious, and traitors punished." Such pronouncements won him the instant admiration of the Radicals. However, despite his rhetoric, Johnson still held to the traditional Democratic doctrines of states' rights and white supremacy. For him, the Civil War had been fought to preserve the Union, not to remake Southern society.

Like Lincoln, Johnson favored a speedy resolution to the problems of Reconstruction, and also like his predecessor,

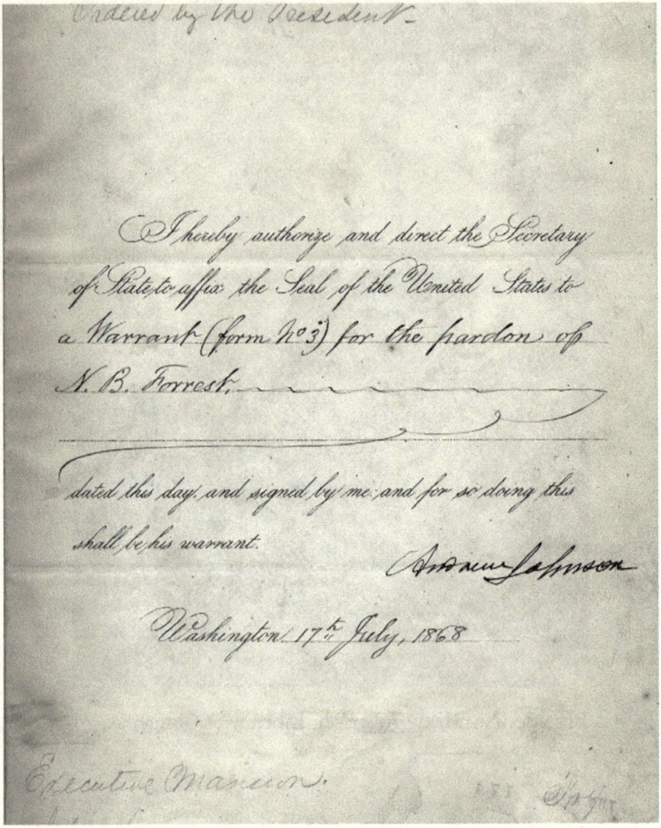

Ordered by the President -

I hereby authorize and direct the Secretary of State to affix the Seal of the United States to a Warrant (form No 3) for the pardon of N. B. Forrest, dated this day, and signed by me; and for so doing this shall be his warrant.

Andrew Johnson

Washington 17th July, 1868

Executive Mansion.

President Andrew Johnson's pardon of Nathan Bedford Forrest. Tennessee State Library and Archives.

he believed the primary responsibility for Reconstruction rested with the executive branch. On May 29, 1865, with Congress out of session, he issued two proclamations that outlined his restoration policy. The first, similar to Lincoln's 1863 amnesty declaration, granted a general pardon to all who would pledge an oath of allegiance and restored complete political rights to the Rebels. But high-ranking Confederate civil, military, and diplomatic officials; those who had resigned a Federal post to serve the Confederacy; and all persons owning taxable property valued at more than $20,000 were denied immediate amnesty. They could, however, appeal to the president for a personal pardon (and those were granted liberally).

The second proclamation applied only to North Carolina originally but was extended to include all Confederate states not previously restored to the Union by Lincoln. (Both Johnson and Lincoln considered Virginia, Tennessee, Arkansas, and Louisiana already restored.) According to its provisions, Johnson would appoint a provisional governor who would register voters for an election of delegates for a state constitutional convention. The convention would nullify the ordinances of secession, abolish slavery, and repudiate all state debts incurred during the rebellion. Next, elections would be held to select a governor, legislature, and members of Congress. These new legislatures would then ratify the Thirteenth Amendment. At this stage, Johnson would recognize the new state government, end martial law, and withdraw Federal troops. In conjunction with these proclamations, he reversed General Sherman's Special Field Order No. 15, which had granted the use of abandoned lands in Georgia to former slaves, and ordered that all abandoned plantations be returned to their former owners. While Johnson intended to uphold the Southern social hierarchy and protect the sanctity of private property, he did suggest that the new state governments offer basic civil rights to the freedpeople and perhaps even a limited franchise to some Black adult males, especially veterans.

White Southerners ignored Johnson's suggestions. The Confederate states quickly followed Johnson's program for readmission to the Union; however, a sense of defiance pervaded the state conventions. Several states "repealed" rather than nullified their secession ordinances, while others refused to repudiate their Confederate debt or to ratify the Thirteenth Amendment ending slavery in the United States. Georgia even reserved the right to seek compensation for the loss of slave property. Perhaps most defiantly, voters also elected prominent Confederate officials to the US Congress, including former congressmen, generals, and even the vice president of the Confederacy, Alexander H. Stephens. An even larger number of former secessionists won election to state offices.

Additionally, the new state governments enacted a series of laws, known as Black Codes, to restrict the civil rights of the freedpeople. The codes varied somewhat from state to state, but typically they prevented Black people from voting, holding public office, serving on juries, testifying against White people, or owning firearms. Also, strict laws limited the occupations open to Black people, and vagrancy laws proclaimed that Black individuals who were considered unemployed could be "hired out" as forced labor. Southern White people clearly intended to limit Black freedom and control Black labor.

Northerners, especially the Radical Republicans, were outraged by the arrogance of the defeated Rebels. Therefore, before Congress convened in December 1865, Northern public opinion demanded changes to Johnson's lenient policies.

Even though the president realized that the former Confederate states had gone too far, he refused to alter his plan. He considered Reconstruction to be a presidential matter and, therefore, complete before Congress met. Johnson's attitude stemmed from his desire to reshape the national political landscape following the war. He hoped to fuse

Conservative Republicans, Southern White people, and Northern Democrats into a new national party that would elect him and ease sectional tensions in a postwar world. Johnson anticipated that this coalition would also isolate the Republican Radicals and prevent them from attempting to reshape the South by granting freedmen some measure of civil rights. Johnson's machinations, however, did not foresee the cohesion mustered by the Republicans. Party leaders realized that if the Confederate states returned to the Union now with slavery abolished, the "Three-Fifths Compromise" would be eliminated and former slaves would be disenfranchised, while ironically giving the former Confederate states a greater number of representatives and thus increased national power. Since the Democratic Party dominated the South, an alliance between Northern and Southern Democrats could easily defeat a sectional party such as the Republicans. Naturally, Republicans were alarmed by Johnson's program, which promised to reward the former Rebels with potential control of Congress.

Tennessee's Radicals

When Johnson left his post as military governor of Tennessee to serve as Lincoln's running mate on the Union Party ticket, he had left William G. "Parson" Brownlow as provisional governor. Brownlow was subsequently elected governor, and in April 1865, he met with the new General Assembly in Nashville. That same month, Lincoln was assassinated, and Johnson was thrust into the presidency.

In this chaotic atmosphere, Brownlow and the legislature began the process of recovering from the war, but unlike recovery for the rest of the former Confederacy, this recovery would be on Unionist terms. In keeping with Lincoln's requirement for reestablishing a state government, the legislature supported the Thirteenth Amendment. However, the cornerstone of the new administration was the disenfranchisement of ex-Confederates.

Brownlow's vision for Tennessee was not shared by all of the state's Unionists. Like Johnson before him, the governor's stubbornness and self-righteousness, along with his need for dictatorial control of the government, drove him into conflict with his fellow loyalists. In fact, his dogged desire to punish the former Rebels became the single biggest factor for the split within the Volunteer State's Unionist coalition. Those who supported Brownlow became known as Radicals, and those who supported a conciliatory attitude toward the defeated Rebels were known as Conservatives. Brownlow faced quite a challenge from Conservative Unionists. Like Johnson, they considered the ex-Confederates as potential allies in building a new Conservative political coalition. These were many of the same men who had split with Johnson earlier when he was military governor over emancipation and his control of the ballot box through his "Damnesty Oath." They now, however, saw Johnson's presidential policies as the right course of action for the state and the nation.

Nonetheless, in June 1865, the General Assembly passed a franchise bill that barred most ex-Confederates from voting for five years (fifteen years for Rebel leaders). The act also established a voter registration system to be administered by county court clerks. Brownlow even offered a reward for the capture of ex-governor Isham Harris. The governor's actions clearly demonstrated that he had not overcome his hatred for the Rebels and was determined to punish them; yet, despite his efforts to control the ballot box, the August congressional elections stunned and embarrassed Brownlow and his supporters. The Conservatives won five out of eight congressional districts across the state. Brownlow declared election irregularities in one district and subsequently replaced the Conservative with his own candidate, but he could not do the same for all districts. The Radicals were further frustrated in the March 1866 county elections when Conservatives did well again, especially in Middle and West Tennessee. Faced with the growing realization that their power base was weak and perhaps dwindling, Brownlow and the Radicals amended the franchise law the following month in April 1866. Previous voter registrations were voided and all new registrations were controlled by election commissioners appointed by the governor. Radicals could now essentially prevent their opposition from voting. Another act banned ex-Confederates from voting for life. Brownlow's new dictatorial powers were designed not only to allow him and his faction to control Tennessee's voting and thus remain in power but also to win the favor of the Radical Republicans in Congress who were soon locked in a monumental struggle with President Johnson over control of Reconstruction policies.

Johnson Versus Congress

When the Republican-controlled Congress convened in December 1865, it promptly refused to seat the eighty Southern representatives and senators, including, of course, those from Tennessee. The Republicans then established a Joint Committee on Reconstruction to hold hearings on the state of affairs in the South while they deliberated on their own Reconstruction program. The party could reach no consensus because the Radicals demanded land confiscations and voting rights for the freedmen, measures the Moderates rebuked. Instead, Moderate Republicans hoped to work with Johnson to secure basic civil rights, except suffrage, for the freedmen and to create a process to prevent the former

Rebels from returning to power. Like Johnson, Moderates wanted to see Southern White Unionists controlling the former Confederate states.

In February 1866, while debating Reconstruction initiatives, Congress passed a bill indefinitely extending the life of the Bureau of Refugees, Freedmen, and Abandoned Lands (Freedmen's Bureau), expanding the agency's legal authority in cases of discrimination, and authorizing the establishment of schools for Black people. The bill passed both houses with virtual unanimous Republican support only to be vetoed by the president. Even more shocking than his veto was Johnson's claim that the measure was unconstitutional because the Southern states, which would be most affected by the bill, were not represented in Congress. Johnson fueled the controversy further by then delivering a speech that attacked the Radicals as traitors for delaying the restoration of the Southern states.

Moderates searched for a solution that would avoid a split with the president and still secure Black rights. In March, passed with near unanimous Republican support, the Civil Rights Act of 1866 essentially nullified the Dred Scott decision and the worst abuses of the Black Codes by granting citizenship to Black people and guaranteeing their civil rights. However, fearing a Northern backlash, Moderates still refused to support Black suffrage as part of the legislation. It mattered little. Johnson again vetoed the act in April on the grounds that it discriminated against native White people and immigrants. His actions did not isolate the Radicals from the Moderates as he had hoped. Instead, he pushed the Moderates closer to the Radical position. That same month, Congress overrode Johnson's veto of the Civil Rights Act and again overrode his veto of a slightly revised Freedmen's Bureau bill in July.

Republicans acknowledged that Johnson would never support their two goals of protecting the rights of Black people in the South and preventing the ex-Confederates from returning to power in the South. Therefore, the Joint Committee on Reconstruction proposed an amendment to the Constitution. In June 1866, after months of deliberation, the Fourteenth Amendment passed both houses of Congress with the necessary two-thirds majority. The result was an awkward compromise between the Radicals and Moderates. Along with the Freedmen's Bureau bill and the civil rights bill, the amendment essentially became the congressional Republican peace terms for the defeated Confederacy. To protect Black people, the amendment defined all native-born and naturalized persons as citizens and prohibited states from denying any person equal protection under the law. Also, while Black men were not granted suffrage, any state that withheld the vote from its adult male citizens would have its congressional representation reduced proportionally. This allowed the Republicans to prevent the former Confederate states from increasing their congressional representation in the absence of the "Three-Fifths Compromise." The Confederate debt was voided, and the amendment stipulated that any person who had taken an oath to uphold the Constitution and then supported the rebellion was now disqualified from federal and state offices (although a two-thirds vote by Congress could remove the disability). The amendment was still conservative in that it did not guarantee Black suffrage, disenfranchise former Rebels, or confiscate land.

For the amendment to become part of the Constitution, it needed a three-fourths vote of approval from the states, including some former Confederate states. However, Johnson discouraged the Southern states from approving the amendment, claiming that it was unconstitutional because Congress had no right to submit an amendment without the Southern states being represented.

Tennessee Radicals Choose a Side

The struggle between the president and Congress over Reconstruction ultimately contributed to the ever-widening split between Johnson and Brownlow. Their relationship had always been cantankerous, and their alliance in Tennessee was solely based on their shared Unionism in the face of secession. Neither man liked the other, and both were blunt, self-righteous, and dogmatic. Their old Whig-Democratic rivalry from the antebellum period had always simmered just beneath the surface, and once the common enemy of secessionism was removed, their animosity and acrimony exploded into hostility.

While Tennessee's Conservative Unionists continued to support the Reconstruction program as outlined by Lincoln and Johnson, Brownlow and his supporters gravitated toward the congressional Republicans, especially the Radicals, who also supported a harsher policy toward the ex-Rebels. Indeed, Brownlow and the Tennessee Radicals endorsed the Fourteenth Amendment, and in July, the Tennessee legislature ratified it despite a last-ditch attempt by Brownlow's opponents to block ratification in the House of Representatives by absenting themselves to prevent a quorum—an attempt the Radicals thwarted by having two absent members arrested, brought to the capitol, held in a room adjoining the House chamber, and then counted as "present but not voting." To Johnson's dismay and embarrassment, his home state of Tennessee became the first Confederate state to ratify the amendment and reenter the Union.

Brownlow immediately telegraphed the US Senate to announce Tennessee's ratification of the amendment, adding, "My compliments to the 'dead dog' of the White House." Congress, then, seated Tennessee's senators and representatives. When the rest of the South rejected the congressional push for the Fourteenth Amendment, Congress imposed military rule on the South, exempting only Tennessee. So, the last state to secede was the first to be readmitted to the Union. Despite his success, Brownlow's dictatorial manner was alienating his own followers. He was creating opponents and enemies and driving potential allies away. Conservatives were planning on challenging Brownlow in the next gubernatorial election. To hold onto power, Brownlow, a virulent racist, now was forced to embrace the idea of enfranchisement for the freedmen.

Johnson's Gambit

Meanwhile, undaunted in his struggle with Congress and the Tennessee Radicals, Johnson embarked on a speaking tour of the Northeastern and Midwestern states to drum up support for his policies, influence the 1866 elections, and promote his new Conservative party. Although this "swing around the circle" as he called it began favorably, he quickly encountered unruly and hostile crowds. The president made matters worse by engaging in arguments with hecklers and denouncing the Republicans as traitors. Newspapers and cartoonists lambasted the president, while Radicals attacked both Johnson and his Democratic supporters as the true traitors to the Union. The press coverage of Johnson's engagement with hecklers was seriously damaging his already weakened political stature, but worse was yet to come.

On May 1 and 2, 1866, a rumor circulated in Memphis that Black soldiers had killed several police officers attempting to arrest one of their comrades. The local military commander, Major General George Stoneman, disarmed the soldiers and confined them to their quarters at Fort Pickering. This left the contraband camps defenseless, and a mob soon descended on them. By the time the two-day riot had ended, forty-eight people had been killed (forty-six of whom were African American), scores of people had been injured, and five women had been raped. Nearly one hundred structures including homes, churches, and schools were burned, hundreds of freedpeople had been robbed and arrested, and almost all other Black people had fled Memphis. The riot clearly demonstrated the volatility within Tennessee's White community. The presence of an occupying force using Black soldiers and the growing demands for civil rights for the freedpeople ignited the simmering frustration and anger of ex-Confederates humiliated by defeat and unwilling to accept a changed social order.

The riot in Memphis and another in New Orleans in July, coupled with Johnson's opposition to the Fourteenth Amendment, persuaded Northern voters that his policies had failed. Johnson found it impossible to convince the Northern public that the ex-Rebels were now eager to support the Union, and thus the Republicans swept the 1866 midterm elections, winning a two-thirds majority in both houses of Congress, all Northern gubernatorial contests, and control of every Northern state's legislature. Johnson's bid for a new Conservative coalition collapsed. Republicans believed they could force a recalcitrant South to accept a more extensive program of Reconstruction. Congress, not the president, now controlled the process.

In Tennessee, the riot in Memphis generated consternation among the state's Radicals, who, eager to have the state reenter the Union, sought to appease the Republicans in Congress. The riot was widely condemned as the act of the ex-Rebels, and the legislature passed the Metropolitan Police Act, which took control of the police away from the municipalities of Memphis, Nashville, and Chattanooga and gave it to commissioners to be appointed by the governor. This was but another attempt by Brownlow to align his administration with the Radical Republicans in Congress. He had hoped that supporting the Fourteenth Amendment as well as the disenfranchisement of the ex-Rebels would ease Tennessee's transition back into the Union and hurt Johnson politically. Brownlow's efforts appeared to be working. The governor even won the praise of arch-Radical Thaddeus Stevens, who, upon Tennessee's readmission to the Union in July 1866, remarked to Congress, "I do not pretend that she [Tennessee] is loyal. I believe this day that two thirds of her people are rank and cure [cruel] rebels. But her statesmen have been wise and vigilant enough to form a constitution which bridles licentious traitors and secures the State government to the true men. And she has an Executive fit to ride upon the whirlwind. . . . She has two or three men in her delegation who would have saved Sodom."

From all perspectives, given the timing and the riots across the South, it was clear to Northerners and Southern Unionists what had been clear to Black people for a long time: current laws and law enforcement provided little protection to freedpeople. For Brownlow, the enfranchisement of Black people, then, offered an opportunity to provide the freedpeople with greater protection through political participation and, perhaps most importantly to him, provide a source of voters to keep his administration firmly in power. Even though Black suffrage would cost Brownlow support among the state's loyalists, he pushed ahead. In February 1867, Radical legislators enacted a law allowing adult Black males to vote. Thus, Tennessee became the first Southern state to enfranchise all Black men. That same month, Brownlow announced to the legislature that Conservative elements were plotting to overthrow the state government. While not true, it provided the General Assembly an excuse to establish a state militia—the State Guard under the control of the governor. Brownlow quickly activated this biracial force and called up some twenty companies to help oversee the upcoming August 1866 election. Brownlow's control of the ballot box through voter registration and the State Guard meant that his challenger, Conservative Emerson Etheridge, did not really stand a chance. Brownlow won seventy-four thousand to twenty-three thousand. Nearly four thousand of Brownlow's votes were from African Americans, demonstrating the emerging power of the Black vote. Moreover, Radicals won all the congressional seats and state senate seats and all but three of the state house seats. Brownlow and his supporters now controlled Tennessee and felt secure and confident enough to implement a slate of policies designed to remake the Volunteer State.

Collapse of the Johnson Presidency

Back in Washington, the conflict between Johnson and Congress was nearing its climax. Although Tennessee had ratified the Fourteenth Amendment, other Southern states had not, and at least some of the unreconstructed states had to ratify it. Therefore, Congress passed the Military Reconstruction Act in March 1867 over the president's veto. The law declared that the ten Johnson-supported state governments were provisional and divided them into five military districts, each commanded by a major general. Congress granted the army authority to supervise the registration of all male voters, including freedmen but excluding ex-Confederates who were barred by the Fourteenth Amendment. Once registered, voters would elect delegates to participate in state conventions where they would frame new constitutions providing for Black suffrage and barring prominent ex-Rebels from holding state and Federal offices. Once Congress approved the new constitutions, elections for state and national office would follow, and the new legislatures would be required to ratify the Fourteenth Amendment. Reconstruction would then end. Although the provisions of the Military Reconstruction Act fell far short of restructuring Southern society as the Radicals envisioned, they did secure the Moderates's two key demands of protecting Black rights and preventing former Confederates from returning to power.

To curtail the president's power, Congress passed two statutes of questionable constitutionality. The Command of the Army Act, a provision of the 1867 Army Appropriations Act, required Johnson to issue all orders to subordinate army commanders through the general in chief of the army, Ulysses S. Grant. The Radicals hoped, thereby, that Grant could control Johnson's actions. The most direct challenge to presidential authority, however, was the Tenure of Office Act, which authorized an official appointed with the Senate's consent to remain in office until that body approved a successor. Ostensibly intended to protect patronage offices, the law, in reality, was designed to prevent the removal of Secretary of War Edwin Stanton, a Radical in Johnson's inherited cabinet. Johnson vetoed the Tenure of Office Act, and although he signed the Army Appropriations Act, he strongly protested its command provisions.

When White Southerners refused to succumb to congressional demands and fought to delay the registration of voters indefinitely, Congress passed a second Military

Reconstruction Act in March 1867 authorizing district military commanders to initiate the process of voter registration, convene the conventions, and schedule the elections. Again, Johnson vetoed the bill, and again, Congress overrode the veto. When Johnson authorized Attorney General Henry Stanbery to issue a ruling that limited military authority in the South to policing duties and prevented commanders from removing civilian officials, Congress passed yet another Military Reconstruction Act in July 1867 declaring the army's supremacy over Southern civilian governments. Meanwhile, White Southerners discovered a loophole in the original Reconstruction Act. Since it mandated that a majority of registered voters was needed to affirm the new constitutions, they thought that by persuading or coercing enough voters to stay home, passage of the constitutions could be prevented. Congress quickly closed the loophole, however, by passing the fourth Military Reconstruction Act in March 1868. This one required ratification of the constitutions by only a majority of those actually voting. By June 1868, six states admitted defeat, finally acquiesced to congressional demands, and rejoined the Union.

Impeachment of Johnson

Johnson was appalled at congressional efforts to enfranchise Black Southerners while disenfranchizing White Southerners he needed to entice into a Conservative coalition for the 1868 election. While he could not prevent the Republican majority from legislating their program, he planned to impede its progress. Despite attempts to restrict Johnson's authority and power, the president retained a considerable capacity to obstruct congressional efforts. As commander in chief, he could appoint Conserva-

Impeachment of President Andrew Johnson.
Library of Congress.

tive generals to administer the five military districts, and as chief executive, he could interpret the Reconstruction Acts narrowly in terms of their enforcement. Radicals recognized Johnson's intent and advocated his removal from office. Their first attempt occurred in January 1867, when the House of Representatives authorized the Judiciary Committee to investigate the possibility of impeachment. However, Moderates dominated the committee and saw no reason to take such an extreme step. While Radicals claimed that the president's thwarting of congressional legislation constituted a misuse of power and grounds for impeachment, Moderates insisted that officials could only be removed from office for indictable crimes.

The Radicals launched another impeachment effort after Johnson suspended Secretary of War Edwin Stanton in August 1867 and began replacing generals who had energetically enforced the Reconstruction Acts. However, Moderates again stood by the president. Johnson's suspension of Stanton occurred when Congress was in recess; therefore, it technically did not violate the Tenure of Office Act, provided Congress agreed with the suspension when it reconvened. Moreover, Democrats had gained ground on the Republicans in the 1867 elections. Black suffrage and the continued occupation of the Southern states were unpopular issues in the North, and the Moderates feared Johnson would become a martyr. The Radicals forced a House vote on impeachment, but without Moderate support, the resolution failed 108–57. Johnson's subsequent actions, however, resurrected the specter of impeachment.

Determined to rid himself of Stanton, the president replaced him in February 1868, this time with Adjutant General Lorenzo Thomas. Since the Senate was in session, Johnson's actions allegedly violated the Tenure of Office Act and prompted another outcry for his impeachment. This time the Moderates voted with the Radicals, and the president was impeached by a party-line vote of 126–47 on February 24, 1868. House prosecutors, known as managers, proffered eleven charges against the president. Eight dealt with his apparent violation of the Tenure of Office Act, while one accused him of attempting to circumvent the army's chain of command in violation of the rider to the Army Appropriations Bill of 1867. The tenth article accused Johnson of bringing Congress into disrepute with his public pronouncements, and the final article drew together charges from the previous ten. Johnson's able legal team claimed that he had committed no crime in testing the constitutionality of the Tenure of Office Act, and they argued that even if the act were constitutional, it did not apply to Stanton, who had been appointed by Lincoln.

Although Moderate Republicans abhorred Johnson, many feared his removal would pave the way for future Congresses with a two-thirds majority to remove any president who disagreed with their proposals, thereby making impeachment a political weapon. Thus, the constitutional balance of power would be destroyed. Moderates also distrusted Radical Benjamin Wade, president pro tempore of the Senate and next in line to the presidency. Using intermediaries, Johnson and the Moderates worked toward a compromise. The president gave no more speeches or interviews denouncing Congress, and he promised to enforce Reconstruction Acts. Johnson also appointed the well-respected Major General John M. Schofield as secretary of war. On May 16, 1868, the Senate voted on the eleventh article of impeachment 35–19. All twelve Democrats and seven Moderate Republicans voted against removal. With a two-thirds majority (36 votes) needed to remove the president from office, Johnson had been saved by one single vote. Votes on articles two and three on May 26 had the same result, forcing the impeachment managers to concede defeat. As for the president's home state, all but one of Tennessee's House delegation had voted for impeachment and denounced the president. In the Senate, David T. Patterson, Johnson's son-in-law, and Joseph S. Fowler would decide Johnson's guilt. Radicals knew that Patterson would vote for an acquittal, but they hoped to persuade, cajole, bribe, or intimidate Fowler. Indeed, members of Tennessee's delegation in the House of Representatives suggested he resign if he could not vote appropriately. Yet both senators voted for acquittal. Thus, when the Radicals failed to remove Johnson by one single vote, they blamed Fowler and labeled him a modern-day Judas.

During his final months in office, Johnson continued to defy Congress by vetoing Reconstruction bills that the Republicans easily overrode and delivering speeches critical of the Radicals. Naively, he clung to the hope that the Democratic Party would nominate him for president in 1868. However, the party threw its support behind New York governor Horatio Seymour, leaving Johnson to be a president without a party and with no influence on national policy.

Radical Policies and Economic Recovery in Tennessee

In Nashville, the Brownlow administration embarked on its agenda to transform the state. Many of the state's Radicals were old Whigs from East Tennessee, so the "Whiggish" support for government aid for internal improvements, business, and education was a key aspect of the policies enacted. Moreover, the war had left Tennessee's economy in shambles, and much aid was needed to help the state's citizens recover. Agriculture, the state's leading industry, had been hit hard by the deprivations of war.

The end of slavery devastated the state's cash crop economy, which had been dominated by the planter class, and the holdings of the larger yeoman class had likewise been severely damaged or destroyed. Across the state, veterans returned to find buildings dilapidated, fences missing, soils deteriorating, work animals either gone or broken down, and scarcely any food. It has been estimated that the state's non-slave property values declined by well over a third because of the war. Tennessee's wealthier farmers had the resources to cope with these losses better than those with small holdings or marginal land. While the elite lost a great deal of their personal property due to pillaging and the end of slavery, they still held onto their land and were thus able to rebuild in a predominantly agrarian society.

Unlike the depopulated and ravaged countryside, many of Tennessee's cities and towns actually grew in size and population. Indeed, the economic potential and safety that the Federal garrisons provided led to an explosion in population in some places. For example, Nashville grew from about seventeen thousand to twenty-six thousand persons in the ten years from 1860 to 1870 and Memphis from twenty-three thousand to forty thousand during the same period. Much of this boom resulted from the influx of the freedpeople abandoning the countryside in search of protection and a better life. Yet Northern businessmen, called "carpetbaggers" by resentful Southerners, as well as many White Tennesseans also sought new opportunities in the growing urban areas. Despite the best efforts of the Radicals, few European immigrants were enticed to come to Tennessee given its limited opportunities for those lacking wealth or skills.

As Tennessee's urban centers grew, so did the state's manufacturing. Most of this growth, however, occurred in small businesses such as lumber mills, smithies, and artisan shops. The few major industries that had existed in the state before the war, such as tobacco processing and iron works, would take time to recover. To support that recovery, Tennessee sought Northern capital. Perhaps the two cities to benefit the most from the influx of the Yankees and their wealth were the East Tennessee towns of Knoxville and Chattanooga. By 1868, Northern transplants in Knoxville owned one-sixth of the city's businesses, and many of these were manufacturing concerns. Chattanooga developed even more than Knoxville, nearly tripling the number of businesses and the number of employees in those businesses by an amazing 1,000 percent. The state's largest cities of

Nashville and Memphis also saw increased manufacturing and development with new iron works, sawmills, gristmills, furniture factories, and so on. By 1870, Tennessee's total manufacturing concerns had doubled compared to 1860, and the value of manufactured items nearly did the same. The number of those employed in manufacturing more than doubled but remained small (only 5,300) when compared to large industrial states of the North.

The 1850s had also been a decade of railroad expansion, and Tennessee, like other states, had loaned money to companies that would build railroads in or through the state. By the beginning of the Civil War, Tennessee was well connected to the rest of the nation via rail, although intrastate travel was underdeveloped. Their widespread destruction during the war meant that the railroads and trestles needed urgent attention. Although the Federal government built new lines and repaired others during the military occupation of the state, the General Assembly needed to do more. By 1869, the legislature had appropriated nearly $14 million raised by bond issue to support railroad companies around the state. Unfortunately, the process led to widespread corruption among the railroad executives and legislators and became a political scandal for the Radicals.

Another key component of the Radical agenda was public education. Before the Civil War, the state lacked a comprehensive system of public schools. Yet education came to be viewed as a means to advance in society, and the ex-Whigs of the Brownlow regime were eager to fund a public school system. In 1867, therefore, the General Assembly established a segregated school system.

The Tennessee Radicals had, indeed, pushed an impressive agenda for the modernization of the state. The cost of such modernization, however, meant that taxes had increased, a move widely condemned by those unwilling to pay for the changes. This was especially true among the disenfranchised ex-Confederates who saw little benefit in paying to support a state government that blocked them from political participation. Worse, from the perspective of the ex-Rebels and Conservative Unionists, part of the Radical agenda to reshape Tennessee included support of Black civil and political rights.

The Freedpeople's Struggle for Equality

In their struggle for equal rights, Black people needed the support of White allies. In Tennessee, as elsewhere across the South, they first exercised basic but profound rights such as adding surnames, searching for family members who had been sold, and establishing churches that became important social institutions in the Black community. Another fundamental right was the freedom to move about. Many Black families moved from the countryside to the towns and cities in search of a better life. Urban neighborhoods such as "Macedonia" on the outskirts of Columbia and "Hell's Half Acre" in Nashville were often located in the old garrison towns where Black people had fled during the Civil War and where contraband camps had been established. The neighborhoods were often overcrowded, diseased, and crime ridden. However, freedpeople wanted to distance themselves from White oversight and control while building a sense of community. These new Black enclaves included churches, fraternal organizations, and even political groups.

The key organization that aided the ex-slaves in their transition to freedom was the Freedmen's Bureau. Major General Oliver O. Howard was appointed bureau commissioner, and Brevet Major General Clinton B. Fisk was appointed assistant commissioner for the Kentucky and

Freedmen's Bureau. Library of Congress.

Tennessee district. In Tennessee, subdistricts were established with headquarters at Nashville, Memphis, Chattanooga, Pulaski, and Knoxville. While the Freedmen's Bureau initially provided food and clothing to thousands of poor African Americans and established orphanages, hospitals, and schools, Fisk made it clear that they would ultimately be responsible for their own economic future.

A key aspect of Fisk's vision and philosophy was education for freedpeople, and many African Americans looked upon education as the means to lift them and their children out of poverty. Across the South, the Freedmen's Bureau set to work educating the Black populace. Idealistic missionaries from the North, male and female, poured into the South with the aim of educating and uplifting the ex-slaves. In Tennessee, by the autumn of 1866, forty-one schools had been established with more than one hundred teachers

Teaching the Freedmen. Tennessee State Library and Archives.

and nearly ten thousand pupils attending. These numbers increased dramatically when the General Assembly took over the expense and administration of the schools. Under Superintendent of Public Instruction John Eaton Jr., a minister, former Union army chaplain, and Freedmen's Bureau agent, Tennessee's public school system grew to include five hundred Black schools with almost twenty-six thousand students by 1869. The most successful and famous of Tennessee's missionary schools was founded in Nashville in 1866 by the American Missionary Association and the Western Freedmen's Aid Commission of Cincinnati. Named for Clinton Fisk, the institution grew and developed into one of the nation's premier Black colleges.

While Black individuals viewed education as an important step toward economic independence, they realized that learning a marketable skill would be critical to their success and security. Some of Tennessee's freedpeople managed to achieve economic independence as artisans, businessmen, or professionals. For example, in Pulaski in 1866, there were numerous Black-owned businesses and scores of Black tradesmen. For them, physical freedom had also brought a measure of economic freedom and the hope for a better future.

While these examples were encouraging, most former slaves lacked marketable skills and relied solely on their labor in agriculture. The key to economic independence in an agrarian society is land. However, neither the Radicals in Tennessee nor their political brethren in Washington possessed the desire or ability to provide that land. As a result, unskilled African Americans found that agricultural labor was their only means of employment, and that employment would be through tenant farming or sharecropping. Although Freedmen's Bureau agents were charged with protecting Black people from unscrupulous White people and unfair contracts, sharecropping was the only choice for the unskilled and impoverished freedmen in Tennessee and across the South.

Under this system, plantations and larger farms were divided up into plots of land where Black families labored to bring in a crop. At harvest time, the crop was sold and the proceeds divided between the land owner and the tenant farmer. However, the farmer also had to pay any debts accrued during the year for food, clothing, shelter, and so on. Once the debts were paid, most found that they either had little money left over or even owed a balance. This meant another season of work in the hope of accruing money or at least avoiding debt. This cycle, known as debt peonage, trapped many Black families in Tennessee and, indeed, across the South into backbreaking work and poverty.

Above all else, Tennessee freedpeople sought political rights, which were key to protecting and advancing all other aspirations. The years between 1866 and 1869 brought many changes and great strides in the political status of African Americans in the state. In 1866, the General Assembly conferred on Black men limited rights of citizenship. Notably absent in these rights were voting, holding office, and marrying a White woman. Desperate for votes, however, by 1867, the Radicals recanted and gave Black men the right to vote and in 1868 the right to hold office and serve on juries.

Although no Black person held state office in Tennessee during the state's Reconstruction years, a number of Black men did obtain local offices. Notable examples include businessman William Bennett Scott Sr., who served as mayor of Maryville in 1869, and saloon owner Edward Shaw, who was elected to the Shelby County Commission. Other than a handful of other municipal positions in Nashville, few Black men ever managed to gain political office. They were still forced to depend on their White allies, the Radicals, to help them achieve the equality and dignity they craved. Unfortunately, their hopes for economic and social betterment and especially their one political achievement, the ability to vote, ignited a savage reaction from the ex-Rebel population of the state.

The White Backlash

Tennessee's governor and his supporters had made it clear that they intended to punish the ex-Rebels and establish a new political, economic, and social order in Tennessee. Brownlow's control of the ballot box led to an overwhelming Radical victory in 1867. This frustrated both the Conservative Unionists and the ex-Rebels who had no influence on political affairs. The resentment of the ex-Confederates was palpable. After suffering through the hardships of war, the sting of defeat, and the economic devastation of peace, few

Two members of the Ku Klux Klan. From *Harper's Weekly*, December 19, 1868.

were willing to endure the indignity of watching Unionists and former slaves control the postwar world.

The great majority of White Tennesseans were former secessionists who, having accepted Confederate defeat and sworn allegiance to the United States, saw no reason why they should be denied political rights. They applauded the lenient Reconstruction policy of President Johnson and excoriated the Republicans he battled in Washington. Likewise, they praised the efforts of Tennessee's Conservative

The Memphis riot of 1866. Tennessee State Library and Archives.

Unionists to repeal the state franchise restrictions while denouncing Governor Brownlow and his Radical Party as a despotic clique ruling by force and fraud.

The ex-Rebels who lived in East Tennessee, where they were a minority, were even more embittered by the treatment they received after the war at the hands of vengeful Unionists. Many former Confederate sympathizers, especially returning Rebel soldiers, were threatened, assaulted, and even murdered in the eastern counties in the postwar months. More than anything else, it was the Black quest for equality that stoked the burning resentment of Tennessee's ex-Confederates, for they remained as devoutly racist as they had been before the war. Acknowledging only that Black people could no longer legally be bought and sold and forced into labor, the former Rebels bristled at any suggestion that the freedmen might be entitled to social, economic, or political equality with the White population.

When verbal abuse and social ostracization failed to deter the freedmen and their White friends, the former Rebels resorted to threats. When threats failed, violence ensued. Black schools were often a target, and more than sixty schools were torched between 1867 and 1869 across the state. White teachers were also targeted by the wrathful ex-Confederates. In Hardeman County, for example, one missionary was dragged from his dwelling, beaten, tarred, and chased from the county.

While random acts of racial violence continued, they were eventually overshadowed by the rise of organized resistance. Many ex-Rebels gravitated to underground movements and eventually became paramilitary forces determined to regain political and economic security for themselves and their families. In Tennessee, the group took the name of Ku Klux Klan, and it spread to other Southern states. Founded as a social fraternity in Pulaski in December 1865 by six young Confederate veterans, the Ku Klux Klan spread in clandestine fashion across the South and developed an elaborate hierarchy of local, district, and state officers. Its organization was formalized at a secret meeting in Nashville in 1867, and there Nathan Bedford Forrest was named supreme commander, or "Grand Wizard."

Incidents of intimidation by Tennessee's Klansmen multiplied after Black men gained the vote in 1867. Sometimes this took the form of late-night visits by robed and hooded horsemen. However, episodes of brutal violence such as arson, beatings, maiming, rape, and murder also occurred. As the 1868 election approached, Klan violence continued to escalate. Determined to deny Tennessee's electoral votes to Republican Ulysses S. Grant and the state's congressional seats to the Radicals, the Klan terrorized the countryside.

Unionists and African Americans who could armed themselves and kept watch at home.

Determined to fight back, Brownlow called a special session of the legislature in July 1868 and asked for more power to combat the Klan. Two months later, the General Assembly passed the Ku Klux Klan Act, providing stiff penalties for political terrorism, and another act that gave the governor sweeping police powers, including command of the reactivated State Guard and authority to declare martial law in any county threatened by the Klan. Brownlow also requested and received a regiment of Federal troops to guard polling places in Middle Tennessee.

With a private army, as well as control of voter registration, Brownlow assured that Grant carried Tennessee in November. Nevertheless, it was clear that the Klan had somewhat succeeded in intimidating the freedmen and Radical Unionists from voting, at least in Middle and West Tennessee. The total vote for Grant in those two regions was only about two-thirds of that garnered by Brownlow fifteen months earlier. Moreover, in two congressional districts, Radical candidates failed to best their Conservative opponents, but Brownlow denied the candidates those seats, claiming election irregularities.

Alarmed by the influence the Klan had exerted on election results, Brownlow declared war on the group. In January 1869, he mobilized the State Guard, and in February he imposed martial law in nine Middle and West Tennessee counties. Moreover, in an effort to obtain some convictions under the Ku Klux Klan Act, the governor hired a Cincinnati man named Seymour Barmore to infiltrate the Klan and obtain incriminating evidence. The Klan discovered the deception and advised him to return to Cincinnati. Ignoring the warning, Barmore disguised himself and managed to get into a Klan meeting in Pulaski early in 1869. He was recognized later as he boarded a train to head back to Nashville, and at Columbia, Klansmen boarded the train and removed him. Six weeks later, his body was found in the Duck River, a rope around his neck and a bullet through his brain.

Not long after Brownlow mobilized the State Guard, Nathan Bedford Forrest ordered the members of the Ku Klux Klan to stop further public demonstrations. This was nothing more than a ploy, however, to prevent Federal interference with the Klan in Tennessee and elsewhere throughout the South. Organized violence against the freedmen and Radical Unionists in Tennessee did not end. And with the 1869 state election approaching, there could be little doubt that more trouble was ahead.

The Waning of Reconstruction

Amid the unrest and violence in Tennessee and the rest of the South, the Grant administration forged ahead with its Reconstruction policies. The 1868 election win by the Republicans served as a referendum of their Reconstruction policy, but it also demonstrated a waning of enthusiasm among the Northern public. While Grant easily defeated his Democratic challenger, Horatio Seymour, in the Electoral College vote, he would have lost the popular vote had it not been for Black votes in the South. The results of the 1868 election, along with earlier Northern state elections, showed that Northern Democrats were winning over voters by campaigning against governmental activism, Black suffrage, and the so-called "bayonet rule" in the South.

Republicans scrambled to strengthen the party. They passed the Fifteenth Amendment to the Constitution in February 1869, nationalizing voting rights for Black men. Despite the unpopularity of Black suffrage in the North, Republicans reasoned that their party's survival, especially in the South, depended on increasing their voter base. While Republicans focused their attention on securing the votes of Southern Black men, they lost more support in the North. Their reformist coalition splintered because of the issue of Black suffrage and the increasing pro-business policies of the party. Therefore, securing votes from Southern Black men became even more crucial to the party's control of the Federal government. The Republican struggle to maintain power took another blow as they lost control of their stronghold in Tennessee.

The Downfall of the Tennessee Radicals

Unable to serve more than two consecutive terms as governor, Brownlow set his sights on the Tennessee senate seat of David Patterson, President Johnson's son-in-law whose term expired on March 4, 1869. Using his influence among the Radicals, Brownlow persuaded the legislature to elect him to the US Senate, and he subsequently resigned as governor on February 25, 1869. His departure for Washington left the governor's office to the speaker of the state senate, DeWitt C. Senter. No one realized it at the time, but the days of Radical rule in Tennessee were numbered. Although Brownlow heaped praise on Senter, calling him "a loyal man, capable, tried, and trusted, who is sound in his principles and who will steadily adhere to them upon the platform of the Union Republican party in Tennessee," he, like many Radicals, would soon be surprised. On the surface, Senter had the credentials of a solid Radical. Like Brownlow, he was an East Tennessean. He had served three terms in the General Assembly prior to the Civil War and had voted against Tennessee's Declaration of Independence from the Union. He had been imprisoned by the Rebels and eventually driven from his home and forced to live in exile in Kentucky. He had returned with the liberation of Tennessee by Union forces and as a state senator supported the Radical agenda, including barring ex-Rebels from the ballot box. However, again like Brownlow, Senter was also politically astute and willing to pivot his position in the face of changing circumstances.

Senter slowly began to relinquish Brownlow's extreme hold on power. He ended martial law. He also made the State Guard subordinate to civil authority and eventually demobilized it altogether. However, his most sweeping reforms came soon after the Radicals held their gubernatorial convention in Nashville in May of 1869. He faced a serious challenge from William B. Stokes, a Union veteran and congressman from the third district. At the convention, supporters of the rival candidates started an argument that quickly escalated into a brawl that had to be broken up by the Nashville police. The convention ended without a clear candidate.

With the internal splintering of the Radical Party, Conservatives saw a chance to increase their influence. Instead of fielding a candidate of their own, they would play power broker to the Radical candidate who offered them the most, either Senter or Stokes. Senter saw his chance and he took it. The proclaimed stalwart Radical now proposed universal manhood suffrage, which was in essence the main thing the Conservatives and ex-Rebels wanted. Even more shocking, Brownlow supported Senter over Stokes. Both men saw that the voting landscape in Tennessee was about to change, partly because of a recent ruling by the Tennessee Supreme Court that the 1865 voter registrations under the 1866 franchise law were unconstitutional. This would allow about thirty thousand Conservatives to vote in the next election. Moreover, the older sons of the ex-Rebels would soon reach voting age, thus again increasing the number of Conservative voters. Time was running out for the Radicals.

Given these additional voters and the continued influence by the Ku Klux Klan to keep Black men and Radical Unionists away from the ballot boxes, Conservative voters now saw the chance to win upcoming state elections. With this shift in the tide, Senter rightly realized the writing on the wall and, like a chameleon, changed his position to reflect the mood of the voters. Stokes, too, tried to garner votes as the election loomed by also promising universal suffrage, but it was too late. Senter won the race to the delight of the ex-Rebels and the Conservatives. Moreover, the Conservatives also won control of both houses of the General Assembly.

When the new legislature met in October 1869, the Conservatives wasted no time in dismantling the Radical political framework. The Ku Klux Klan Act and the State Guard Act were repealed, and the entire school system was swept away. The legislators also repealed laws that banned segregation in public transportation. In addition, the Conservatives drastically cut taxes, which had quadrupled during Brownlow's time in office. While much of the money had funded the public school system, millions of dollars had been squandered in widespread railroad corruption. Perhaps the legislature's most significant action, however, was a referendum calling for a convention to write a new state constitution. That December, the citizens of Tennessee, Unionists and ex-Rebels, approved the convention by a five-to-one margin and elected seventy-five delegates, of whom only four were Radicals and none were Black. The convention met in Nashville on January 10, 1870, and the delegates elected John C. Brown, a former Confederate general and Ku Klux Klan member, as chairman. The new constitution, essentially the same as the current one, was ratified in March.

Stunned by the Conservative resurgence, freedpeople and Radical Unionists appealed to the Federal government to invalidate the election and put the state under military rule. Their efforts were in vain, however. Neither Grant nor Congress would intervene. Reconstruction was over in Tennessee.

Reconstruction Collapses Across the South

The Volunteer State's termination of Reconstruction was followed by that of other former Confederate states across the South. The inability to control organized violence against Unionists and Black people, coupled with waning enthusiasm for maintaining military rule in the South, wore away at Northern and even Republican resolve.

In 1873, an economic depression swept the nation. Northern voters registered their dissatisfaction with Republican economic policies by giving the Democrats control of Congress. Many Republicans remained committed to Black rights and pushed through Congress the 1875 Civil Rights Act, which outlawed segregation. This was the last piece of Reconstruction legislation. Most White Northerners believed that the three amendments to the Constitution were enough because the freedpeople now had legal equality.

The presidential election of 1876 brought down the final curtain on Reconstruction. Republican candidate Rutherford B. Hayes ran against Democratic hopeful Samuel Tilden of New York. Although Tilden won the popular vote, the electoral votes of South Carolina, Florida, and Louisiana were disputed. If Hayes won all three states, he would win the presidency. The Republicans struck a deal. Known as the Compromise of 1877, the informal pact stipulated that if the Democrats agreed not to challenge Hayes's claim to the presidency, the Republicans would remove the remaining Federal troops from the South and not oppose new Democratic state governments. Without Federal support, the remaining Republican state governments in the South collapsed, and Democrats gained control of the Southern political process. White Southerners gradually established laws to segregate the Black population and disenfranchise them through poll taxes, literacy tests, intimidation, and violence. The US Supreme Court supported their efforts by issuing conservative rulings. An 1883 decision, for example, declared the Civil Rights Act of 1875 unconstitutional except in cases of juries, and the landmark 1896 *Plessy v. Ferguson* decision sanctioned segregation through the doctrine of separate but equal. Although the Union had been preserved, the two Republican goals following the Civil War of protecting Black civil rights and preventing ex-Confederates from regaining power had failed. What that failure meant for Tennessee and the rest of the nation would play out over the coming century and a half.

EPILOGUE

The Civil War era fundamentally changed Tennessee and, indeed, the entire nation. During the period, the Volunteer State experienced unprecedented political, economic, and social upheaval. Tennesseans regardless of class, race, or gender had to adjust to the transformation that the war and its aftermath brought to the state and nation.

The human cost of the calamity had been truly horrific. Thousands of Tennessee soldiers, both Federal and Confederate, had been killed or wounded, while thousands more succumbed to disease and malnutrition. Many of these men would carry both physical and emotional scars throughout the rest of their lives. Worse still, the civilian populace had been exposed to a savage modern war. Most had suffered greatly as both armies foraged across the land while guerrillas and brigands brought terror, depredations, and even death to many. Animosities engendered by four years of conflict and guerilla atrocities ensured that Tennesseans would go through a long and contentious period of recovery. The deep wounds of the conflict in many cases would never truly heal.

Likewise, the war devastated the state's economy, essentially erasing the impressive gains of the first half of the nineteenth century. Widespread destruction in the agricultural sector meant that farm production and property values would not reach the 1860 levels again until 1900. The national economic depression of the early 1870s only made postwar economic challenges even more difficult. Wartime destruction, emancipation, and a lack of capital converged in the bankruptcy and breakup of antebellum plantations into small tenant farms. The old elites needed labor, and the freedpeople and poor Whites needed land. This created a system of sharecropping that existed well into the twentieth century. As Tennesseans struggled to rebuild their farms, their towns, and their lives, many (especially those in the cities like Nashville and Chattanooga) hoped that by embracing the edicts of the northern-inspired commercial ethos of the "New South," a renaissance of prosperity would uplift the state and South as a whole. Some new industries, often funded by Northern capital, did develop around extracting the state's abundant timber and mineral wealth. These industries did not, however, generate the wealth hoped for by the native population. Even as the state gradually embraced efforts at modernization and urbanization, Tennessee remained predominantly rural and agricultural into the twentieth century.

While the economic impact of the war degraded Tennessee's wealth from its antebellum high, the state's national political influence all but disappeared. After Johnson's tumultuous presidency, Tennessee never regained its foremost place in the nation's political arena. Like the rest of the former Confederacy, Tennessee would essentially become a one party (Democratic) state. Indeed, not until the mid-twentieth century did the South and its politicians again exert a major influence on national politics. Tennesseans, however, never again enjoyed the influence their state commanded in the Jacksonian period.

The only positive outcome to emerge from the devastation of war and political turmoil was that 275,000 formerly enslaved Tennesseans achieved their freedom. Indeed, Tennessee was at the forefront of the political and social changes that resulted in emancipation for African Americans. Early occupation by Federal forces allowed the Lincoln administration to gradually develop its position on reconstruction and emancipation. The intensity of the rebellion eventually forced the North to decide to end the institution by 1863. Slavery was legally abolished in Tennessee even before the war officially ended. Early in April 1865, the Tennessee General Assembly unanimously ratified the Thirteenth Amendment to the US Constitution. During the Reconstruction period, Tennessee's former slaves continued the transition to freedom that had begun during the war, establishing communities outside of the rule of slavery. They created churches, cemeteries, and schools, and sought to establish their own means of economic support.

In response to the assertive efforts of Black Tennesseans to take full advantage of their new civil liberties, Whites stripped many of these rights from African Americans before they could be exercised fully. Legal means of repression such as poll taxes or segregation of public facilities were often backed up by threats or use of violence. Early evidence of White hostility toward Black freedom can be found in the intimidation of Black residents exacted by the Ku Klux Klan. While the Klan and its activities largely faded in the post-Reconstruction period, the group did not disappear, nor did episodes of racial violence such as lynchings, used to spread terror and submission throughout the Black community. Not until the civil rights movement of the 1950s and 1960s, often called the Second Reconstruction, would Tennessee's African Americans gain the freedom to exercise the political rights granted a century earlier.

For most White Tennesseans, Black freedom and the call for equal political rights was disturbing. Yet perhaps more disturbing than Black freedom or even the economic turmoil was having to come to terms with the defeat and tremendous loss of life. Like most places in the South, there was a need to understand the war's meaning and to commemorate the sacrifices of the dead. This process would be complicated in Tennessee because of the large number of Unionists in East Tennessee who saw not defeat but victory in the war's outcome. Regardless, during the early postwar years, women spearheaded efforts by former Confederate and Union supporters to mark the graves of soldiers.

As time passed, and as the economy improved in the state, commemorative activities became increasingly elaborate and politicized. Tennesseans honored both the Confederate and Federal dead through the creation of state and national military parks and the erection of monuments near county courthouses. Residents created new institutions to venerate Tennessee's Civil War heritage, including state and local branches of the United Daughters of the Confederacy, the Grand Army of the Republic, and the Sons of Confederate Veterans. Veterans' homes and other facilities provided medical care and retirement services for former soldiers, and many schools memorialized the war by changing their names to reflect army leadership.

The desire to remember the fallen and find a way to heal the wounds of the war led both former secessionists and loyalists in Tennessee and the nation to work toward reconciliation. Part of that process involved creating a national narrative to give meaning to the suffering. Southern proponents of the so-called "Myth of the Lost Cause" were integral in developing this narrative, and amazingly they won the war of historical interpretation. What emerged was a tacit agreement to depict the war as a great tragedy in which all soldiers fought for their vision of the Union. In this way, the sacrifice and heroism exhibited by both sides could be portrayed as deserving of praise and remembrance. The war, then, essentially came to be viewed both as a power struggle between the states and the national government and as an economic struggle between industrialization and agrarianism. Such an interpretation obviously ignored slavery's role in the origins the conflict. Beginning in the 1960s, however, civil rights groups began challenging this sanitized view of the war, as the Lost Cause mythos, Confederate symbols, and memorialization of the Confederacy came under scrutiny. Decades of controversies over flags, monuments, and place names followed, and, indeed, the debate continues today as Americans still grapple with what the Confederacy represented and how it should be remembered.

In the end, Tennessee's experience during the tumultuous years of the Civil War era was exactly as Sallie Gannaway Jamison predicted. It was, indeed, "the greatest calamity" that could befall her and her fellow Tennesseans. Yet, all of the pain, destruction, and brutality of the war can be viewed as an evolution from an older form of republic to a newer one that formed a stronger sense of national identity and racial equality and offered hope for a brighter future. The republic had survived and would continue to develop as part of an ongoing process, the constant shaping and molding that defines our great republican experiment.

BIBLIOGRAPHIC ESSAY

The literature focusing on Tennessee during the Civil War era is rich and extensive. It includes a wealth of primary source material found in the state's depositories such as the Tennessee State Library and Archives, the various university special collections holdings, and the National Archives in Washington, DC. Also, hundreds of valuable monographs as well as articles found in academic journals such as the *Tennessee Historical Quarterly*, the *Journal of East Tennessee History* (formerly *East Tennessee Historical Society's Publications*), the *West Tennessee Historical Society Papers*, and the *Journal of Southern History* cover the period in detail. Moreover, numerous unpublished dissertations and theses offer even more insights into the era. This essay will primarily list only monographs since they are readily available to those who wish to delve deeper into the state's Civil War experience.

General History

Any study should begin with a general history of the state to place the Civil War era into context. Appropriate sections of Philip M. Hamer's *Tennessee: A History, 1673–1932*, 4 vols. (New York: The American Historical Society, Inc., 1933) would be a good place to start, as would John Trotwood Moore and Austin P. Foster, *Tennessee: The Volunteer State, 1769–1923*, 5 vols. (Chicago: S. J. Clarke Publishing Company, 1923). Also valuable are Robert E. Corlew and Enoch L. Mitchell, *Tennessee: A Short History* (Knoxville: Univ. of Tennessee Press, 1976) and Paul H. Bergeron, Stephen V.

Ash, and Jeanette Keith, *Tennesseans and Their History* (Knoxville: Univ. of Tennessee Press, 1999). *Tennesseans and Their History* is especially valuable because Bergeron and Ash are noted scholars of the antebellum, Civil War, and Reconstruction periods in Tennessee.

Antebellum Tennessee

Tennessee's division into three often competing sections greatly affected the state's history during the Civil War era. These divisions, resulting from the state's geography, influenced economic and political developments. For the antebellum period and the coming of the Civil War in the Volunteer State, the important economic influences can be seen in Stanley John Folmsbee, *Sectionalism and Internal Improvements in Tennessee, 1796–1845* (Knoxville: East Tennessee Historical Society, 1939); Donald L. Winters, *Tennessee Farming, Tennessee Farmers: Antebellum Agriculture in the Upper South* (Knoxville: Univ. of Tennessee Press, 1994); Blanche Henry Clarke, *The Tennessee Yeomen, 1840–1860* (Nashville: Vanderbilt Univ. Press, 1942); and Tracy McKenzie, *One South or Many? Plantation Belt and Upcountry in Civil War-Era Tennessee* (New York: Cambridge Univ. Press, 1994). An interesting examination of the period's urban development can be found in Lisa Tolbert, *Constructing Townscapes: Space and Society in Antebellum Tennessee* (Chapel Hill: Univ. of North Carolina Press, 1999).

The political aspects of the sectional divide are covered well by Mary Emily Robertson Campbell, *The Attitude of Tennesseans Toward the Union, 1847–1861* (New York: Vantage Press, 1961); Daniel W. Crofts, *Reluctant Confederates: Upper South Unionists in the Secession Crisis* (Chapel Hill: Univ. of North Carolina Press, 1989); Paul H. Bergeron,

Antebellum Politics in Tennessee (Lexington: Univ. Press of Kentucky, 1982); and Jonathan Atkins, *Parties, Politics, and the Sectional Conflict in Tennessee, 1832–1861* (Knoxville: Univ. of Tennessee Press, 1997). Bergeron's and Atkins's works are similar in their coverage but not necessarily in their conclusions. They offer the best overviews of the political developments in Tennessee during the state's most influential period in national politics. Atkins also offers a fine examination of the secession crisis in Tennessee. For a comprehensive overview of arguments over secession, see Dwight Pitcaithley, editor, *Tennessee Secedes: A Documentary History* (Knoxville: Univ. of Tennessee, 2021).

East Tennessee Exceptionalism

The exceptional Unionism of East Tennessee has attracted a good deal of scholarship, and among the most important early works are Thomas William Humes, *The Loyal Mountaineers of Tennessee* (Knoxville: Ogden Brothers & Company, 1888); Oliver P. Temple, *East Tennessee and the Civil War* (Cincinnati: The Robert Clarke Company, 1899); and James Welch Patton, *Unionism and Reconstruction in Tennessee, 1860–1869* (Chapel Hill: Univ. of North Carolina Press, 1934). Three more recent monographs are Noel C. Fisher, *War at Every Door: Partisan Politics and Guerrilla Violence in East Tennessee, 1860–1869* (Chapel Hill: Univ. of North Carolina Press, 1997); W. Todd Groce, *Mountain Rebels: East Tennessee Confederates and the Civil War, 1860–1870* (Knoxville: Univ. of Tennessee Press, 1999); and John D. Fowler, *Mountaineers in Gray: The Nineteenth Tennessee Volunteer Infantry Regiment, C.S.A.* (Knoxville: Univ. of Tennessee Press, 2004). Groce's path-breaking book explored the long-neglected Confederate population within the region. Fowler's work, while based on the experiences of a regiment, also provides a socioeconomic profile that offers insights into the social, economic, and political differences between the region's Unionists and Confederates.

Military Studies

The list of military studies of the Civil War in Tennessee is far too long to cover in brief. It includes general studies, campaign studies and works focused on specific battles, unit histories, soldier diaries and reminiscences, archeological studies, and a range of other works. While all of these cannot be covered in this essay, several books are key to understanding the war. The general reader should examine Randy Bishop, *Civil War Generals of Tennessee* (Gretna, LA: Pelican, 2013); Myers E. Brown, *Images in America: Tennessee Confederates* (Charleston, SC: Arcadia, 2011); *Tennessee's Civil War Battlefields: A Guide to Their History and Preservation* (Gretna, LA: Pelican, 2008); and James B. Jones Jr., *Tennessee in the Civil War: Selected Contemporary Accounts of Military and Other Events, Month by Month* (Jefferson, NC: McFarland & Company, Inc., 2011). A straightforward, blow-by-blow military account of the major battles fought in Tennessee can be found in three works by Jack Lepa, including *The Civil War in Tennessee, 1862–1863* (Jefferson, NC: McFarland & Company, Inc., 2011); *Grant's River Campaign: Fort Henry to Shiloh* (Jefferson, NC: McFarland & Company, Inc., 2013); and *Breaking the Confederacy: The Georgia and Tennessee Campaigns of 1864* (Jefferson, NC: McFarland & Company, Inc., 2011). An excellent general resource that offers information on the organization of the infantry, cavalry, and artillery units raised in Tennessee (both Union and Confederate) as well as a brief history of those units is *Tennesseans in the Civil War*, 2 vols. (Nashville, Civil War Centennial Commission, 1964).

It also lists all known Civil War participants from Tennessee at the time of printing. Finally, one of the best memoirs of the Civil War comes from Tennessean Sam R. Watkins, *'Co. Aytch': A Side Show of the Big Show* (New York: Collier Books, 1962 [1882]). It is a raw and vivid example of a soldier's experiences. While many of these reminiscences exist, this one is a must read.

The starting place for a deeper examination of the military aspects of the war in Tennessee is Thomas Lawrence Connelly's superb two-volume history of the Army of Tennessee, *Army of the Heartland: The Army of Tennessee, 1861–1862* (Baton Rouge: Louisiana State Univ. Press, 1967) and *Autumn of Glory: The Army of Tennessee, 1862–1865* (Baton Rouge: Louisiana State Univ. Press, 1971). Connelly's book explains the strong Tennessee connection to the origins of the army as well as the importance of Tennessee and the rest of what he christens as the Confederate Heartland. Other general works on the Army of Tennessee include Larry J. Daniels, *Cannoneers in Gray: The Field Artillery of the Army of Tennessee, 1861–1865* (Tuscaloosa: Univ. of Alabama Press, 1984); Larry J. Daniels, *Soldiering in the Army of Tennessee: A Portrait of Life in a Confederate Army* (Chapel Hill: Univ. of North Carolina Press, 1991); Stanley F. Horn, *The Army of Tennessee* (Norman: Univ. of Oklahoma Press, 1941); and Richard M. McMurry, *Two Great Rebel Armies: An Essay in Confederate Military History* (Chapel Hill: Univ. of North Carolina Press, 1989). McMurry's book is vital in helping to explain why the Army of Tennessee performed so poorly during the Civil War. Two long-neglected Union counterparts to these studies are Steven E. Woodworth, *Nothing but Victory: The Army of the Tennessee, 1861–1865* (New York: Knopf, 2005) and Larry J. Daniel, *Days of Glory: The Army of the Cumberland, 1861–1865* (Baton Rouge: Louisiana State Univ. Press, 2004).

A general study of the Western Theater that contains pertinent information on the struggle in Tennessee is Earl J. Hess, *The Civil War in the West: Victory and Defeat from the Appalachians to the Mississippi* (Chapel Hill: Univ. of North Carolina Press, 2012). Steven E. Woodworth has also authored three important works in that vein, including *Decision in the Heartland: The Civil War in the West* (Lincoln: Univ. of Nebraska Press, 2011); *Jefferson Davis and His Generals: The Failure of Confederate Command in the West* (Lawrence: Univ. of Kansas Press, 1990); and *No Band of Brothers: Problems of the Rebel High Command* (Columbia: Univ. of Missouri Press, 1999).

The collapse of the Confederate defensive line in the Western Theater in 1862 opened Tennessee to Union invasion. The best overall campaign study covering the early struggle for Tennessee is Stephen D. Engle, *Struggle for the Heartland: The Campaign from Fort Henry to Corinth* (Lincoln: Univ. of Nebraska Press, 2001). Focusing on the Battles of Fort Henry and Fort Donelson, Benjamin F. Cooling's *Forts Henry and Donelson: The Key to the Confederate Heartland* (Knoxville: Univ. of Tennessee Press, 1987) and *Fort Donelson's Legacy: War and Society in Kentucky and Tennessee, 1862–1863* (Knoxville: Univ. of Tennessee Press, 1997) offer solid accounts of the engagements at the forts and their consequences for Tennessee and the Upper South. Perhaps the best single volume on the capture of the forts is Timothy B. Smith, *Grant Invades Tennessee: The 1862 Battles for Fort Henry and Donelson* (Lawrence: Univ. Press of Kansas, 2016).

Two lesser known but important battles in the collapse of the 1862 Confederate defensive line are covered by Larry J. Daniel and Lynn N. Bock, *Island No. 10: Struggle for the Mississippi Valley* (Tuscaloosa: Univ. of Alabama Press, 1996) and Kenneth A. Hafendorfer, *Mill Springs: Cam-*

paign and Battle of Mill Springs, Kentucky (Louisville: KH Press, 1993).

For an examination on the Battle of Shiloh, one should consult Wiley Sword, *Shiloh: Bloody April* (New York: William Morrow & Co., 1974); James Lee McDonough, *Shiloh: In Hell Before Night* (Knoxville: Univ. of Tennessee Press, 1977); Larry J. Daniel, *Shiloh: The Battle That Changed the Civil War* (New York: Simon & Schuster, 1997); and Timothy B. Smith, *Shiloh: Conquer or Perish* (Lawrence: Univ. Press of Kansas, 2014). Smith's work is an impressive attempt to cover the battle in detail and offers fresh insights into one of the war's bloodiest early battles.

The Confederate Kentucky campaign and the subsequent Stones River campaign are well covered in Earl J. Hess, *Banners to the Breeze: The Kentucky Campaign, Corinth, and Stones River* (Lincoln: Univ. of Nebraska Press, 2000). For a detailed account of the battle of Stones River, see James Lee McDonough, *Stones River: Bloody Winter in Tennessee* (Knoxville: Univ. of Tennessee Press, 1980); Peter Cozzens, *No Better Place to Die: The Battle of Stones River* (Urbana: Univ. of Illinois Press, 1990); and Larry J. Daniel, *Battle of Stones River: The Forgotten Conflict Between the Confederate Army of Tennessee and the Union Army of the Cumberland* (Baton Rouge: Louisiana State Univ. Press, 2012).

Currently, the best account solely focused on the Tullahoma campaign is Michael R. Bradley, *Tullahoma: The 1863 Campaign for the Control of Middle Tennessee* (Shippensburg, PA: Burd Street, 2000). Steven E. Woodworth, in his *Six Armies in Tennessee: The Chickamauga and Chattanooga Campaigns* (Lincoln: Univ. of Nebraska Press, 1998), offers a great overview of the later campaigns for control of Chattanooga and lower East Tennessee.

The battle of Chickamauga has attracted a good bit of scholarly attention and is perhaps one of the most written about battles of the Western Theater. Important works covering this engagement include Glenn Tucker, *Chickamauga: Bloody Battle in the West* (Indianapolis: The Bobbs-Merrill Company, Inc., 1961); Peter Cozzens, *This Terrible Sound: The Battle of Chickamauga* (Urbana: Univ. of Illinois Press, 1992), and David A. Powell, *The Chickamauga Campaign*, 3 vols. (El Dorado Hills, CA: Savas Beatie, 2014–16).

The struggle for Chattanooga is well covered in James Lee McDonough, *Chattanooga: A Death Grip on the Confederacy* (Knoxville: Univ. of Tennessee Press, 1984) and Wiley Sword, *Mountains Touched with Fire: Chattanooga Besieged, 1863* (New York: St. Martin's, 1995), but a more detailed account is Peter Cozzens, *The Shipwreck of Their Hopes: The Battles for Chattanooga* (Urbana: Univ. of Illinois Press, 1990).

Until recently, Digby Gordon Seymour's *Divided Loyalties: Fort Sanders and the Civil War in East Tennessee* (Knoxville: Univ. of Tennessee Press, 1963) offered the best and only in-depth coverage of Longstreet's campaign in East Tennessee. However, Earl J. Hess, *The Knoxville Campaign: Burnside and Longstreet in East Tennessee* (Knoxville: Univ. of Tennessee Press, 2012) now offers the first scholarly account of the campaign.

The Nashville campaign has captured the interest of scholars since the end of the war largely due to the Lost Cause belief that the Confederacy missed an opportunity for a victory at Spring Hill that would have altered the course of the war. In reality, no such opportunity existed at Spring Hill or elsewhere, and John Bell Hood's campaign was a needless waste of lives. Among the most important works covering the campaign are Thomas Robson Hay, *Hood's Tennessee Campaign* (New York: Neale, 1929); Wiley Sword's two volumes, *Embrace an Angry Wind: The Confed-*

eracy's Last Hurrah: Spring Hill, Franklin, and Nashville (New York: Harper Collins, 1992) and *The Decisive Battle of Nashville* (Baton Rouge: Louisiana State Univ. Press, 1956); James Lee McDonough and Thomas Lawrence Connelly, *Five Tragic Hours: The Battle of Franklin* (Knoxville: Univ. of Tennessee Press, 1983); James Lee McDonough, *Nashville: The Western Confederacy's Final Gamble* (Knoxville: Univ. of Tennessee Press, 2004); and Anne J. Bailey, *The Chessboard of War: Sherman and Hood in the Autumn Campaigns of 1864* (Lincoln: Univ. of Nebraska Press, 2000). Bailey's work is part of the Great Campaigns of the Civil War Series and is the best at placing Hood's ill-conceived and ill-fated campaign into proper context.

Biographies

Several biographies have been written of key military and political leaders from Tennessee who heavily influenced events in the state during the period. For those concerning Union officers, see William S. McFeely's *Grant: A Biography* (New York: W. W. Norton & Company, 1981) and two works by Brooks D. Simpson, Grant's most ardent champion: *Let Us Have Peace: Ulysses S. Grant and the Politics of War and Reconstruction, 1861–1868* (Chapel Hill: Univ. of North Carolina Press, 1991) and *Ulysses S. Grant: Triumph Over Adversity, 1822–1865* (New York: Houghton Mifflin, 2000). Both volumes offer detailed and quite positive views of Grant's military and political career. Another recent hagiographical tribute to Grant can be found in Ron Chernow, *Grant* (New York: Penguin Books, 2017). Important biographies of other Union generals include three recent works on George Thomas, arguably the Union's finest general: Benson Bobrick, *Master of War: The Life of General George H.*

Thomas (New York: Simon & Schuster, 2009); Christopher J. Einolf, *George Thomas: Virginian for the Union* (Norman: Univ. of Oklahoma Press, 2010); and Brian Steel Wills, *George Henry Thomas: As True as Steel* (Lawrence: Univ. of Kansas Press, 2012). Stephen D. Engle, *Don Carlos Buell: Most Promising of All* (Chapel Hill: Univ. of North Carolina Press, 1999) is the most even-handed monograph covering this important and often overlooked commander. Finally, William M. Lamers, *The Edge of Glory: A Biography of General William S. Rosecrans, U.S.A.* (Baton Rouge: Louisiana State Univ. Press, 1999) and David G. Moore, *William S. Rosecrans and the Union Victory: A Civil War Biography* (Jefferson, NC: McFarland & Company, Inc., 2014) cover a gifted general whose reputation is much maligned. Indeed, Frank P. Varney's *General Grant and the Rewriting of History: How the Destruction of General William S. Rosecrans Influenced Our Understanding of the Civil War* (El Dorado Hills, CA: Savas Beatie, 2013) has demonstrated Grant's visceral and disingenuous attacks on Rosecrans and his reputation, which skewed the historical perception of generations of historians.

Biographies of important Tennessee Unionists include Thomas Alexander, *Thomas A. R. Nelson of East Tennessee* (Nashville: Tennessee Historical Commission, 1956), and E. Merton Coulter, *William G. Brownlow, Fighting Parson of the Southern Highlands* (Chapel Hill: Univ. of North Carolina Press, 1937).

The most famous and influential Tennessee Unionist was, of course, Andrew Johnson, who served as a US Senator until Lincoln appointed him military governor of the state from 1862 until 1865. Johnson went on to become one of the most controversial presidents in American history. The best overall biography of Andrew Johnson is Hans L. Trefousse, *Andrew Johnson: A Biography* (New York: W. W.

Norton, 1989), and the best brief biography is James E. Sefton, *Andrew Johnson and the Uses of Constitutional Power* (Boston: Little, Brown, 1980). Clifton R. Hall, *Andrew Johnson, Military Governor of Tennessee* (Princeton: Princeton Univ. Press, 1916) is a solid account of Johnson's critical role in easing Tennessee back into the Union. Albert Castel's *The Presidency of Andrew Johnson* (Lawrence: University Press of Kansas, 1979) is a solid account of Johnson's struggle with Congress during Reconstruction, while David W. Bowen, *Andrew Johnson and the Negro* (Knoxville: Univ. of Tennessee Press, 1989) covers Johnson's ideas on race. Eric L. McKitrick, *Andrew Johnson and Reconstruction* (Chicago: Univ. of Chicago Press, 1960) is an older look at Johnson and his ideas on restoration. The impeachment of Johnson is covered in two Watergate-era works, Michael Les Benedict, *The Impeachment and Trial of Andrew Johnson* (New York: W. W. Norton, 1973) and Hans L. Trefousse, *Impeachment of a President: Andrew Johnson, the Blacks, and Reconstruction* (Knoxville: Univ. of Tennessee Press, 1975). A more recent and even harsher critique comes from David O. Stewart, *Impeached: The Trial of President Andrew Johnson and the Fight for Lincoln's Legacy* (New York: Simon & Schuster, 2009). An important examination of Johnson's wartime career and presidency is provided by Paul H. Bergeron's aforementioned *Andrew Johnson's Civil War and Reconstruction*. Bergeron's study is perhaps the most balanced and thoughtful analysis of the man. This is undoubtedly because of Bergeron's extensive time spent as the editor of the Johnson Papers, which remain an important resource for those interested in Johnson and the Civil War and Reconstruction eras, especially as they relate to Tennessee (Leroy P. Graf, Ralph W. Haskins, and Paul H. Bergeron, eds., *The Papers of Andrew Johnson*, 16 vols. (Knoxville: Univ. of Tennessee Press, 1967–2000).

The biographical literature for political and military Confederate leaders is equally rich. Among the most important works covering Confederate generals are Charles P. Roland, *Albert Sidney Johnston: Soldier of Three Republics* (Austin: Univ. of Texas Press, 1964); Charles P. Roland, *Jefferson Davis's Greatest General: Albert Sidney Johnston* (Abilene: McWhiney Foundation Press, 2010); Judith Hallock, *Braxton Bragg and Confederate Defeat* (Tuscaloosa: Univ. of Alabama Press, 1991); Earl J. Hess, *Braxton Bragg: The Most Hated Man in the Confederacy* (Chapel Hill: Univ. of North Carolina Press, 2016); Richard McMurry, *John Bell Hood and the War for Southern Independence* (Lexington: Univ. of Kentucky Press, 1982); Brian Craig Miller, *John Bell Hood and the Fight for Civil War Memory* (Knoxville: Univ. of Tennessee Press, 2010); Stephen M. Hood, *John Bell Hood: The Rise, Fall, and Resurrection of a Confederate General* (El Dorado Hills, CA: Savas Beatie 2013); Joseph H. Parks, *General Edmund Kirby Smith, C.S.A.* (Baton Rouge: Louisiana State Univ. Press, 1954); Christopher Losson, *Tennessee's Forgotten Warriors: Frank Cheatham and His Confederate Division* (Knoxville: Univ. of Tennessee Press, 1989); and Sam Davis Elliott, *Soldier of Tennessee: General Alexander P. Stewart and the Civil War in the West* (Baton Rouge: Louisiana State Univ. Press, 1999).

Confederate cavalrymen are examined in John W. Dubose, *General Joseph Wheeler and the Army of Tennessee* (New York: Neale, 1912); John P. Dyer, *"Fightin' Joe" Wheeler* (Baton Rouge: Louisiana State Univ. Press, 1941); James A. Ramage, *Rebel Raider: The Life of General John Hunt Morgan* (Lexington: Univ. of Kentucky Press, 1986); Brian S. Wills, *The Confederacy's Greatest Cavalryman: Nathan Bedford Forrest* (Lawrence: Univ. Press of Kansas, 1992); and Jack Hurst, *Nathan Bedford Forrest: A Biography* (New York: Vintage Books, 1994).

Not enough has been done to cover Tennessee secessionists, but Sam Davis Elliott's *Isham G. Harris of Tennessee: Confederate Governor and United States Senator* (Knoxville: Univ. Press of Tennessee, 2010) is an excellent biography of the state's most influential secessionist. Joseph Howard Parks's *John Bell of Tennessee* (Baton Rouge: Louisiana State Univ. Press, 1950) looks at the erstwhile Unionist who, while not initially a secessionist, fought to keep Tennessee in the Union but was forced in the end to succumb to secession.

Home Front

The literature on the Tennessee home front is not as developed as that covering the military aspects of the state's struggle, but it contains several notable and important works. Any serious study should begin with Mark Grimsley's *The Hard Hand of War: Union Military Policy Toward Southern Civilians, 1861–1865* (Cambridge: Cambridge Univ. Press, 1995) and Stephen V. Ash's *When the Yankees Came: Conflict & Chaos in the Occupied South, 1861–1865* (Chapel Hill: Univ. of North Carolina Press, 1995). Ash's work covers the entire South, allowing for Tennessee's experience to be placed within context. Additionally, Ash's *Middle Tennessee Society Transformed, 1860–1870: War and Peace in the Upper South* (Baton Rouge: Louisiana State Univ. Press, 1988) gives an impressive overview of how one of the state's grand divisions struggled through the tumultuous Civil War and Reconstruction years. It serves as an excellent model for future studies. Another work covering Middle Tennessee is Peter Maslowski, *Treason Must Be Made Odious: Military Occupation and Wartime Reconstruction in Nashville, Tennessee, 1862–1865* (Millwood, NY: KTO Press, 1978), which provides a good introduction to Federal attempts to quickly bring Tennessee back into the Union. While not as comprehensive as Ash's work, the aforementioned monographs by Noel Fisher, *War at Every Door*, and Todd Groce, *Mountain Rebels*, offer insights into the home front conditions in East Tennessee. Additionally, Robert Tracy McKenzie, *Lincolnites and Rebels: A Divided Town in the American Civil War* (New York: Oxford Univ. Press, 2006) provides an interesting examination of one of the chief towns of the region during the war. West Tennessee needs a book-length study to complement the work on the other grand divisions.

Slavery and the Black Experience

The collapse of slavery and the African American experience in Tennessee are other areas that beg for greater research. Currently, the best single volume on the collapse of slavery is John Cimprich, *Slavery's End in Tennessee, 1861–1865* (Tuscaloosa: Univ. of Alabama Press, 1985). Four older but still valuable works include Caleb Perry Patterson, *The Negro in Tennessee, 1790–1865* (Austin: Univ. of Texas Press, 1922); Alrutheus Ambush Taylor, *The Negro in Tennessee, 1865–1880* (Washington, DC: Associated Publishers, Inc., 1941); Chase C. Mooney, *Slavery in Tennessee* (Bloomington: Indiana Univ. Press, 1957); and Lester C. Lamon, *Blacks in Tennessee, 1791–1970* (Knoxville: Univ. of Tennessee Press, 1981). Bobby L. Lovett's *The African-American History of Nashville, Tennessee, 1780–1930: Elites and Dilemmas* (Fayetteville: Univ. of Arkansas Press, 1999) provides an effective portrait of the plight of African Americans in Tennessee's capital during the period.

Works focusing on the Freedmen's Bureau and its critical role in the Reconstruction period include George Bentley, *A History of the Freedmen's Bureau* (Philadelphia: Univ.

of Pennsylvania Press, 1955); William S. McFeely, *Yankee Stepfather: General O. O. Howard and the Freedmen* (New Haven: Yale Univ. Press, 1968); Donald G. Nieman, *To Set the Law in Motion: The Freedmen's Bureau and the Legal Rights of Blacks, 1865–1868* (Millwood, NY: KTO Press, 1979); Ronald E. Butchart, *Schooling the Freed People: Teaching, Learning, and the Struggle for Black Freedom, 1861–1876* (Chapel Hill: Univ. of North Carolina Press, 2010); and Robert C. Morris, *Reading, 'Riting, and Reconstruction: The Education of the Freedmen in the South, 1861–1870* (Chicago: Univ. of Chicago Press, 1981). While none of these works focus exclusively on Tennessee, they contain critical information on the bureau's experience in Tennessee.

Finally, John Cimprich, *Fort Pillow, a Civil War Massacre, and Public Memory* (Baton Rouge: Louisiana State Univ. Press, 2005) is an excellent volume covering the most infamous racial massacre of the war.

Reconstruction

Tennessee's restoration to the Union was unique among the Confederate states largely due to Andrew Johnson and the large Unionist population that managed to control the state during Reconstruction's early stages. Tennessee became the first readmitted state with its ratification of the Fourteenth Amendment. However, Tennessee was also the first of the former Confederate states to see its Unionist government collapse to be "redeemed" or replaced by former Confederates. For placing Tennessee's experience into proper context, Dan Carter, *When the War Was Over: The Failure of Self-Reconstruction in the South, 1865–1867* (Baton Rouge: Louisiana State Univ. Press, 1985); Kenneth M. Stampp, *The Era of Reconstruction, 1865–1877* (New York: Alfred A. Knopf, 1966); and especially Eric Foner, *Reconstruction:*

America's Unfinished Revolution, 1863–1877 (New York: Harper & Row Publishers, 1988) are indispensable monographs on this topic. Several older but still valuable works that are specific to Tennessee include J. W. Fertig, *The Secession and Reconstruction of Tennessee* (Chicago: Univ. of Chicago Press, 1898); John R. Neal, *Disunion and Restoration in Tennessee* (New York: Knickerbocker Press, 1899); James Welch Patton, *Unionism and Reconstruction in Tennessee, 1860–1869* (Chapel Hill: Univ. of North Carolina Press, 1934); and Thomas B. Alexander, *Political Reconstruction in Tennessee* (Nashville: Vanderbilt Univ. Press, 1950).

White reaction to disfranchisement and Black freedom led to the formation of paramilitary groups to intimidate both the African American population and White Unionists. The Ku Klux Klan that formed in Tennessee is discussed in Stanley F. Horn, *Invisible Empire: The Story of the Ku Klux Klan, 1866–1871* (Boston: Houghton Mifflin Company, 1939) and Allen W. Trelease, *White Terror: The Ku Klux Klan Conspiracy and Southern Reconstruction* (New York: Harper & Row Publishers, 1971). The Unionist state government pushed for a military component to battle not only the Klan threat but also its political opponents. This topic is covered in Ben H. Severance, *Tennessee's Radical Army: The State Guard and Its Role in Reconstruction, 1867–1869* (Knoxville: Univ. of Tennessee Press, 2005). Stephen V. Ash's *A Massacre in Memphis: The Race Riot That Shook the Nation One Year After the Civil War* (New York: Hill and Wang, 2013) is also an important work describing the seething racial tensions in postwar Tennessee.

The collapse of Reconstruction in Tennessee can be gleaned from Roger L. Hart, *Redeemers, Bourbons, and Populists: Tennessee, 1870–1896*. (Baton Rouge: Louisiana State Univ. Press, 1975) and William Gillette, *Retreat from*

Reconstruction, 1869–1879 (Baton Rouge: Louisiana State Univ. Press, 1979). Two interesting personal accounts of Reconstruction in Tennessee, one from a Unionist and the other from a secessionist, are John David Smith and Michael J. Larson, eds., *Grant, Lincoln, and the Freedmen: Reminiscences of the Civil War by John Eaton* (Knoxville: Univ. of Tennessee Press, 2022) and Sam D. Elliott, *John C. Brown of Tennessee: Rebel, Redeemer, and Railroader* (Knoxville: Univ. of Tennessee Press, 2017).

Clearly, there is not a shortage of excellent works covering Tennessee's experience during the Civil War era. These monographs along with the myriad articles in academic journals; theses and dissertations prepared by graduate students; important primary sources in the form of diaries, letters, and reminiscences produced by those who lived through the tumultuous period; and, of course, military records such as the Compiled Service Records for the various regiments from Tennessee, the Official Records of the War of the Rebellion, and the Naval Records of the War provide students of the war a huge cache of material with which to explore and understand the nation's greatest calamity. This volume is an attempt to provide a short overview of the era and serve as a portal for more detailed study.

INDEX

Bold numbers indicate illustrations; *italic numbers* indicate maps.

abatis, 73
abolitionists, 15–16, 19, 21
acoustic shadow, 117–18
Alatoona Pass, Battle at (GA), 191
Alexander's Bridge, 153–54
ambushes, 208–9, 223, 235, 240
American Missionary Association, 275
American Party, 15
amnesty, 241, 249, 252–53
anarchy, 227, 235
Anderson, Samuel, 36
Anthony's Hill, 209
Appomattox, VA, 210
aristocracy, 22, 30–31, 35
Arkansas, 23; Reconstruction of, 253
Army Appropriations Act (1867), 265, 268
Army of the Cumberland (USA), 82, 120, 131–32, 134, 141, 143–45, 153–54, 158, 162–64, 171, 176, 183. *See also* Army of the Ohio
Army of Mississippi (CSA), 82–83, 112, 118
Army of the Mississippi (USA), 103, 105–6
Army of Northern Virginia (CSA), 153, 155, 157, 167, 185
Army of the Ohio (USA), 50, 71, 79, 97, 102, 105–6, 111, 115, 120, 131, 183. *See also* Army of the Cumberland
Army of the Potomac (USA), 49, 163, 166
Army of Tennessee (CSA), 121, 125, 128, 132–36, 140–42, 147, 149, 151–53, 159, 163, 178, 181–84, 189–94, 197, 199, 202, 205, 207–9, 216, 233, 239; incompetence of officers of, 120–22, 153; insubordination by officers of, 120–22, 135, 150–53, 157, 186; power struggles in, 120–21, 134–35, 163–64, 190, 198; surrender of, 210
Army of the Tennessee (USA), 70, 74–75, 82–84, 97, 102, 105, 183, 191, 194
artillery, 44, 58–60, 68, 73–75, 89–90, 93–94, 108, 124, 129, 132, 174, 176, 179, 198, 209
artisans, 271, 276
Ash, Stephen, 225
Atlanta, GA, 183–85, 189–90; campaign for, 183–86, 188–89

Baird, Absalom (USA), 150–51
Bank of the US, 12

Barmore, Seymour, 281–82
Bate, William B. (CSA), 196–97, 199, 203
Bean's Station, Battle at (TN), 181
Beatty, David "Tinker Dave," 224
Beauregard, Pierre G.T. (CSA), xiv, 52, 61, **70**, 71–72, 80–82, 106–9, 121, 136; and Division of the West, 190, 193; and Shiloh, 83–84, 87, 89–90, 92, 95–98, 100–103; throat ailment of, 108
Beech Grove, KY, 56–58, 60
Bell, John, xiv, 11, 16–17, **18**, 26–27, 31
Bell Buckle Gap, TN, 136
Big Creek Gap, 37
Big South Tunnel, 112
Black Codes, 254, 258
Blacks, 278; churches for, 273; citizenship for, 258–59; civil rights for, 250, 253–55, 257–59, 273, 287; community for, 273; disenfranchisement of, 287; enfranchisement of males, xv, 250, 253, 257–59, 261, 263–66, 268, 277, 280, 282–83; equality for, 279–80, 286; as farm laborers, 276; migration of, 271, 273; as office holders, 277; political rights for, 276–77; schools for, 230, 258, 272, 274–75, **275**, 280; as soldiers, 188, 204, 218, 231–32, **232**, 233, 243, 262; violence against, 280, 282, 287; and voter interference, 285
blankets, 73–74
blockhouses, attacks on, 203–4
"Bonnie Blue Flag," 127, 199, 223
Booth, John Wilkes, 250
Bowling Green, KY, 48, 50, 61–62, 70–71, 73, 79, 115
Bragg, Braxton (CSA), xiv-xv, 81–83, 88–89, **113**, 237, 240; as administrator, 135; army reorganization by, 121, 157, 159, 163–64; and Chattanooga siege, 159, 161–63, 166–67; and Chickamauga campaign, 149–53, 155–57, 159; as commander, 108, 110, 112–14, 121–22, 134–38, 140–45, 148–49, 171–73, 176, 178, 181, 239; criticism of, 120, 133–36; insubordination by officers of, 121–22, 135, 150–53, 157; Kentucky invasion by, 115–20, 181–82; as military advisor, 178; resignation of, 178; at Shiloh, 88–89, 95, 98, 101; and Stones River/Murfreesboro, 124–25, 128–29, 131–33
Bragg, Mrs. Braxton, 136
Brannan, John M. (USA), 158
Breckinridge, John C. (CSA), 16–17, 82–83, 135, 164, 167, 172–74, 176, 178; and Shiloh, 89, 95, 98–101; and Stones River/Murfreesboro, 124–25, 129–30, 132
Breezy Hill, 199

Bridgeport, AL, 162–63, 166, 191
bridges, 37, 68, 153, 162, 193, 195, 198, 209; burning/destruction of, 55, 112, 173, 175, 195, 201, 235–36. *See also* pontoons
Brown, John C. (CSA), 196–202, 285–86
Brown, Neill S., 215
Brownlow, William G., xiv, 17, **18**, 22, 29–31, 33, 213, 220–21, 236, 241, 260, 264, 284; attitude of toward Johnson, 260–61, 263; as governor, 255–57, 261, 263–64, 270, 272, 277, 279, 281–83, 285; newspaper propaganda of, 242; personality of, 242, 256–57, 261; as treasury agent, 241–42; as US senator, 283
Brownlow, Mrs. William G., 56, 236
Brown's Ferry, 165–67, 171
Buchanan, James, 72
Buckner, Simon Bolivar (CSA), 48, 73, 76–78, 143, 148, 150, 163, 237
Buell, Don Carlos (USA), xiv, 49–51, 56, 60–62, 71, 79, 82–83, **86**, 105–6, 111–15, 119–21, 216; Kentucky campaign by, 115–19; and logistics problems, 111–12; and Shiloh, 84, 90, 94, 96–100, 102
Bureau of Refugees, Freedmen, and Abandoned Lands. *See* Freedmen's Bureau
Burnside, Ambrose E. (USA), 142–43, 147–49, 167–68; and East Tennessee campaign, 147–48, 168, 171, 177, 181, 238, 241–42
bushwhackers, 223, 235, 240. *See also* guerillas
businesses, Black-owned, 276

Cairo, IL, 46, 242
Cameron, Simon, 25–26
Camp Andrew Johnson (Barbourville, KY) (USA), 53
Camp Buckner (Pineville, KY) (CSA), 52–54
Camp Cheatham, TN (CSA), 36
Camp Trousdale, TN (CSA), 36
Camp Wildcat, KY (USA), 53–55
Campbell's Station, 168
cannon, 44, 68, 74, 89, 94–96, 103
Carondelet (ironclad), 63, 74, 104
carpetbaggers, 271
Carroll, William (CSA), 11, 56–59
Carter, John C. (CSA), 202
Carter, Samuel P. (USA), 240–41
Carter, William B., 55, 240
Carter, Mrs. William B., 56
Cartmell, Robert H., 234
cartridges, 44
Caswell, William, 36–38
cattle, 44
cavalry: CSA, 72–73, 89, 101, 112, 122–25, 136–37, 139–40, 151, 153–55, 162, 171, 178, 186–89, 193, 195–96, 198–99, 208, 216, 223, 233; USA, 152, 154, 184, 188, 204–6, 208–9

Chattanooga, TN, 43, 112, 114–15, 120, 141–42, 153–54, **185**, 232–33, 243; Battle of, xiv, 168–69, *170*, 171–76, 182–83, 239–40; campaign, 142–44, 148; campaign casualties, 177–78; CSA evacuation of, 144, 149; economy of, 271; as logistics hub, 182–83; siege of, *160*, 162–63, 165, 168–69, 239; USA occupation of, 144, 149, 158–59, 171
Chattanooga Creek, 171, 173
Chattanooga Valley, 171, 176
Cheatham, Benjamin F. (CSA), xiv, 125–27, 164, 190, 194, 196–99, 201–2, 205–7, 210
Cheatham, Richard B., 215
Chickamauga: Battle of (GA), xiv, 152–55, **156**, 156–59, 239; campaign, 149–53, *154*, 154–55; casualties of, 159
Chickamauga Creek, 152–53, 155, 169, 175, 177
children, 238
Cincinnati, OH, 242
Cincinnati (ironclad), 63, 68
Civil Rights Act: (1866), 258–59; (1875), 286–87
Civil War, Western Theater of, *26*
Civil War Tennessee: Battles and Leaders (Connelly), xi
Clarksville, TN, 230–31
Cleburne, Patrick (CSA), xiv, 125, 128, 135, 150–51, 172, 174, 177, 196–201; death of, 200, 202
clothing, 44, 73–74, 181, 208–9, 274
coats, 73–74
Columbia, TN, 137, 195, 208, 231, 273
Columbia Pike, 196–201
Columbus, KY, 61–62, 70, 79; CSA evacuation of, 80, 103; CSA occupation of, 46–47, 51, 79
Command of the Army Act (1867), 265
Compromise: of 1850, 14; of 1877, 286–87
Compton's Hill (Shy's Hill), 205–6
conciliation policies, xv, 248–49
Conestoga (gunboat), 63, 74
Confederacy, tyranny of, 30–31, 33, 35, 37
Confederate debt, 253–54, 259
"Confederate Heartland," xiv, 42, 45, 79, 110, 182, 189, 212
Confiscation Acts (1861, 1862), 228–29
Congress, and Reconstruction, 250, 254, 257–62, 264–67
Connelly, Thomas, xi, xiv, 42
constitutional amendments, on slavery, 23, 25, 253–54, 256
constitutional conventions (state), 253–54, 265–66
Constitutional Union Party, 16, 20
contrabands, 228, 230–31, 233–34; camps for, 230, **231**, 239, 243, 262, 273; as laborers, 230–31, 243

Cook, Henry Howe (CSA), **46**
copper mines, xiii, 44
Corinth, MS, 80–82, 85, 101, 103, 106–7; Battle of, 118–20; evacuation of, 108–9; as hospital center, 107; siege of, 107–8
corn, 6–7, 44
Corse, John M., 191
cotton, 7–8
"Cracker Line," 164, *165*, 166–67
Crawford, Robert A. (USA), 241
Crittenden, George (CSA), 56–60, 82
Crittenden, Thomas L. (USA), 97, 116, 121, 123–24, 128, 138, 140, 142–44, 150, 152–53, 155, 158
Crittenden-Johnson Resolution, 228–29
Crockett, David, 11
Cumberland Gap, 37, 48, 52, 54, 112, 114, 119, 148–49, 180
Cumberland Plateau, 3, 54, 142
Cumberland River, xiii, 3, 5, 40–42, 47, 51, 56–57, 67, 73, 79, 110–11, 181; flooding of, 57–58
Cummings, David H. (CSA), 59

Dalton, GA, 177, 184
Dalton's Ford, 153–54
Davis, Charles Henry (USA), 108–9
Davis, Jefferson, 30, 35, 37–38, 42, 45–46, 48, 56, 80–81, 106, 108, 110, 120–22, 135–36, 149, 163, 167, 178, 185, 189–92, 210, 236
Davis's Ford, 195
debt peonage, 276
Delaware, 23
Democratic Party, 11–12, 14–16, 19, 21, 24, 35, 250, 255, 268, 270, 286–87. *See also* Peace Democrats; War Democrats
Department of the Cumberland (USA), 120
Department of East Tennessee (CSA), 112
Department of Missouri (USA), 49
Department of the Ohio (USA), 49, 147
deprivation, on home front, 211, 226, 243–44
deserters, 144–45, 240
disease, 53, 107–8, 121, 273; casualties from, 107
disenfranchisement: of Blacks, 287; of ex-Confederates, 256–57, 259, 263, 265–66, 279, 284, 287
disloyalty, crackdowns on, 225, 236
Division of the West (CSA), 190
"Dixie," 127, 199, 223
Donelson, Daniel S. (CSA), 40–41, 237
Douglas, Stephen A., 16–17
Dover, TN, 41, 61, 74–75
Dred Scott decision, 16, 258
Dry Valley Road, 153, 156
Duck River, 195–96

Dug Gap, 150–51
dysentery, 107

East Tennessee, xiii-xiv, 1, 3–4, 20, 35; agriculture in, 5–10, 35, 44; Blacks in, 238, 243 (*see also* Blacks; East Tennessee, slavery in; slaves); campaign for, 145, 147–48; CSA conscription in, 236–38; CSA raids in, 234, 238; CSA troops in, 31, 36–37, 39–40, 143, 234, 236, 238; confiscation in, 242; defense of, 37–40; economy of, 5–10, 30, 35, 44, 234, 242–44, 271; ex-Confederates in, 279–80; geography of, 3–6, 35, 148, 235, 238; guerillas in, 234–40, 242, 244; home guards in, 241; and internal conflict, 35, 244; liberation of Unionists in urged, 50–51, 54–55, 111, 119, 147; martial law in, 236; political power in, 10–12, 35, 244; and Reconstruction, 240; revolt in, 55; secession efforts in, 31–32; secession resisted in, 3, 22, 29–33, 213–24; and separate statehood, 33; slavery in, 8–9, 35, 238–39; Unionist anti-Confederate activities in, 37–40, 235, 237, 239; Unionist conciliation attempts in, 38–40, 236–37, 239; Unionist revenge in, 244; Unionist women in, 238; Unionists in, 22–23, 29–33, **34**, 35, 37–40, 220, 234, 244, 248; Unionists expelled from, 56, 236; Unionists flee from to Kentucky, 235–36, 238; Unionists hanged in, 55; Unionists mistreated in, 235–36, 239; USCT recruitment in, 231–32, 243; USA control of, 181, 225, 238, 240; USA troops from, 33, 38; USA troops in, 142
East Tennessee and Georgia Railroad, 5–6, 32, 42–43, *43*
East Tennessee and Virginia Railroad, 6, 31–32, 42–43, *43*
East Tennessee Relief Association, 243
Eaton, John, Jr., 275
economic depression, 286
education. *See* Blacks, schools for; schools; Tennessee, schools in
elections, 1860 (presidential), 16–17, 19, 249; 1861 (TN), 40; 1863–64 (TN), 216, 219; 1864 (presidential), 219–20, 229; 1865 (TN), 221, 256–57; 1866 (TN and midterm), 257, 261–62, 264; 1867 (TN), 268, 277, 281; 1868 (presidential), 266, 270, 280–82; 1869 (TN), 282, 284–85; 1876 (presidential), 286
elitism, 22
Ellet, Charles, Jr., 109

emancipation policies, 244, 249–50
Emancipation Proclamation, xv, 217, 219, 229, 233, 237, 239, 249
entrenchment(s), 84, 106, 131, 174, 195, 199–200, 203, 205
erysipelas, 107
Essex (ironclad), 63, 68–69
Etheridge, Emerson, 264
ex-Confederates, 277–78, 285; disenfranchisement of, 256–57, 259, 263, 265–66, 284, 287; mistreatment of, 279; political rights of restored, 249, 253, 255; violence by, 280–82

Ferguson, Champ, 223–24, **224**
Fifteenth Amendment, 282, 286
firearms manufacturing, 44
"Fire-Eaters," 14–15
Fisk, Clinton B. (USA), 273–75
Fisk University, 275
flanking movements, 184, 195–96, 199
Fleming, John, 22
Florence, AL, 192–94
Floyd, John B. (CSA), 71–73, 75–78
foodstuffs, 44, 60, 80, 107, 209, 225–27, 243, 270, 274
Foote, Andrew H. (USA), 60–61, 63, **64**, 66–70, 74–77, 79, 103–4, 108
Foote, Henry S., 31
foraging, 225, 227, 242
forges, 7
Forrest, Nathan Bedford (CSA), xiv, 72–73, 78, 80, **95**, 96, 101, 112, 122, 137, 152, 155, 186–89, 193, 195–96, 198–99, 203–4, 208, 223, 233, **252**; and Ku Klux Klan, 280, 282
Fort Donelson, TN, xiv, 41, 51–52, 61–62, 67, 72–73, 75, 231; Battle of, 69–70, *71*, 72–77, 82; casualties of, 75, 77; CSA escape plan from, 75–78; surrender of, 77–79, 82
Fort Harris, TN, 37
Fort Heiman, TN, 41, 51–52, 65–66
Fort Henry, TN, xiv, 41, 51–52, 60–63, *65*, 65–66, 75; Battle of, 63, 65–66, **66–67**, 67–70, 73–74; surrender of, 68–70, 79, 82
Fort Pickering, TN, 262
Fort Pillow, TN, 37, 108–9; massacre at, **187**, 187–88, 233
Fort Randolph, TN, 37
Fort Sanders, TN, 178–79, **179**, 180–81
Fort Sumter, SC, xiii, 25, 27, 29, 32
Fort Wright, TN, 37
Fortress Rosecrans, TN, 203
foundries, 44
Fourteenth Amendment, xv, 259–63, 265, 286; ratification of, 260–61, 264
Fowler, Joseph S., 269
Frankfort, KY, 115, 117

Franklin, TN, 198–99; Battle of, xiv, 198–202; casualties of, 200–202
Fredericksburg, Battle of (VA), 147–48
Freedmen's Bureau, 258, 273–74, **274**, 276; bill (1866), 258–59
"Fry," **39**
furloughs, 209
furniture factories, 272

Gallatin, TN, 112, 231
Garesché, Julius (USA), 128–29
garrison towns, 225–27, 230, 243, 271, 273
Georgia, Reconstruction in, 253–54
Gettysburg, Battle of (PA), 142, 159, 182
Gilbert, Charles Champion (USA), 116
governors, provisional, 253, 255
Grand Junction, TN, 230
Granger, Gordon, 138–40, 155
Granny White Pike, 205
Grant, Ulysses S. (USA), xiv, 46, **64**, 71, 78, 86, 103, 105–6, 114, 118, 239; criticism of, 102–3; as division commander, 164, 168, 171–72, 176–77, 181; and election of 1868, 280–81; and Fort Donelson, 69–70, 73–77, 84, 89; and Fort Donelson surrender, 78–79; and Fort Henry, 60–61, 63, 65–66, 69, 73; as general in chief, 183, 192, 204, 265; promotions of, 79, 82, 164, 183; and Reconstruction, 282, 286; and Shiloh, 83–84, 87, 89–90, 92, 94, 96–98, 100, 102; at Vicksburg, 138, 142, 148
Greeneville, TN, Unionist convention in, 33
grist mills, 7, 272
guerillas, 53, 211, 216, 236; raids by, 37, 39, 112, 186, 223–25, 227, 235, 237–38, 240, 242
gunboats: (CSA), 68, 108–9; (USA), 60, 63, 65–67, **67**, 68–70, 73–75, 79, 94, 96, 103–4, **104**, 108–9
gunpowder mills, xiii, 43–44
Guy's Gap, TN, 136, 140

"Hail Columbia," 127
Halleck, Henry Wager (USA), xiv, 49–52, 60–62, 68–69, **69**, 72, 78–79, 82, 84, 87, 102–5, 108; as chief of staff, 183; as general in chief, 109–12, 116, 119, 121, 133, 137–38, 144, 163; Western command by, 105–8, 110
hanging, of Unionists, **39**, 55
Hardee, William J. (CSA), 48, 71–72, 82, 88–89, 98, 100–101, 120, 123–25, 128–29, 135–36, 139–41, 171–73, 178, 184, 190; insubordination by, 120–22, 135
Hardeman County, TN, 280
harnesses, 44
Harpeth River, 198

Harris, Isham, 256; in Civil War, 91, 100–101; as TN governor, **19**, 20–21, 25–27, 30, 32, 35–38, 40, 42, 47, 220
Hawes, Richard (CSA), 116
Hayes, Rutherford B., 286–87
Hazen, William B. (USA), 129, 166
Heiman, Adolphus, 41
"Hell's Half Acre," 273
Henry, Gustavus Adolphus, Sr., 31, 41
"Hensie," **39**
Highland Rim, 3–4, 136
Hill, D.H. (CSA), 163
Hindman, Thomas C. (CSA), 150–51, 163
hogs, 6–7, 44
home guards, 241
"Home Sweet Home," 127
Hood, John Bell, xiv, 184–86, 189–92, 208–9; and Nashville campaign, 191–99, 201–5, 207, **207**, 227; relieved of command, 209
Hooker, Joseph (USA), 163, 166, 171, 173, 175, 177
Hoover's Gap, TN, 136, 140–41
"Hornet's Nest," 91, 93–94
horses, 7, 44, 163, 204, 208–9
Horseshoe Ridge, 159
hospitals, 107, 225, 274
Howard, Oliver O. (USA), 273
hunger, on home front, 211, 226–27, 243
Hurlbut, Stephen A. (USA), 82, 90, 94, 97, 100
industrialization, 7, 21–22, 43
infantry, mounted (USA), 140–41, 143
internal improvements, 12, 270
iron works, xiii, 43, 271–72
ironclads (gunboats), 63, 67–70, 74–75, 103, **104**, 109
Island No. 10, xiv, 103–4, **104**, 105, 108
Iuka, Battle of (MS), 118–19

Jackson, Andrew, 10–11
Jackson, John K. (CSA), 167
Jamestown, TN, 37, 54
Jamison, Sallie Gannaway, xi
Johnson, Andrew, xiv, 22, **24**, 24, 30, 32, 55, 212, 236, **251**; attitude of toward Brownlow, 260; and Conservative fusion party, 255–56, 261–62, 266; and emancipation, 217–19; family of, 56, 215, 236; impeachment of, **267**, 267–69; as military governor of TN, xiv, 212, 215–19, 221, 224–25, 248, 255–56; opposition to, 261, 263, 265–69; and pardons, **252**, 252–53; personality of, 215–19; political background of, 250–51; as president, 221, 250, 255, 258, 267; property of, 215; and Reconstruction, 221, 250–58, 260–61, 264–67, 278; and secession(ists), 213–16; slaves of, 215; speaking style of, 261, 270; and "swing around the circle," 261;

Johnson, Andrew (*cont'd*)
as Unionist, 212–15, 217–18; and Unionists, 217–18; vetoes by, 258, 264–66, 270; and vice presidency, 220–21, 255
Johnson, Mrs. Andrew, 56, 215, 236
Johnson, Bushrod R. (CSA), 41, 78, 153
Johnston, Albert Sidney (CSA), xiv, 45–46, **47**, 48–49, 52–53, 60, 62, 70–72, 75, 79–84, 87, 89; criticism of, 80; death of, 91, 102; and Shiloh, 83–84, 87, 89–91
Johnston, Joseph E. (CSA), 120, 122, 132, 135–36, 138, 178, 184–85, 190, 209–10
Joint Committee on the Conduct of the War (USA), 188
Joint Committee on Reconstruction, 257, 259
Jones, Samuel (CSA), 237

Kansas-Nebraska Act, 15
Kelly Farm, 156, 159
Kelly's Ferry, 166
Kennesaw Mountain, Battle of (GA), 184
Kentucky, xiii, xv, 17, 23, 37; CSA support in supposed, 112–13, 115–17, 119; contrabands in, 239; invasion of, 113–20; neutrality of, 36, 41, 46–48, 52; raids in, 187; refugees joining US army in, 235; Unionists in, 53, 214, 235; Zollicoffer's campaigns in, 52–54, 56, 58
Kentucky-Tennessee border, 37, 39–41, 47, 148
Kirby Smith, Edmund. *See* Smith, Edmund Kirby
Knoxville, TN, 5–6, 143, 148, 167–68, 233, 243; CSA campaign against, 167–68, 171, 178–80, *180*, 181, 240; economy of, 271; Union occupation of, 148–49; Unionist convention in, 32
Knoxville Whig, 17, 21, 30–31
Knoxville Whig and Rebel Ventilator, 242
Ku Klux Klan, xvi, **278**, 280–82, 285–86
Ku Klux Klan Act, 281, 285

LaFayette, GA, 144, 149, 152–53
LaFayette Road, 153, 155–56
land, confiscation of, 257, 259
latrines, 107
La Vergne, TN, 203
Lee, Robert E. (CSA), 142, 147, 167, 178, 181, 185, 210
Lee, Stephen D. (CSA), 190, 195, 201, 205, 207
Lee and Gordon's Mill, 152–53, 155–56
Lexington, KY, 115, 117
Lexington (gunboat), 63, 96
Liberty Gap, TN, 136, 139–40
Lincoln, Abraham, xii; administration of, xv, 23–24, 211, 216, 218, 269; and amnesty

proclamations, 241, 249, 252; and Andrew Johnson, 212–14, 216–17, 219–20; assassination of, 221, 250, 255; election of, xiii, 16–17, 19, 220; and emancipation, 217, 229, 239; and the military, 50–51, 62, 82, 102–3, 111, 116, 119, 121, 133, 137, 147–48, 162–64, 183, 192, 239; and Reconstruction, 248–50, 253, 260; and secession, 214; and slavery, 22, 25, 228, 248–50; as tyrant, 25, 32, 35; and war preparations, 25, 29, 32;
livestock, 7–8, 44
logistical problems, 142, 193, 209
Longstreet, James (CSA), xiv, 153, 157–59, 166–68, 171–72, 178, 180–81, 240
Lookout Mountain, 143–44, 150, 166, 169, 171–73, 175; "Battle Above the Clouds," 173
Lookout Valley, 165–66
looting, 225, 227, 240
Louisiana, Reconstruction of, 253
Louisville, KY, 115–16, 242
Louisville (ironclad), 74
Louisville Journal, 243
Louisville and Nashville Railroad, 48, 50
lumber mills, 7, 271
Lynnville, TN, 231

"Macedonia," 273
malaria, 107
malnutrition, 107
Manassas, VA, First Battle of, 48
"March to the Sea," 192
market economy, 4–10
martial law, 253, 281, 284
Maryland, 17, 23
Maynard, Horace, 22, 30, 32, 220, 236
Maynard, Mrs. Horace, 56, 236
McClellan, George B. (USA), 48–49, 51, 55, 60–61, 72, 82, 109, 219, 229
McClernand, John A. (USA), 65, 74–76, 82, 94, 100, 106
McCook, Alexander M. (USA), 97, 116–17, 121, 123–24, 128, 138–39, 143–44, 150, 152, 158
McCown, John P. (CSA), 125, 128, 237
McKenzie, Tracy, 8
McLemore's Cove, GA, 149–51, 154–55
McMinnville, TN, 137, 231
McPherson, James B. (USA), 105, 183
measles, 107
Memphis, TN, 233, 263; capture of, 109–10, 181; contraband camp at, **231**, 231; economy of, 5, 44, 226, 272; growth of, 271; gunboat battle at, 109; munitions manufacture in, 44; raid on, 188–89; riot at, 262–63, **279**; wartime conditions in, 226
Memphis and Charleston Railroad, 6, 112

Memphis and Ohio Railroad, 68, 70
Memphis Appeal, 21
Memphis Enquirer, 17
Metropolitan Police Act, 263
Mexican War, 13
Middle Tennessee, 1, 3–5; agriculture in, 7–8, 44, 122; CSA evacuation of, 80, 141–42; CSA invasion of, 113, 119; CSA troops in, 36, 122; defense of, 40; economy of, 7–10, 44; geography of, 3–4, 142; intimidation in 281; political power in, 10–11, 15; Reconstruction in, 214–15; secession sentiment in, 20, 25, 29, 32–33, 244; slavery in, 8–9, 21, 40; Union control of, 223; USCT recruitment in, 231, 233
Military Department No. 2 (Western Department) (CSA), 45, 48
military districts (Reconstruction), 264, 266–67
Military Division of the Mississippi (USA), 164
military equipment, manufacture of, 44
military governors, 248. *See also* Johnson, Andrew
Military Reconstruction Acts (1867–68), 264–66, 268
military rule, during Reconstruction, 261, 286–87
militia (TN), 264
Mill Springs, KY: Battle of, 57–60, 235; campaign, 56–58
mines: explosives, 63; minerals, 7
Missionary Ridge, 143, 149, 169, 171–75, **175**, 176–77, 239–40
missionary teachers, 230, 280
Mississippi River, xiii, 4–5, 37, 42, 80, 103, 108, 110, 181
Missouri, 17, 23, 50
Mobile, AL, 112
Moccasin Bend, 165–66
Montgomery, James E. (CSA), 108–9
Montgomery, AL, 112
Morgan, George (USA), 112
Morgan, John Hunt (CSA), xiv, 112, 122
mud, 83, 208
Mulberry, TN, 225
mules, 7, 44, 162–63, 208–9
Munfordville, KY, 115
munitions factories, xiii, 43–44
murder, 280
Murfreesboro, TN, 80–81, 112, 122, 124, 136, 231; Battle of. *See* Stones River, Battle of; campaign, 123–24; CSA retreat from, 133–34; raid on, 203
musicians, 127
muskets, 44

Nashville, TN, 231, 233, 243, 273, 275; Battle of, xiv, 204–6, **206–7**, 233; campaign for, 191–95, 199, 202–3; capture

of, 50–51, 110, 181; casualties, 207; CSA evacuation of, 79–80; defense of, 40, 71–72, 79, 194, 202–3, 216; economy of, 5–6, 43–44, 272; growth of, 271; as logistics hub, 182–83, 202; munitions manufacture in, 44; prostitution in, 226
Nashville and Chattanooga Railroad, 112, 141
Nashville convention (1850), 14
National Guard of Tennessee, 241
Nashville Republican Banner, 13, 17
National Union Party, 220, 255
Native Americans, 3
Negley, James S. (USA), 149–50
Nelson, Thomas A.R., 30, 32–33, 213, 237, 241
Nelson, William "Bull" (USA), 90, 94, 97
New Jersey, 17
New Madrid, MO, 103
New Orleans, LA, 43, 110; riot in, 262
no-man's land, 227
Noble Ellis (steamboat), 60
North Carolina, 16, 23, 45, 209; Reconstruction of, 253
Nullification Crisis (1833), 13–14

oaths of allegiance, 219, 225, 236, 241, 249, 253, 256, 259
occupation policies (USA), 244
Opposition Party, 15, 24, 213
Orchard Knob, 172, 176
Ord, Edward (USA), 118–19
Ordnance Department (CSA), 44
outlaws, 211, 223–24, 227, 234, 240, 242
overcrowding, 226–27, 273

Paducah, KY: raid at, 187; US occupation of, 47
Palmetto, GA, 189
pardons, 241, 249, **252**, 253
patronage, 265; for Tennessee, 24, 212–13
Patterson, David T., 269, 283
Peace Democrats, 229
Pemberton, John C., 122, 138
percussion caps, 44
Perryville, Battle of (KY), 117, 120, 135
Phelps, S.L. (USA), 68
pickets, 85, 128, 132, **169**, 209
Pigeon Mountain, 149–50
Pikeville, TN, 23
pillaging, 221–22, 225, 227
Pillow, Gideon J. (CSA), 14, 36, 73, 75–78
Pittsburg Landing, TN, 82–84, 89–91, 94, 105, 108
Pittsburgh (ironclad), 74–75, 104
Plessy v. Ferguson (1896), 287
police, 263
Polk, James K., 13
Polk, Leonidas (CSA), xiv, 45–48, 79–80, 82–83, 88–89, 98, 101, 120, 124–26, 129–30, 132–33, 135–36, 140–41, 152–53, 157, 159, 163, 184; death of, 190; insubordination by, 120–22, 153

Polk, William H., 40
pontoons, 161–62, 169, 193, 209. *See also* bridges
Pope, John (USA), 79, 103–6, 108
popular sovereignty, 16
Porter, William D. (USA), 68
Prentiss, Benjamin M. (USA), 82, 87, 90–93; surrender of, 93–94
Preston, William (CSA), 91
Price, Sterling (CSA), 114, 118–20
prisoners of war, 178
Proclamation of Amnesty, 241, 249
prostitution, 226
Provisional Army of Tennessee (CSA), 44
Pulaski, TN, 194–95, 208–9, 230–31, 276, 280

racists, 279
raids, by cavalry, 53, 121–23, 141, 186–89, 216, 223, 233
railroads, xiii, 5–7, 9, 39, 42–43, *43*, 48, 50, 79, 81, 111–12, 121–22, 167, 193; and corruption, 272, 285; destruction of, 61–62, 68, 112, 148, 186, 191–92, 203–4, 223, 272; growth of, 272; repair of, **137**, 186, 191
rainstorms, 57–60, 65–66, 69, 74, 81, 83, 96–97, 104, 123–24, 127, 132–33, 140, 162, 168, 172, 189, 193, 204, 206, 208
rams (gunboats), 109
rape, 221, 227, 262, 280
Ready, Alice, 222
Rebel yell, 128, 193
Rebels. *See* Confederates; ex-Confederates
Reconstruction: end of 285–86; Southern defiance of, 254; in Tennessee, xv, 214–15, 220–21, 247–48, 285–86; wartime, 244, 248–50
Reed's Bridge, 153–54
refugees, **212–13**, 221–22, 226, 242–43
Republican Party, 214, 282–83, 286–87
Republicanism (political theory), 12; threats to, 22, 30, 35
Republicans: Conservative, 250; Moderate, 229, 250, 257–59, 265, 267–69; Radical, 221, 229, 250–51, 254–55, 257–65, 267–70, 276, 283–84
retaliation, 225, 240, 242, 244, 279
Richardson, Richard V., 223
Richmond, VA, 43
rifles, 84
Ringgold Gap, 177
riots, anti-Black, 262–63
River Defense Fleet (CSA), 108–9
Rosecrans, William, xiv, 105, **118**, 118–20, 122, 133–34, 137–38, 145, 149, 164–65; and army reorganization, 120–21, 138, 142; and Chattanooga campaign, 142–44, 148, 237; and Chattanooga siege, 162, 164–65, 239; and Chickamauga cam-

paign, 152–53, 155–59; and Stones River/Murfreesboro campaign, 123–24, 128–29, 131–33, 137; and Tullahoma campaign, 138–42, 148
Rossville, GA, 155, 171
Rossville Gap, 159
Rossville Road, 172–73
Rousseau, Lovell (USA), 203
Rutherford Creek, 196

sabers, 44
saddles, 44
St. Louis (ironclad), 63, 74
Salisbury, NC, 210
saltpeter, 44
Sand Mountain, 143
Sanders, William P. (USA), 148, 178
sawmills, 272
Schoepf, Albin Francis (USA), 56–57
Schofield, John (USA), 183, 194–99, 202, 205–6, 269
schools, 272, 274–75, 285; destruction of, 280
Scott, William Bennett, Sr., 277
Scott, Winfield (USA), 49
scurvy, 107
secession: efforts for, 13–14, 20–21, 25, 31–32; invalidated, 247; referendums on, 20, 22, 24, 27, 29, 31–33; repudiation of, 13, 17, 19, 21, 32–33; of Southern states, 17, 19–21
secessionists: expulsion of, 241; imprisonment of, 225, 241
segregation, 285–87
Senter, DeWitt C., 220, 283–85
Seward, William H., 25
Seymour, Horatio, 270, 282
sharecropping, 276
sharpshooters, 74–75
Shaw, Edward, 277
Shelbyville, TN, 133, 136, 138–40, 231
Sheridan, Philip (USA), xiv, 105, 129
Sherman, William T. (USA), xiv, 82, **85**, 85–86, 90, 105, 163, 168–69, 171–76, 181, 194, 253; and Atlanta campaign, 183–92; and "March to the Sea," 192–93, 209–10; and Shiloh, 85–87, 94, 96–97, 100–101
Shiloh, Battle of (TN), xiv-xv, 83–85, 87, *88*, 88–92, **92–93**, 93–99, *99*, 100–102, 105, 181; casualties of, 102
Shiloh Church, 90, 101
shoes, 193, 204, 208
Shy, William M. (CSA), 205
Shy's Hill (Compton's Hill), 205–6
"Slaughter Pen," 129
slave aristocracy, 22
slavery: expansion of opposed, 16, 19, 25; in Tennessee, xv, 8–9, 13, 15–16, 247; threats to, 22, 25, 228–29
slaves: confiscation of, 228–29; freed, 233–34, 244–45, 247; runaway, 226, 228, 230, 239

small arms, 44
smallpox, 243
Smith, Andrew Jackson "A.J." (USA), 194, 205–6
Smith, Charles F. (USA), 65, 74, 76–77, 82
Smith, Edmund Kirby (CSA), 112–14, 120–21, 235–37; Kentucky invasion by, 114–17, 120, 237
Smith, William F. "Baldy" (USA), 164–65, 168–69
smithies (blacksmiths), 7, 271
smuggling, 223
snow, 74, 76, 81, 193–94, 204, 208
songs, 127
South Carolina, 13, 17
Southern rights, 15, 19–20
Special Field Order No. 15 (Sherman), 253
spies, 223, 238
Spring Hill, TN, 195; Battle of, 196–97
Stanbery, Henry, 266
Stanley, David S. (USA), 121, 138, 143
Stanton, Edwin M., 137, 163, 192, 265, 268–69
State Guard (TN militia), 264, 281, 284–85
Steedman, James B. (USA), 204
Stephens, Alexander H., 254
Stevens, Thaddeus, 263
Stevens Gap, 151–52
Stevenson, Carter L. (CSA), 167, 172
Stevenson, AL, 191
Stewart, Alexander P. (CSA), 190, 194, 196, 198–99, 202, 205–7
Stokes, William B., 284–85
Stoneman, George (USA), 262
Stones River, TN, 124–25, 129; Battle of, xiv, 124–26, *126*, 127–29, **130**, 131, *131*, 132–34; casualties of, 133–34
stragglers, 90, 94, 101, 108
Strawberry Plains, TN, 31
suffrage, universal manhood, 284–85. *See also* enfranchisement
"Sunken Road," 90–91
supplies, 84, 142–43, 145, 155, 164–65, 178, 186, 191, 193; destruction of, 112, 123, 162, 187–89; shortage of, 53, 60, 117, 119, 121, 133, 149, 164, 168, 180, 189, 204, 209; shortage at Chattanooga, 162–63; shortage for civilians, 226, 243

tanneries, 7
tariffs, 12–13
taxes, 272–73, 285
Taylor, Richard (CSA), 209
Temple, Oliver P., 22, 33
"Ten-Percent Plan," 250
Tennessee: agriculture in, xiii, 3–8, 270–71; attitudes toward Johnson in, 214–19; Black male suffrage in. *See* Blacks, enfranchisement of males; Civil War key role of, xii-xv, 42–45, 110, 244; civilian gov-

ernment for, 220–21; conciliation in, 222–24, 235, 241, 243; Confederate loyalty in, 214, 222–24; Conservative Unionists in, 256–57, 260, 273, 277–78, 284–86; constitutional convention in, 285–86; declaration of independence by, 27; East. *See* East Tennessee; economy of, 4–9, 12, 30, 270–72; General Assembly (legislature) of, 255–56, 260, 264, 272, 275, 277, 281, 283, 285; geography of, 3–6, 35; "Grand Divisions" of, 1, 4, 6, 10, 20, 23; industrialization in, xiii, 7, 43–44; Middle. *See* Middle Tennessee; Northern immigrants in, 271; and patronage, 24, 212–13; Radical Unionists in 256–57, 260, 270, 272–73, 276–86; raw materials in, 44; readmission of, 263; Reconstruction in, xv, 214–15, 220–21, 247–48, 253, 260, 285–86; rural devastation in, 270–71; schools in, 230, 272, 274–75, **275**; secession of xiii-xv, 1, 2, 20–22, 25–27, 32–33, 36, 214; and secession referendums, 20, 22, 24, 27, 29, 31–33, 213–14; secession repudiated, 13; slavery in, 8–9, 13, 228–29, 249; slavery ended in, xv, 217–19, 228, 234, 270; State Guard, 264, 281, 284–85; taxes in, 272–73; troops from (CSA), xiii, 44–45, 244; Unionism in, xiii, xv, 13, 16–17, 20–27, 29, 31; Unionists post-war split, 256–57; Unionists and slavery, xv, 25, 217–18, 238–39; as "Volunteer State," xii-xiii, 1; voter registration in, 256–57, 281; war preparations of, 36, 41–44, 47–48; West. *See* West Tennessee; zones of occupation in, 225–27

Tennessee Cavalry, 12th (CSA Partisan Rangers), 223

Tennessee Infantry, 19th (CSA), 37, 40, 59, 107, 127, 193

Tennessee-Kentucky border, 37, 39–41, 47, 148

Tennessee River, xiii, 3, 5, 40–42, 47, 51, 63, 79, 82, 110–11, 141–43, 161–62, 169, 172, 181, 192–93, 208–9; flooding of, 65–66, 68

tents, 44

Tenure of Office Act, 265, 268–69

Texas, 45

textile mills, xiii

Thedford's Ford, 153–54

Thirteenth Amendment, 253–54, 256, 286

Thomas, George H. (USA), xiv, 54–55, 57, 59, 105, 116, 119, 121, 123–24, 138–41, 143–45, 149–50, 152, 155, 157–59, 164–65, 168–69, 171–72, 176–77, 183; and Nashville campaign, 194, 202, 204–5

Thomas, Lorenzo (USA), 231, 268
Three Star Series, xi-xii
Tigress (gunboat), 90, 94
Tilden, Samuel, 286
Tilghman, Lloyd (CSA), 52, 66–68
tobacco, 6–8, 271
torpedoes (mines), 63
troops: armament of, 36, 44; call for by Lincoln, 25, 29, 32, 35; recruitment of, 36, 231, 233
Tullahoma, TN, 134–36, 141; campaign for, 138–39, *139*, 140–42, 182
Tunnel Hill, GA, 172–73
Tupelo, MS, 108, 110, 112, 209
Turchin, John B. (USA), 166
turnpike, 54–55
Tuscumbia, AL, 193
Tuttle, James (USA), 97
Tyler (gunboat), 63, 74, 94, 96
typhoid fever, 107

uniforms, 44
Union, preservation of, 228–30, 251
Union City, TN, 36
Unionist coalition, 22–25, 29
Unionist conventions, 32–33
US Colored Troops (USCT), 188, 204, 231–32, **232**, 233, 243, 262; casualties in, 233
US Supreme Court, 287
US troops, and emancipation, 229–30
urbanization, 5–6, 271

Van Dorn, Earl (CSA), 106, 114, 116–20
vegetables, 44, 107
venereal disease, 226
Vicksburg, MS, 114, 122, 136, 138, 142, 148, 163, 182
violence, racial, 280, 282, 286–87
Virginia, xiii, 16–17, 23; Reconstruction in, 253
"Volunteer State" nickname, xii-xiii, 1
voters: control of, 277, 279, 285, 287; registration of, 264–66, 284

Wade, Benjamin, 269
wagons, 162, 208–9
Walden's Ridge, 162
Walke, Henry (USA), 74
Walker's Ford, Battle at (TN), 180
Wallace, Lew (USA), 74, 76, 82, 84, 87, 90, 96–97, 100, 102, 106
Wallace, W.H. L. (USA), 82, 90, 93, 97; wounding of, 93
Walthall, Edward C. (CSA), 208–9
war crimes, 223–24
War Democrats, 217, 219–20
warehouses, 44
Wartrace, TN, 136, 141, 231
Washburn, Cadwallader C. (USA), 188
water, contamination and shortage of, 107
Watkins, Adam, **232**

Watkins, Hannah, **232**
Watkins, Sam (CSA), 202
Wauhatchie Station, 166–67
West Tennessee, 1, 4–5; agriculture in, 8; CSA evacuation of, 80; CSA invasion of, 114, 118; CSA troops in, 36–37; defense of, 37, 47; economy of, 8–10; intimidation in 281; political power in, 10–11, 15; raids in, 187, 223; secession sentiment in, 20, 25, 29, 32, 244; slavery in, 8–9, 21; US control of, 225; USCT recruitment in, 231, 233
Western and Atlantic Railroad, 143, 177, 186, 189–92
Western Department (Military Department No. 2) (CSA), 45, 48
Western Freedmen's Aid Commission, 275
Western Theater commanders (USA), 105
wheat, 6–7, 44
Wheeler, Joseph (CSA), 122–23, 136, 178, 186, 193; raid by, *161*
Whig Party, 11–12, 14–17, 21–24, 35, 38, 213, 217, 270, 272
White, Hugh Lawson, 11
Wilder, John T. (USA), 140, 143
Wilson, James H. (USA), 205–6
Winstead Hill, 198–99, 201
Withers, Jones (CSA), 125–27
women, 238, 241
Wood, Thomas J. (USA), 152, 158
Wood, William B. (CSA), 56
Worsham, William J. (CSA), 127, 193, 202
wounded soldiers, 107, 131, 133, 201
Wright, Moses H., 36

Yancey, William, 31
"Yankee Doodle," 127

Zollicoffer, Felix K. (CSA), **38**, 38–40, 48; death of, 59; Kentucky campaigns of, 52–58
zones of occupation, 225–27